AF326525

THE JOURNEY

MARGARET HAWKINS

Contents

I hope you enjoy my story, one of resilience, humanitarian service, and the perpetual journey of self-discovery and growth.

• -Margaret Hawkins

CHAPTER 1

Eight decades have passed yet the memories of the Journey from the Old World to the New come flooding back in waves of great clarity.

The year was 1933 and my mother, Matilda, born in 1905, a tall, beautiful and gregarious woman, decided to leave her beloved village Szakasz, now known as Ratesti, Romania. In the Treaty of Trianon (1920) after WW1 parts of the Austro-Hungarian empire were carved up and this area was given to Romania. Consequently, although our ancestry was Hungarian we were now considered Romanian citizens. With her little five year old daughter Margit – me! – in tow she was determined to join her husband, Peter, in a remote little Pulp and Paper Town in Northern Ontario, Canada. The journey didn't feel entirely mysterious to her for she had been carefully and deliberately coached by her older brother Nicholas, who, with his wife and two young children had recently returned from Canada, in fact from the same Northern town, Smooth Rock Falls, that her husband Peter had settled in. Nicholas loved life in the New World, the advantages as well as the challenges, but his wife sadly succumbed to feelings of loneliness and isolation and yearned to return to her large extended family. Nicholas warned my mother in a stern and foreboding voice, "Matile, (Matilda) you pack up, take your little girl and go to Peter as soon as possible for he is lonely and rumour has it that he intends to look up his red-headed childhood sweetheart in Cleveland, Ohio". My mother needed no other incentive – a fantasy rumour worked its magic and plans for the journey began almost immediately. But how did Peter have a childhood sweetheart in Cleveland, you might ask?

Like so many European men of that era my paternal grandfather, George Tarcza emigrated to Cleveland where he worked as a labourer, returning to Szakasz every other year for a happy reunion with his beloved wife, my grandmother, Maria and his young son Peter, my father, for a month, then returned to America and his work. When he finally saved enough money for their passage they left their native land in 1912. Father was eleven years old at the time. Preparations for that journey, I was told, included weeks of labour for my grandmother sewing new outfits for herself and young son Peter. She was an accomplished seamstress and having a keen eye for design the two were decked out in their Sunday best for the long journey to join my grandfather and other relatives in America.

Coincidentally, my maternal grandfather Nicholas Zvonik did the same, only his pursuit for work was further south, to São Paulo, Brazil, where he worked as a gardener, returning every two years to the family at which time another child would be conceived, eight in all, the ninth being born in Brazil after the family emigrated there in 1924. I remember some years ago attending a lovely musical "Tango Under The Stars", with a good friend in Toronto. As a prelude the history of the Tango was explained as a combination of European and South American music that had its genesis when lonely European men without their families would find solace and warmth dancing with beautiful South American women. An 'aha' moment occurred as I thought about my grandfather Nicholas!

My grandmother and father set sail from Bremen, Germany on December 7, 1912 on the s.s. Bulow which carried 2042 passengers traveling first, second and third or steerage class. They landed at Ellis Island on December 19th where they were processed and then continued to Cleveland, Ohio where my grandfather George eagerly awaited them at 9308 Sophia Avenue.

Some years ago I toured Ellis Island and as I walked along the great empty passageways, aware of huge hanging pictures of arriving immigrants with only one or two suitcases, it moved me to tears thinking of how courageous and daring they were to undertake such a daunting journey. Unable to speak the language and also not knowing what lay ahead of them in the vast new country they were entering. Many, sadly, were also refused entry for health and other reasons and were shipped back to their country of origin.

However, grandmother and my father, with mixed feelings of fear and elation, were grateful to finally arrive in the "land of the free and the home of the brave". I still get very emotional each time I hear "America the Beautiful" and "The Star Spangled Banner" – my eternal tie to my beloved grandparents and to my father.

My grandparents, George and Maria, both worked full-time in factories close to their home; he at the National Malleable Steel Casting Company, in existence from 1868 to 1943. My father attended public school and within a year had a paper route delivering two hundred papers a day after school. He also had the additional chore of prepping vegetables for the evening meal which his mother prepared after a gruelling day at the factory. I always attributed my father's culinary skills (and they were impressive) to his mother's early lessons in the kitchen. After completing public school at fourteen my father joined his father as a labourer in the same foundry to supplement the family income. He also had an evening job setting up pins for ten-pin bowling and eventually became an excellent bowler winning championships and thus augmenting the family coffers significantly. It occurred to me on reflecting on my father's life, that, like so many other young immigrants at that time, he was really deprived of what we would today consider a proper childhood. Although he was a bright student with dreams of becoming an accountant it was impossible for him to pursue this goal for the extra family income was needed to survive.

At age eighteen he had saved three thousand dollars and also presented his mother a lovely fur coat for Christmas. The three thousand dollars, however, was sent by my grandmother to two of her eight brothers back in the Old World for new roofs for their houses. Sadly, this seemingly kind act created a lifelong rift between mother and son with my father accusing his mother of, "caring more for her family of origin, than for him". The loan was never repaid.

In 1920 a shock not unlike a thunderbolt hit the Tarcza family. My grandmother, at the age of 39, gave birth to a son, Joni, and in 1922 in a repeat performance her third son, Bela, was born. Given her age and unable to cope with the trauma of caring for two infants my grandmother decided the family should return to Szakasz where love and support were abundant. It was a hard sell convincing my father to join them. At age 22 he had grown up an American, loved his life there and particularly loved his red-headed girlfriend! However, parental authority prevailed with my grandmother's assurance that he could return to America in the future if he wished. So the family of five returned to Szakasz. in 1923. This move turned out to be a grave error in judgement bordering on tragedy when WWII broke out.

My father often recounted the story of first seeing my mother working in the vineyards of Szakasz with her red and white polkadot kerchief tied around her hair. The moment he saw her he was smitten and thought to himself, "someday I'm going to marry that girl". And that he did in 1924. My mother and her sister, Mari, were married in a double wedding ceremony prior to my maternal grandparent's, (Nicholas and Matilda) departure with their six children and son-in-law, to start a new life in São Paulo, Brazil. My mother and her brother, Nicholas stayed behind and never saw their family of origin again. Later in life, Mother confided in me how difficult her childhood had been. Being the eldest girl in a family of eight children and given the consistent absence of her father she shared many of the responsibilities of parenting with her mother by caring for her siblings. Consequently she loved and was closely bonded with her mother and paternal grandfather whom she described as a kind and gentle man. Her father however, was a different story. She remembered him as a short tempered, impulsive man (unlike his own father) whom she feared, showing me a scar on her ankle where he had kicked her when she took too long to fetch water from the well, at age nine! One of the reasons she was happy not to be emigrating to Brazil. She desperately missed her mother and siblings but during the years that followed they communicated with letters and photographs and open hearts as they shared each others' life stories.

In 1926 Matilda and Peter had their first child, a son born with a heart defect who died ten days later. Mother said how heartbroken and sad they were over their loss . For years each time she talked about the loss of little Feri tears would flow relentlessly. There is no pain greater than the pain of losing a child and parental grief seldom if ever ceases but with time often changes in intensity and manner of expression. As the years passed, tears were replaced by a sad and faraway look. Finally, as my mother lay dying of cancer (in her early eighties), in an effort to console her, I said she finally would be reunited with her beloved family and her little baby Feri. Her reply, "did I have a son?" convinced me that veiled memory finally had removed the burden of pain she carried her whole life regarding little Feri. I said a silent prayer of thanksgiving as I cried and held her.

My father, who was and still felt American, could not adjust to life in Romania and slowly prepared to return to Cleveland. His application, however, was denied as the immigration quotas were filled at that time and he had not attained citizenship before leaving America. Consequently he emigrated to Canada in April of 1928, a month before my birth. His travel plans arranged by an agent stated his destination as a rural area south of Edmonton Alberta where he was to be given work as a farm labourer. When he arrived at his destination after a long, tiring journey he found no one there by that name and realized he was a victim of a scam. Fortunately, he spoke English fluently and was able to get help. He was advised to go to Northern Ontario where they were looking for workers for a new pulp and paper mill. After a long harrowing journey by rail he arrived in Smooth Rock Falls, Ontario where he was employed by the Abitibi Pulp and Paper Company for the next thirty-eight years.

So, the saga of the red-headed girlfriend, although interesting, was not to be.

There are certain memories of Szakasz which remain vividly in my mind although I was only five when we left. One was our white stucco house which my mother inherited when her family emigrated to Brazil and my grandparents' similar home nearby. Up the main street of the little village stood the Roman Catholic and Greek Catholic churches side by side shaded by beautiful chestnut trees. My mother attended the former, my father and his family the latter. In the distance and on a slight incline, were the vineyards bordered by fruit trees where my mother took me each day in a little wooden cradle while she performed her daily work to earn a living. Beyond the vineyards lay the vague outline of the Transylvania Mountains.

I also remember two little playmates a girl and a boy with whom I played almost daily from age three on. When I returned more than a half century later for a happy and memorable visit with my surviving relatives, they both came over to reminisce about the past. How wonderful and moving it was to see them all! One of my little friends, now an adult, was a teacher, the other worked on his family's farm. I had great difficulty describing my profession, a Social Worker, but succeeded in communicating the fact that I help people with various problems in their lives. As for my little village it seemed as though time stood still and nothing much had changed. But back to the journey.

My mother had diligently saved every penny she could in hopes of joining my father as soon as possible. So, earnestly saving the money she earned from selling her farm produce, grapes and fruit, along with regular money she received from my father in Canada she had more than enough saved for our passage and other expenses.

In fact she had more than was allowed to bring into Canada at the time. Not to be outdone *Nagymama* (grandmother) devised a grand strategy. A triangle was cut out of a large round loaf, the money inserted and the crust replaced. Needless to say the money and the loaf made it safely to Canada! She was also advised by *Nagymama* who had previously made the journey and was experienced, to include in her 'must haves', feather pillows and duvets for the cold North American winters. Duck down, by the way, from her own flocks.

To avoid any upset to the grand plan Mother and *Nagymama* had cunningly devised, a telegram was sent to my father in Canada advising him of our arrival date after arrangements were complete. The steamer trunk was finally packed and sealed, and two smaller suitcases carrying the clothing we would need en route made ready. My grandfather hitched the horses to the wagon and we were soon on our way to Szatmar rail-station (SatuMare in Romanian), to begin the long journey, first by train to Le Havre, then by boat to Canada. *Nagymama* accompanied us to Szatmar assuring us all the way that we were, "leaving a bad life behind for a better one in Canada." Nevertheless, the tears continued to flow like a river, mine included, but I was crying only because I saw my loved ones doing so. At the last moment my favourite uncle, Bela, who was only six years older than I, came running out in pyjamas for a tearful goodbye. At our 1991 reunion he confessed that he wept for days after our departure, "for you not your mother," until finally *Nagymama* admonished him and with a smarting slap on his backside declared, "now you have something to cry about." So like my stoic grandmother!

I was very attached and closely bonded with *Nagymama*, a feisty little woman only five-foot two and found the separation painful. As we boarded the train in Szatmar she kept returning and covering us with kisses and tears. The final time she announced to me, "see that little bench, Margit-ka? When you return *Nagymama* will be waiting right here for you." On every bench we passed from Szatmar to Smooth Rock Falls I searched in vain for

Nagymama who was obviously not there. And the tears flowed endlessly.

In contrast, my memories of my Grandfather are less vivid. I remember him as a tall, thin moustached gentleman, rather introverted but always gentle and kind. Men in that era, I suspect, had more defined roles which did not include child rearing. Also my grandfather would be absent from the family circle from dawn to dusk hard at work in the fields, another reason I wasn't as closely bonded with him as with my grandmother. This pattern prevailed in my own family for I didn't meet my father until I was five years old. For various reasons we had what I would call a distant relationship until many years later when I finally felt emotionally close to him. When he was seventy-eight he had an unfortunate and painful brush with cancer. In the process of seeking and obtaining help for him our relationship changed to an emotionally close one and remained so for the following fifteen years until his death at age ninety-three.

After a lengthy journey by train we finally arrived in Paris, France where my mother had the good fortune to meet an interesting woman, who, with her little girl, age six, was also emigrating from Berlin to Timmins, a mining town in Northern Ontario. *Szuszi-neni* (Auntie Susan) as I was to call her, spoke both German and Hungarian, so they became fast friends. Living in an urban area all her life she quickly took my mother, "under her wing", and led us on a wonderful shopping spree! New heavier wool coats for us both, a few more fashionable dresses, new shoes and French berets worn at a saucy angle. And for me what we would call a, "Sassoon", haircut (bangs with a short blunt cut). "What a big surprise your Peter will get," *Szuszi* laughed.

Three things stand out in my memory of Paris – the shopping spree, my new little playmate, *Szuszi* (Susan) and an incident in our hotel room. We were escorted to our room with our luggage and while my mother was trying to communicate with the bellboy I noticed an interesting button on the wall near the doorway and proceeded to push it holding my finger on it for some time. Suddenly a man dressed in uniform came in, looked at me sternly and slapped my hand releasing it from the bell. Of course, it was a call-bell for service.

With our new look and our French berets worn at a tilt we boarded the last train from Paris to Le Havre where we embarked on the White Star Line s.s. Ascania. As we lay in our bunks that evening I vividly recall the first movement of the boat as it left the harbour heading for the open sea.

CHAPTER 2

The predominant memory of our long journey across the Atlantic ocean is my mother's isolation in our cabin due to severe sea-sickness. I had my little friend Szuszi as a distraction each day when her mother would take us into the dining-room for meals. The smell of freshly baked rolls pervaded the air from morning to night. I also remember being frightened by a quivering red blob on a plate set before me to eat. I pulled away thinking it was something alive and refused to eat it. On the same occasion there were floating balloons, many sticking to the ceiling, and I was mesmerized having never seen them before. The trauma obviously faded fast as I learned to love what was in fact moulded Jello and floating balloons for celebrations.

It always saddened me to see my mother so ill when I returned to our cabin. I would wipe away her tears and keep repeating *Nagymama's* advice, "don't cry, you are leaving a bad life behind to go to a better one in Canada." Mid-way in our crossing Mother had to leave our cabin, as did all the other passengers. We donned our life-jackets and climbed to the boat deck, something we had practiced once before in sunshine, but this time the sky was laden with ominous clouds and a rough stormy sea made the vessel pitch. I don't remember being frightened as my mother's warm hand entwined mine, comforting me. Being a devout woman all her life she chose prayer as a form of consolation and prayed quietly during the whole exercise. When we finally returned to our cabin Mother knelt down, me beside her, with prayers of thanksgiving.

My happiest memory, beside playing with my little friend Szuszi, was the day after the bad storm. We were on the boat deck on a bright sunny morning and absolutely enchanted watching a school of porpoises joyfully leaping in and out of the water, so like a present day Disney production, only this was spontaneous, beautiful and unforgettable live theatre.

We disembarked from the "Ascania" on September 7th,

1933, in the port of Halifax much to my mother's relief. We were then laboriously processed through immigration. I particularly recall the medical examiner, a kind smiling man, tweaking my chubby cheeks as much as to say, 'you're a healthy specimen'! Not so when I was nine months old. My mother recounted the story of how I contracted pneumonia and after seven days she was told I was unlikely to survive – no antibiotics then. A grave was dug and the local priest contacted, but miraculously on the tenth day as the church bells were peeling the Angelus I suddenly opened my eyes and started to nurse again. Mother, who lost her first child, was overjoyed and convinced my recovery as the church bells were ringing was God's answer to her prayers. I've always regarded it as the genesis of Margit's survival instinct which would come into play many times down the bumpy road of life.

It was also in Halifax that we said a tearful goodbye to Szuzi-neni and my little friend Szuszi as their travel schedule was different from ours. However for the next decade we had many happy reunions in Timmins, Ontario until they eventually left to settle in the west in Alberta.

Finally admitted into Canada, we sat in the Halifax railway station awaiting the next lap of our journey, when what I call 'the banana eating incident' occurred. Mother and I were seated on a bench waiting patiently when a handsome middle-aged man sitting across from us smiled and tried to communicate, unsuccessfully of course. Giving up, he handed Mother two bananas as a friendly gesture and motioned with his hand that we should eat them. So mother took the first bite, skin and all, and quickly spat it out into her hankie warning me not to eat mine as it tasted terrible! Meanwhile the generous gentleman laughing uncontrollably proceeded to peel another banana to show us how to eat it. We followed his instructions and thoroughly enjoyed our first banana ever on Canadian soil.

The gruelling journey took several days with two more train changes before our final arrival at Cochrane, some forty miles from Smooth Rock Falls where my father, Peter, was to meet us. With the train stopped, we gathered our belongings and waited near the exit. After some time Mother became panicky for my Father was nowhere to be seen. We walked through the next few coaches and suddenly she shouted excitedly, "Péter!" In seconds they were embracing each other after their long separation, over five years, while I stood thinking, who is this strange man kissing my mother? He finally picked me up, twirled me in the air and covered me with kisses. A reunion never to be forgotten.

The train continued on to Jacksonboro, known locally as 'the junction', where we left the Northland train to ride the Company owned Mattagami Railway for the three mile trip to Smooth Rock Falls. Built in 1916 Mattagami Railway was the shortest chartered standard gauge railway in Canada. At its peak in 1947 it carried eleven thousand passengers, forty years later it was down to fifty. Better roads and the automobile were the main reason but also the decline of the pulp mill itself was a factor. Friends were waiting with a truck and car to transfer our luggage and take us to our first Canadian home in Frenchtown where we spent the next two years.

CHAPTER 3

———

Smooth Rock Falls with a population of 1031 was Incorporated as a town in 1929. The main industry, the Abitibi Power and Paper Company established in 1927, was originally the Mattagami Pulp and Paper Company, circa 1916. It was a mainstay of the newsprint industry during the first half of the twentieth century. All the houses in town were originally built and owned by the Company including a large bunkhouse which housed and fed men without family. Houses were rented, for a nominal sum, with free power and water. The town had two churches, St. Gertrude's, Catholic, predominantly French-speaking, was affiliated with the Separate School and Trinity United for Protestants, predominantly English-speaking affiliated with the Public School and attached Continuation School grades 9 to 12. A general store called Mercantile Stores, was built in 1926 and later, in 1947, became the Hudson's

Bay which included a pharmacy. Any clothing we needed was ordered from Eaton's or Simpson's mail order catalogues. Wags will tell you that many a country outhouse contained last year's catalogue with the warning not to use the shiny pages. A large Community Hall located near the United Church welcomed all residents, a venue where movies and live concerts, produced by the locals, were presented. Another favourite landmark was The Inn, built in 1918, operated by the Caradine family when we arrived. Several stories high, it housed employees of the Mill, teachers and travellers. It also had an office for sending and receiving telegrams and provisions and large parcels delivered from the Mattagami Railroad on a large hand-pushed wagon. The Royal Bank, established in 1927, was located in the Mill office. A post office, opened in 1916, was a favourite meeting place for young and old. It was where we awaited letters from friends and loved ones, clothing from the catalogues (alas! a two week wait if they did not fit) and gifts and cards at Christmas. There were no home telephones. There was one physician, Dr Munn but no hospital or dentist at that time. A visiting dentist came from Cochrane twice a year to attend to our needs.

The Mill, its pyramids of logs and obnoxious odours dominated the town. A dam built by the Company provided power for everyone. Below the dam was a fisher's paradise where my father, an avid fisherman, caught a five foot long sturgeon in 1939. With his good friend and neighbour Ugo Mattussi they carried the huge fish home by placing a thick branch through the sturgeon's gill, then each carrying one end of the branch on their shoulder. As they proudly marched home by foot, as neither owned a car, a small group of men and children followed behind not unlike the story of the Pied Piper and according to "tall tales" the catch was so heavy they had to stop five times to rest before reaching home in Hollywood (a newly developed area where we lived). Sturgeon steaks were enjoyed by many for several days!

In the outskirts of town the suburbs included Clouthierville, Mooreville and Unionville where people could build and own their own homes and businesses. Unionville had a little business area of eateries, a bakeshop, a general store Bordeleau's and a grocery store called Gravels. It also housed the renowned Elite Hotel, a favourite watering hole of immigrant men, built in 1935 and owned by the Litniki family.

Our first home in Smooth Rock Falls, located in Frenchtown, was a tar paper shack, very poorly constructed, with three small rooms. A kitchen with an eating area, table and chairs, a sink with no running water (which meant outdoor toilets or "outhouses") and a wood stove with an oven. The living room had a sofa, two chairs and a wood/coal heater. A small bedroom contained a double bed for my parents, a dresser and a small cot for me. Many nights I cried myself to sleep feeling thoroughly dislocated. How disappointing it must have been for Mother having to leave her spacious home and lovely vineyards in Szakasz to come to this. No complaint came from her however, for she was so happy to see land again and to be with her husband.

In the first month she transformed the tar paper shack into a cosy little home with newly made curtains, her feather duvets, colourful embroidered tablecloths and cushion covers from the Old World. She scrubbed and polished the three little rooms all the while singing her beloved Hungarian songs with intermittent tears, of course. Both my parents had beautiful voices, my father often performed in community concerts singing Al Jolson songs. Family patterns die hard for years later my sister Helen and I, being members of the school choir, always sang in harmony while we helped with household chores.

Shortly after we arrived, my Father gave us what I refer to as 'his patriotic lecture'. 'This is your New Country now and it is a beautiful country full of good people. You must try to forget the Old Country, learn English so you can talk to people and make new friends. We will NEVER go back for this is our new home now'. Even at age five the message became deeply embedded as Father's tone was most serious. I have never forgotten his lecture and am a proud Canadian who adheres to patriotic protocol to this day. Father became a naturalized citizen as soon as possible appearing before a citizenship judge in Cochrane. Mother's and my name were added a few years later. When I turned eighteen, while in Toronto, I applied for my own citizenship papers which I treasure to this day. My parents never returned to the Old Country for a visit, but spent their time integrating into their new society. For my father it wasn't difficult for he already spoke English and adopted Canadian customs and habits eagerly. Having been raised in America he wasn't regarded as a real immigrant. He immediately joined sports activities including baseball and bowling in a mixed ten-pin bowling league where he excelled due to his teenage experiences in Cleveland and fit in with both English and French easily.

Mother and I had a more difficult time. On leaving the house we found no Hungarian immigrants, although a few came later, and the majority spoke Ukrainian and Polish. Not to be defeated by anything, Mother immediately began learning Ukrainian so that she could meet new friends. Simultaneously she would take my 'John & Mary' reader, which I brought home from school and laboriously study the words each night, writing them out and trying to pronounce them with my help. No ESL in those days! Within a year we were speaking both broken Ukrainian and English well enough to make new friends. The Ukrainian/Polish immigrants were our closest friends as we had similar backgrounds. We were all in the 'same boat' so to speak. Many of these friends ended up being life-long friendships. One particularly, Hope Zawadski, walked with me to school every day. We became best friends from the time we met and remain so to this day. Hope had an exceptional career teaching nursing in Peterborough where she eventually married and with her husband Ken

Hotston raised three lovely children and also successfully maintained her career until retirement.

Sadly, in 2016 Hope passed away. Husband, Ken, died the following year. Thus a life-long friendship came to an end but leaving me with countless happy memories.

Father chose to send me and later, my sister, Helen, to Public School so that we would learn English. Consequently I often attended Sunday School at Trinity United. My devout Mother didn't attend church, as immigrants, in the early days, were not made welcome by the general public (perhaps due to the language barrier); however the Parish Priest Father Forget was affable and friendly with everyone. Some years later St Gertrude's introduced Nuns to the religious community to teach school and catechism at which time the atmosphere became more friendly toward immigrants. Mother then attended church regularly.

The thirties, often referred to as the dirty thirties, had Canada and most industrialized countries in a deep depression. The stock market crashed and many people, particularly in large towns and cities were unemployed, homeless and hungry. My aunt Bertha, one of the first graduating female lawyers in Canada, a devout and most generous and loving woman, recounted tales of hungry unemployed begging for food. When they called at her door in north Toronto she never sent them on their way without first sitting on the back step where she fed them thick sandwiches and a big glass of milk.

Fortunately the impact was not as devastating in our little town. The Mill continued to operate with slight cutbacks to four or five days a week, instead of the usual six. Father worked five days a week and Mother, of course, was a wonderful manager making small amounts of money stretch by baking her own bread, preserving all kinds of fruit for winter, while Father contributed with his vegetable garden and fishing. Mother also sewed all our, as well as her own, clothing and made curtains, bedspreads and other household items. Therefor we didn't feel the impact of the depression as much as city folk.

In 1933 mince beef was 25c a pound, milk 8c a quart, a postage stamp 1c, a cup of coffee 5c, a haircut 50c for adults and 35c for us kids. Admission to movies was 25c and airplane rides 1c a pound as I found out the hard way !! Every cent counted and Mother was a strict saver from early adulthood to old age. Father, on the other hand, was the opposite. He loved to spend. So it was a bone of contention in their marriage and the crux of many a battle during their lifetime.

All was not dire in the immigrant experience for there were some lighter and even hilarious moments. Like the time my mother, in the very early phase of learning a second language, was visiting a Ukrainian neighbour, Mrs Bosa, who had just acquired a lovely new floor model Stewart-Warner radio. She proudly turned on the radio to show Mother the marvels of it and tried to communicate with words and hand gestures that sometimes there was Hungarian music on the radio. Misunderstanding the message Mother went to the radio and began shouting excitedly her request for a particular Hungarian song. Mrs Bosa, in the meantime, was rolling on the floor with laughter as Mother continued demanding her request – but nothing happened. Over a cup of tea, Mother realizing her *faux pas* , they laughed heartily and then continued their language lesson. To add insult to injury Mother recounted the tale to my Father that evening and he was mortified (embarrassed?) and explained the concept of radio and its operation to her. What did my good natured Mother do? She could see the humorous side of the event and she laughed and laughed (but didn't roll on the floor). She recounted the story many times in several languages and it never ceased to be funny. Lessons were learned the hard way often at our own expense.

The first winter snowfall in Smooth Rock was magical. Having never seen snow before I watched beautiful huge snowflakes fall and tried to catch them in my hands but they melted instantly. Then I found a better way. With head tilted back I'd catch them with my tongue and laugh with delight at the cold sting it produced. Whenever I gaze at A. Y. Jackson's painting "First Snow" I associate it with this lovely childhood memory.

Winter could also be a brutal experience. With heavy snowfalls the snowbanks sometimes rose to ten feet or more. The townsite workers cleared the roadway eventually but often we trudged to school knee deep in snow arriving there with wet and cold feet. Other days we couldn't get through the drifts so absenteeism wasn't unusual during the hard winter months. The fun side however, included tobogganing and skiing down snowy hills on weekends and holidays. No fancy ski gear, then only a simple harness that would spring shut over our boots and off we'd go. Another favourite winter sport was skating on home-made rinks in the back yard by the light of the moon, pretending we were Sonja Henie. As I mention the moon I recall how terribly I missed my Grandmother those first few years and at some point I made the connection that we probably were looking at the same moon. So at bedtime as I lay in my bed crying for her I would suddenly see the moon shining brightly through the curtain and think *Nagymama's* looking at the same moon! It became my connection to her and comforted me greatly.

Summer games when we were very young included kick the can, hide-and-go-seek and hopscotch. There were also unique and innovative games. Like the time our neighbours in Frenchtown, the Ruddick brothers with their friends, built a wonderful "merry-go-round consisting of a large wooden pole in the centre with eight ropes fastened to it securely and at the end of the ropes they attached a bushel basket, making a total of four seats on this hand-propelled merry-go-round. How excited we were anticipating our first ride on this wonderful contraption! However there was a price to be paid. The boys informed the eager girls that in order to get our ride we must first go up to their tree house and pull our panties down (show and tell time I presume). We girls all protested, and sister Alice went even further with "I'm telling Mom" and she did. Mrs. Ruddick, a dear friend of mother's, immediately made the boys tear down the merry-go-round AND the tree house and the boys were properly punished. So much for the Circus that never was!

As we got older we progressed to tennis, baseball, volleyball and hockey. There were no swimming pools nearby until many years later. Consequently, I never learned to swim even after signing up for swimming lessons at Central Tech in Toronto many years later. One of the first requirements was to do the "deadman's float" across the pool which I failed miserably. Not wanting to lose my tuition fee I opted for sewing lessons instead and became an accomplished seamstress like *Nagymama* and Mother. Many dresses, gowns, drapes and bedspreads later, I thought to myself "what a brilliant move that was"!

A few months after our arrival and shortly after our 'patriotic lecture' my Father took Mother and me to the local barbershop for what he called a stylish haircut. Mine was uneventful and looked much the same – a Sassoon like look; however, Mother's was a different story. She had beautiful long brown hair that fell below her shoulders and each day she would brush it, braid it and pin it into a

French roll at the nape of her neck – she looked absolutely beautiful and so trusting with her large hazel eyes and warm smiling lips. As the barber started his awful deed down came the French roll. With scissors he aggressively chopped her hair to below ear length with a side-part and in ten minutes completely changed her appearance. I could see the tears welling in the corner of her eyes as she bent down to retrieve the chopped off hair, bundled it tenderly in a napkin and placed it in her purse then in the steamer trunk where it remained for many years. Father was pleased that she looked more stylish – less Hungarian – and patted me on the head indicating he liked my new look. Arriving home Mother looked in the mirror and burst out crying at which time I did too, seeing her so unhappy. I sassed my Father with, "I'll tell *Nagymama* what you made us do." He roared with laughter at my cheekiness. A few years later we progressed to curly hair when 'perms' became fashionable. Mother finally adapted – or capitulated? – and agreed short hair was much easier to care for.

CHAPTER 4

On June 18th, 1934 on a warm sunny day a most traumatic/ joyful event occurred in all our lives. My sister, Helen Elizabeth, arrived with a loud wail. Remember our little tar-paper shack with one bedroom? It became the delivery room. With no door, only a curtain across the doorway, Dr. Munn and his able assistant, nurse Suzy Davis, attended Mother, with my Father and me on the other side of the curtain. Father translated the doctor's instructions, (bear down etc.) for what seemed like an eternity. Then out came the wonderful sound of a baby's cry. Nurse Davis swaddled my little sister and brought her out for us to see. She then placed her on the covered kitchen table where she proceeded to wash her, attend to her eyes, diaper her and finally showed me how to kiss her on the cheek – and I did! As an aside, years later in 1956, when my sister, an RN, worked in the Smooth Rock Falls hospital for the summer months, before returning to Toronto for post-graduate studies, had a horrifying experience. She was told by the same nurse, Suzy Davis, how disappointed her Mother and Father were that she wasn't a boy. To console my sister I laughingly told her they probably wished I had been a boy too after the heartbreak of losing little Feri. Actually they were overjoyed to have us both.

Mother remained in bed several days while her Ukrainian friends came for daily visits bringing love, food and support. She also had a loveable Scottish friend, Maggie Wilson, who made daily visits and was so kind and supportive. Maggie, her husband John, a very humorous and witty man and their daughter, Mary, remained friends for many years that followed. Mother's ability to make friends with several English-speaking women was an interesting phenomenon as this didn't generally happen with most immigrant women. I think my Father's fluent English and his general comfort with both French and English citizens may have facilitated this. Also the fact that Mother was making a great effort to learn to read and write English and reach out to people were additional factors. Many immigrants, both men and women, never learned to speak nor write English fluently but only learned the basic essentials necessary to communicate. A contributing factor could have been their self-ghettoization – it was easier to stick together as a group thus squashing the incentive to learn. Another factor no doubt was the initial rejection of them by the indigenous population – both French and English. My father was often asked to help with translations at work or letter writing when it was required.

After a week or so, when Mother was up and about, I gathered together all my friends who came streaming in to see my baby sister in her new pram. Helen was beautiful and such a showpiece. No sibling rivalry there – so far!

Around this period my Mother's health started to deteriorate. She developed, what we now call, a strep throat. No medication was available so Maggie Wilson showed her how to make Vicks poultices to put around her neck. She also became very thin and developed a stomach ulcer. In retrospect quite possibly she was suffering postpartum depression, probably not diagnosed or treated in those days. There were frequent visits to Dr Munn's office for ulcer treatment and later years to Timmins to consult a specialist. After a year went by she adjusted and our home was filled with song again. Mother busied herself with embroidering lovely pieces, knitting scarves and mittens and sewing all her (fashionable) and our clothing on her new Singer sewing machine – a manual model operated by a foot treadle. The first words Helen learned were, "'ellow pink", the colour of the embroidery thread Mother used in her work.

From the first time I kissed my newborn baby sister on the cheek I felt a sense of elation knowing I now had someone to love and play with. I don't remember ever feeling jealous (sibling rivalry) even when she became closely bonded with Father, a security I lacked as a child growing up. I have always felt affection and a sense of protectiveness toward her. An example of this is when Helen, a pre-schooler about age four innocently asked Mother "where did I come from?" Mother who had a great sense of humour which I suspect often served as a survival mechanism but sometimes got out of hand, replied "we found you in a cabbage patch and brought you home." My little sister burst into tears and cried and cried. The more she cried the harder Mother would laugh. It seemed bizarre so I ran to my sister's defence, cradled her in my arms and told her that wasn't true because I was present behind the curtain with Father when she was born. I told her how nurse Suzi Davis diapered her and let me kiss her on the cheek. Feeling comforted, the tears finally ceased and Mother stopped laughing. The next time my sister posed the question Mother's reply was "we found you in a goldfish bowl". Helen laughingly replied "no you didn't because I can't swim!" That really set Mother off on a laughing spree. Again, a reluctance to talk about the process of procreation openly. It was easier (and more appropriate) to cloak it in fairy tales or mythology.

My other favourite memory of my sister as we were growing up, was how we always sang together as we helped with household chores. We harmonized with songs like "Flow gently sweet Afton", "Santa Lucia" and other favourites learned in school choir practice. She had a beautiful voice and was often chosen for solos in school concerts dressed to the T in costumes Mother made on her Singer sewing machine. We always applauded loudly encouraging her with her gift of singing but in the end she chose Nursing and teaching Nursing and had an exceptional career at St. Michael's Hospital in Toronto.

In 1935 the tar-paper shacks were burned to the ground by the Company and the residents, mostly immigrants, were temporarily housed in huge semi-detached square houses with large verandahs. The Bechard's, a French-speaking family, lived in the house attached to ours. Immediately beside us were the Dubas's, a blended family with two teenage boys and two young daughters, Mary and Fedora. Mrs Dubas, a close friend of Mother's, came over one day and tearfully begged her to take in her eighteen year old son Mike because her husband, Mike's step-father, was very abusive with him causing great turmoil in their home. Mike was already working and would pay room and board. Soft hearted Mom could not say no to a friend so Mike spent the next few years living with us until he married and established a home of his own. Many years later Mike attended Mother's funeral in Brantford, Ontario to bid a tearful goodbye to 'his second mother'. He never forgot her kindness.

I would be remiss not to talk about the family dynamics in our home, for despite the time lapse I remember it well. From a family systems perspective we functioned more like a single parent family for my Father was absent most of the time while we were growing up.

He was away to work early in the morning with his lunch pail but was present for the evening meal and even though he slept at home he would be out most of the evening doing his various activities and come home long after Helen and I were tucked up in bed. As soon as the "honeymoon period" was over, after our arrival, I hardly remember our Father participating in the family except for emergencies and disciplinary issues. He was a gregarious man, liked people and fit in with both the English and French-speaking population. He participated regularly in sports activities like baseball, bowling in leagues and fishing Sundays and weekends. But more than that he was the ideal 'community' person and took part in building the Canadian Legion, in 1950, of which he was made an honorary member and where he cooked many wildlife meals and the skating arena in 1952. He also was one of the primary instigators forming the Workers Union at Abitibi

Pulp and Paper mill. Organization was done secretly until they attained the required number of members to warrant certification. For many years he served as the collector of Union dues from the workers – Treasurer? In the 1950's, with Paul Gagne, he attended a delegate conference in Toronto. The town's gain was most certainly our, the family's, loss for we saw so little of him growing up. How lonely it must have been for Mother being abandoned in that way!

The only memory I have of Father being home consistently was from 1940 to 1942. A few years after his arrival in Smooth Rock a kind English gentleman, Mr Price, a few years away from retirement, taught Father how to operate the crane, an essential operation at the mill unloading coal, sulphur and other commodities for use in the manufacture of paper. He became a very skilled crane operator and after a few years approached his supervisor, Ted Richmond, a very affable and highly respected man, for a raise as a crane operator rather than as an unskilled worker. Ted Richmond smiled at him and replied, "Peter, I would love to give you a raise but I can't because you are not certified as a crane operator." Father needed no other incentive. He went to Kapuskasing, enrolled in a correspondence course to train as stationary engineer and crane operator and came home with two great piles of books and began his home study. For two years he gave up extra-curricular activities and studied diligently. Then he returned to Kapuskasing, wrote the required examinations and qualified as stationary engineer and crane operator. It didn't take long to present Ted Richmond with the papers at which time his salary doubled. Father didn't know who was happier, he or Ted Richmond. Despite the fact that I saw Father so little I attribute this event and his constant railings about the importance of education as inspiration for my own journey toward higher education. I really had mixed feelings for my father. On the one hand I resented his constant absence from our home and mother's resulting loneliness but admired his gregarious personality and his total involvement in his community. Growing up American he probably felt more at ease with the French and English population in Smooth Rock in the early years than he did with us.

In 1937 profound tragedy struck our little town. Five young people, three male, two female, boating on Departure Lake all drowned while canoeing. The Litnicki family, owners of the The Elite Hotel, lost two sons Anthony 23 and Edward 15, their only children. Our neighbours, the Sicards, had a large family but lost their lovely daughter Juliette, 18. The other two youngsters were unknown to us. The whole town was shocked and wracked with grief. In those days there were no funeral parlours in town so the open coffin was placed on a stand in the middle of the living-room surrounded by candles and other religious symbols. Friends would then gather to extend their condolences to the family, mourn with them and pay their last respects to the deceased. Since the Sicards were good neighbours and friends my parents did just that. Only nine at the time, this was my first experience with death. We filed passed the coffin at which time people touched the crossed hands of the deceased, I, therefor, followed their example and remember the utter shock at feeling a cold unresponsive, stiff touch and pulled my hand back quickly. Both families suffered for years and the Litniki family bereft and so saddened sold the Elite hotel a few years later.

A second encounter with death a few years later was more personal and therefor more painful. At age eleven I was put in charge of walking little neighbours to school and home again safely, including my sister who was in kindergarten. One of my charges was a young Russian immigrant, Vasha, who contracted pneumonia and died suddenly. It was the Christmas season and the airwaves were filled with Christmas carols and for years I associated Christmas with this sad occasion. I remember crying for days for my little friend and at that time I suffered several severe nosebleeds requiring Dr. Munn's attendance. Each time this would happen I was sure I too would die like Vasha and mother would hug me and reassure me that I would survive. My first recollection of fear of death. Sadly Vasha's parents eventually parted. The intense grief tore them apart, not unusual in those days, because professional help was not available to assist families dealing with the tragic loss of a child. However, friends and neighbours brought food, love and support and local clergy provided spiritual support. We were a very close-knit and supportive community when trouble prevailed.

CHAPTER 5

In the primary grades in school I had a good friend, Maxine, who often came to my rescue in Frenchtown, the battleground of name calling and stone throwing. Maxine had an unfortunate accident when very young. She saw her parents rolling cigarettes and not quite getting it right rolled cigarette paper only into a cigarette, lit it and of course the paper caught fire and burned and scarred one side of her face badly. Walking to school one day she informed me that she was going for an airplane ride with her uncle and that I was coming too. The plan was that she would come with me after school to the Royal Bank at the Mill where I would withdraw ninety cents, my weight at one cent per pound, from my Penny Bank account. I rarely said no to Maxine for despite being a friend I always found her a little intimidating – she was a 'little toughie'. So, off we went money in hand to the light plane on skis parked on the frozen river where her uncle awaited us. We got comfortably settled with a window each as the plane took off high into the sky, circled the town and flew as far as Driftwood, a few miles from Smooth Rock Falls. The view of snow covered terrain, pine trees, rivers and houses was stunning. The plane landed in the same area that it took off leaving me both thrilled and a little shaken. I never flew again until I was in my forties. Was it the fear of flying or the memory of the consequence?

When I returned home Father, who saw me going to the Bank with Maxine asked, "my dear, why were you at the RBC today?" I replied, innocently, that I withdrew ninety cents from my Penny Bank account and went for an airplane ride with Maxine and her uncle. My mother gasped and turned white. My father took his razor leather strap hanging behind the kitchen door and I received two stinging lashes across my bottom for what I had done. And well deserved it was! I can only wonder what trouble an adult would be in now taking a minor for an airplane ride without permission of the parents.

Another time, when I was about eight, my mother sent me to the Mercantile Store to buy a pound of loose tea and I returned with a half pound package of Lipton's loose tea and a bag of cream filled chocolates which I proudly handed to Mother stating I got both with the money she gave me. This time there was only laughter and a warning, 'never to do that again'. It seems I was a precocious child.

A week before Christmas we had an annual ritual where

Father would take a toboggan, place me on it and we would go looking for the perfect Christmas tree. Father was very fussy so it would take an hour or more to find a perfectly shaped tree, usually spruce. He would chop it down, place it on the toboggan, tie it down and together we would pull it home. The tree would be placed outside to settle, then it would be shaken to get rid of excess snow. The next day it was hammered on to a home-made cross-bar and placed in the living room where it would be decorated. The memory of this family ritual must have stayed with me, for a few years later I wrote the following assignment for one of my English classes in Public School.

Once upon a time in a wooded patch in the valley lived a beautiful perfectly shaped evergreen tree. It was happy in its home with its parents and many tree and animal friends always around it. One bright and sunny morning a woodsman came into the peaceful valley and with his cruel axe chopped down the little tree, placed it on a toboggan and began to leave the forest. The little tree cried and cried for it would never see its mother and father and all its little friends in the forest again.

After a long ride over the snowy hills the little tree was placed against the wall of a house where it shivered from the cold and cried all night because it was lonely. The next morning the woodsman took the little tree, shook the snow from its branches and carried it into a cosy little house. The little tree felt better but was still sad when suddenly it heard the laughter of children who were very excited by the little tree.

The next day the children gathered together beautiful shiny ornaments and strings of beads and popcorn and placed it all over the little tree. On the very top the woodsman placed a lovely silver angel with shimmering wings. Finally, strings of bright twinkling lights were placed all over the branches. Now the little tree felt beautiful and was no longer lonely because it made the children feel so happy. For days they gathered together, danced around the tree and sang lovely Christmas songs while the little tree trembled with joy.

Many years later on a beach in Sarasota, Florida I met a lovely woman who was a professor of English literature and also an author at Pennsylvania State University. We were discussing writing and I told her about the story I wrote at age nine about a little tree. She was enchanted by the story and proceeded to continue it.

And after all the decorations were removed the little tree felt bare as it was placed outside again but when Spring came, beautiful, colourful birds flew by, loved the little tree and built their nest and made their home there while the little tree happily sang wind-songs.

We both marvelled at the magic of imagination.

CHAPTER 6

My first memory of public school was that of a mini-battleground. While the English and French were religiously divided and seemed to dislike each other, neither liked the immigrants – US! This resulted in fights on the way to school, on the way home from school and even in the schoolroom. One incident I recall vividly in kindergarten. I turned around to look at my fellow classmate's drawing a black house and received a hard punch in the nose. I remember my lovely teacher Miss McDermott taking me on her knee trying to stop the bleeding and consoling me with words I didn't entirely understand. Her actions however I did and remember to this day!The perpetrator had to stand in the corner for sometime as punishment. Other forms of punishment for misbehaviour included standing in the cloakroom (isolation), standing in the waste paper basket (humiliation) or a wrap on the knuckles with a ruler and the most serious the hand strap, usually administered by the Principal (corporal punishment). If you pulled your hand away you earned an extra strap for belligerence. I don't remember experiencing any of the above at school. How things have changed over the years regarding child protection, making us a better and somewhat more humane society. We must never become too complacent, however, for often one form of abuse replaces another i.e., bullying and cyber bullying which are prevalent and so disturbing at the present time.

The battles and name calling continued until we eventually matured and became the best of friends, appreciating rather than fearing our differences. In retrospect, looking at this period as an adult, I think this behaviour would be classified as bullying (no less harmful of course) rather than discrimination against immigrants. While the French and English battles were based on religious and language differences. Nevertheless, in real time as a child it was a most unpleasant experience.

I always enjoyed my school years, eagerly anticipating what new knowledge each day would bring. In public school I particularly enjoyed our teacher Mr. Gerhardt reading stories to us with great expression and feeling. My favourite was Ann of Green Gables which transported me to a different world so unlike my own, titillating the imagination.

Besides the curriculum there were other important

lessons taught. For instance in our home economic class our Principal Mr. Fells suggested we undertake a project knitting different coloured squares and sewing them together to make a large multicoloured Afghan to send to a Native Indian Mission school in James Bay. It would help the residential children keep warm. I was put in charge of assembling the squares and constructing the Afghan and it was a great success. We received a thank you note from the children acknowledging the gift.

As WWII broke out we knit mittens and sox for the Red Cross who in turn gave them to needy war victims. These were all early lessons on how to be community minded and care about others less fortunate than ourselves. In addition to teaching us knitting skills it also developed character, empathy, caring and giving of oneself, all important qualities for successful adulthood. In later life this pattern which I learned from these dedicated teachers (as well as from my parents) became a constant in my life whether it was volunteering in our church, in the community or beyond in Third World countries with Organizations like CESO (Canadian Executive Services Overseas). It is said that doing volunteer work one often receives more than one gives. I believe this to be true as you acquire new skills with each project and meet interesting people from diverse cultures. It therefore becomes a growth enhancing experience unlike any other.

Music was an enjoyable part of our education. My sister and I were both members of school choirs where we learned about music and how to harmonize. She had a beautiful voice and often sang at concerts and later at weddings and on the radio. I wasn't gifted that way but at age eleven I received a Hawaiian guitar for Christmas together with ten lessons taught by Mr. Ponder. I mastered it enough to play Rock of Ages, The Old Rugged Cross and other beautiful hymns which made my mother very happy. Hawaiian music and current popular songs were also a part of my repertoire.

When I reflect on our teen years in Smooth Rock I can only marvel at our innocence. Early teens meant bobby sox, plaid shirts and learning to jitterbug. My dearest friend Hope and I would go to the Community Club, the favourite meeting place for bowling and dancing to the juke box. We picked only the boys who could dance the best so they could teach us – not necessarily the most handsome ones. Usually they were recent arrivals from larger towns or cities. Our hair-dos consisted of sausage type rolls across the top, down the sides and at the back, gone were the Sassoon style cuts. It was after one of these dancing sessions that I had my second encounter with the famous strap. We had a curfew, nine o'clock on week nights. One Friday night after a two hour session of jitterbugging Hope and I scurried home trying not to violate the curfew. Half way home I realized my glasses were missing, left back at the Community Hall. We ran all the way back to retrieve them and consequently I was ten minutes late arriving home. As I entered the front door, breathlessly, Father sprung out with strap in hand and I received two mandatory lashes for breaking the rules. I was fourteen and that was my last corporal punishment – unforgettable, no less.

Reminiscing about other adolescent capers, I remember our first attempt at smoking. We bought a small packet of 'Spuds', a cheap packet of ten cigarettes, tried smoking them and nearly choked. Then the dilemma of who would hide the cigarettes. Of course I was chosen. I hid them under the mattress thinking it was a very safe and secret place. When Mother changed the beds weekly out flew the Spuds. I was punished, no Community Club for two weeks – that hurt, no community jitterbugging.

We were not allowed officially to date boys but were permitted to meet in groups – safety in numbers I suppose – for dancing and bowling. Sex education or discussion by parents or teachers was absent. Mother's only warning was, "don't let anyone touch you there," no mention where there was. In my own mind I took it to mean breasts and genitals. Stolen kisses were innocent. No French kissing occurred. If a student was unfortunate enough to become pregnant, as a few were, she was quietly sent away to stay with 'an auntie' and the baby usually put up for adoption. Of course there was peer gossip and conjecture to sort out, in our own way, and adolescent games of 'show and tell'. That will never change! Sex education was so absent that when I had my first child at twenty-one I wasn't certain as to how she would be born. I could not imagine a baby coming through the vagina so I was sure they would cut open my abdomen and retrieve the baby. When I think of our naiveté and compare it with the sexual freedom rampant today at a much too early age, it makes me very sad. Sex without responsibility leads to disaster for so many young teenagers as well as for the families who have to pick up the pieces for many years to come. Surely there is a more healthy balance somewhere and we must try to find it. Perhaps in senior grades of Public school teaching parenting courses and the responsibility entailed in bringing a child into the world could be a good beginning.

My last memories of Frenchtown were not pleasant. Having so many Ukrainian friends we adopted a lot of their customs, one being that on New Year's day we would go from house to house – immigrant homes only – throwing rice for good luck while singing a little Ukrainian song. People would give us candy in return. I ended up getting more than candy, for a neighbour's German Shepherd and her pup escaped from their garage and ran after Hope and me. The mother dog bit me on the back of the leg just above the knee while Hope escaped with just a nip from the pup. When we got home Mother gave me a banana to quieten me then put iodine and a bandage on the wound and took me to the doctor the next day. No anti-rabies shots then! The experience left me with a fear of dogs and a good-sized scar as a constant reminder. Needless to say we never repeated that New Year's tradition again!

From Frenchtown we moved from our semi-detached house to a brand new detached one in an area called Hollywood, a subdivision built by the Company. Mike, our boarder, moved with us for he was now a part of the family. We occupied four large rooms and a bathroom downstairs and Mike and two friends he invited to live with him occupied the two large upstairs rooms and toilet. There was no bath tub until Father installed one upstairs two years later. Bath night consisted of a big round steel tub placed near the kitchen stove that was used to heat the water. The oven door would be left open to generate more heat. The men upstairs ate their meals at the bunkhouse and used the Company bunkhouse shower after work.

Our three guests, Mike, Nick and Yarmovich played the violin, saxophone and accordion so after dinner each evening we were treated to lovely music, both Ukrainian and the latest tunes on the hit parade, often accompanied by Mother singing. It was a happy time. Eventually Mike and Yarmovich married local girls and left, while Nick moved to The Inn. Helen and I then moved to the upstairs bedrooms. Father soon installed a bathtub in a large hallway near the staircase and we could enjoy the luxury of a real bathtub at last. The bedrooms had dormer windows and that is where Helen would stand on her bed leaning her elbows on the window sill waiting for Father to come home. Of course she fell asleep in the process more often than not.

With our new large backyard Father was able to plant a beautiful, large vegetable garden although the growing season was short. To compensate, each fall vendors would come from Southern Ontario with truckloads of fruit and vegetables so Mother would stock up with a bushel each of apples, peaches, pears and tomatoes as well as baskets of cucumbers and peppers. She would then do her magic making tasty jars of preserved fruit and delicious relishes and dill pickles which we feasted on all winter. She continued this wonderful tradition for many years after their retirement using the bounty from their garden and fruit trees in Brantford. An avid gardener, Mother took great pride in her rose bushes often producing a hundred roses each. She also had beds of mixed flowers of every variety. Helen and I would take large bouquets for our teachers before they froze, usually in mid-September. It was from Mother that I learned the art and gift of gardening, a hobby that I found joyful and fulfilling all my adult life, and still do to this day. In my garden today I have Mother's peonies transported in 1990 from their garden in Brantford. I always feel her presence when I work with them. In turn I have passed on flowers from my garden to two grand-daughters, Lisa and Jessica, who are also keen gardeners. Hopefully they will feel my presence working in their gardens long after I'm gone.

CHAPTER 7

In High School we, (the girls), wore uniforms – navy blue tunics with white blouses. I particularly remember Miss Quinlan who taught English and made it so interesting. We studied many of the great poets and writers including Shakespeare and often had to memorize and recite poetry in class. She made learning a pleasure. I also studied Latin and French together with the rest of the curriculum. I was an avid student studying diligently and usually placed top or near top of the class, a position not conducive to popularity. I was considered a 'browner'. When it came to receiving term results, posted at the back of the room, I knew from experience with my name being the longest that I could see my position from where I sat and so had no need to leave my seat and aggravate my classmates.

Like most northern towns sports were central to daily life and taught as Physical Education (PhysEd). We had both boy's and girl's baseball, hockey and volleyball teams. In hockey we competed with teams in neighbouring Cochrane where we were billeted with a student family for meals and a sleepover. They returned the visit when we did the same. Smooth Rock Falls proudly boasts two NHL players, Marcel Parizeau and Richard Mattussi, a close family friend. As WWII broke out in 1939 boys in Senior High School began leaving to serve in the armed forces. Some that I can remember were Hope's brother, Bill, who joined the Navy with his friend Walter Lebedick and Forrest Richmond also in the Navy and his sister, Myrtle, who joined the WAACs. Jerry Kit joined the RCAF as did Robert Poe who sadly lost his life serving his country. Being an only child it was an especially sad loss for his parents. A good cross-section of immigrants, French and English in our little town proudly served their country. When Mr Hill, Principal of the High School, also went off to war he was replaced by Miss Quinlan. It was Miss Quinlan who, when she heard Father pulled me out of school at the end of Grade 11 to attend Shaw's Business School in Toronto, admonished Father and told him he must bring me back to complete Grade 12 as I was their top student. He disregarded the advice, of course. Many years later I regretted not informing the teachers I admired so much, Miss Quinlan being one, that I completed my undergraduate studies at York U, BA, BSW 1979 and graduate studies when I was awarded a Fellowship at University of Toronto, MSW 1984. They were the wonderful dedicated group of teachers who planted the seed, taught, guided and encouraged and inspired the little immigrant girl so many years before to believe that she could do it!

When war ended and Mr Hill returned, Miss Quinlan sadly was downgraded. A not uncommon outcome in those days.

Prior to entering High School both Hope and I had our first summer job working in a bakery in Unionville. We would meet every morning at 5.30 and walk together in the dark, a perilous journey as it meant passing the local dump where bears were known to rummage for scraps. We'd arrive at the bakeshop eager to help Steve the baker. Within a week we became adept at slicing bread by machine and wrapping and stacking the loaves on racks. Our last jobs before returning home, around four o'clock in the afternoon, were to grease all the pans for next day's baking and scrub the bakery floor. For our labour we received a free delicious lunch cooked by Steve the baker, a dollar a day and all the bread we wanted to take home.

Within two weeks Steve taught us to slice and weigh the dough after which he would knead it, shape it, score the top of French sticks and push them into the oven on long paddles. That first job taught us discipline, responsibility and also a valuable skill. Great lessons at such a tender age. Prior to the bakery job the main source of income came from babysitting which earned us twenty-five cents and perhaps an apple, or housecleaning which consisted of tidying up, sweeping each room with a broom and using a pail of soapy water and a rag mop to wash the kitchen and bathroom floors. The reward for a day's work was between seventy-five cents to a dollar – an almost Dickensian regimen – but we were eager to earn anything.

CHAPTER 8

As I reflect on the short period, twelve years, spent in Smooth Rock Falls, although annual visits continued until my parents retired in 1966, I am amazed and most grateful for the cultural diversity that surrounded me growing up.

Forced by circumstance to learn two additional languages Ukrainian and English by the age of seven, seems like a daunting task in itself, but even more so when you consider we also adopted and practiced the social customs and habits of each culture as well as our own – Hungarian.

Our social life included attendance at Ukrainian weddings, Christmas celebrations and New Year's traditions where we learned Ukrainian songs and dances and enjoyed delicious Ukrainian food. It was easy to become acculturated.

Similarly, because there were only a few Hungarians,

mostly single men until much later, the few gathered together and attended summer picnics in Driftwood, twelve miles away where there was a larger Hungarian population. The outdoors was magically transformed to resemble a Hungarian village. Many of the young people would dress in their traditional brightly embroidered costumes for the occasion, with ribbons on their hair. The men donned high boots and sheepskin vests. They constructed a large platform for dancing and the musicians, mostly with violins, accordions and their beloved cimbalom (xylophone), would play tirelessly until after sundown. Mother made us lovely organza tiered, ruffled dresses to wear on these occasions. The day was spent dancing the *csarda* and waltzes and singing beautiful Hungarian melodies, while the younger children joined hands and danced in circles. It was so heartening to see Mother dancing and singing and thoroughly enjoying herself. She was enlivened by the music and dancing which probably brought back sweet memories of her youth in Szakasz.

At sundown we sat at long tables to enjoy wonderful Hungarian cuisine and pastries, returning home after dark tired but happy. Mother's distant cousin Margit and her husband Joe would take us there for Father rarely, if ever, attended. A few Polish and Ukrainian people living in Driftwood also attended these festivities, the most renowned being 'Big Joe Verbowski' a well know Polish bachelor who was loved by all for his generous and good deeds. He also had a keen eye for beautiful women. We made several lasting friends during the celebrations – the Toth family (Turos Basci) who came to Smooth Rock selling his cottage cheese, cream and garden produce. Kalman Toth, his handsome son, who I had a secret crush on, also joined the Canadian army and took part in the ill-fated raid on Dieppe, which thankfully he survived but with a badly injured leg. I received several letters from him from Overseas and a beautiful porcelain be-flowered necklace but the pen pal romance died quite suddenly when he married a young English lass and soon after became a father!

Our other memorable social event was our annual vacation time visiting my godparents, the Rists, in Timmins, Ontario. Mari Rist was one of Mother's childhood friends who emigrated with her husband, a gold miner, and daughter, Mary, two years before us. Their son, Michael, was born in Timmins. Mother and Mari were like schoolgirls at their first reunion laughing and crying as they recalled old memories. We loved visiting Timmins because it was, to us, a big city full of adventure and new things to see. We had our first family photograph taken there to send to relatives in Szakasz and Sao Paulo. We also took the opportunity to visit Szuszi-neni and little Szuszi in their new home on each visit. The Rists would spend their annual vacation in Smooth Rock with us. We shared wonderful times together. It was our godmother who sent us beautiful dolls each Christmas and little ribbon headbands that we loved so much.

While living in Toronto I was able to visit my godfather in Sunnybrook Hospital before he died in the early 50's and my godmother in St Michael's Hospital where she died in the late 60's. Michael died tragically at age twenty-three and only Mary and her two sons survive in Timmins.

In order to be able to communicate with my beloved *Nagymama* I decided to learn to write Hungarian. That took at least two years and I can't tell you how thrilled grandmother was to receive my first letter. I also wrote letters in Hungarian to my maternal grandparents the Zvoniks whom I had never met. Photographs and letters kept coming and going, keeping us in touch with our loved ones. My brother-in-law, Gerald Flaherty, Helen's husband, attended a General Counsel conference in Sao Paulo and accompanied by a young lawyer who spoke both English and Portuguese visited my Mother's family. They welcomed him like the prodigal son, covered him with kisses and were overjoyed to meet him. In 1985 on a Varig flight to Costa Rica, I met a young Brazilian student attending University of Toronto (my Alma Mater) and in the course of our conversation I mentioned that I had many relatives in Sao Paulo whom I had never met but that we communicate by letter. She asked me where they resided and when I showed her my Aunt's address she said she lived just one block away. I excitedly wrote a letter to my Aunt which the young student delivered personally.

To my surprise and delight a reply was waiting for me on my return to Canada. It is a small world after all!

Mother's parents and siblings eventually died, she outliving all of them died at age eighty-two. Regarding Father's parents, his father died at age sixty and *Nagymama* at eighty-nine. His two siblings are both gone and Father, who died at ninety-three, predeceased his younger brother, Bela, who died a few years after him. Unfortunately I do not keep in touch with either family presently although I think about them often. Family ties break easily if effort is lacking.

My memories of those days are that I lived in a global village going back and forth between languages and cultures. However, as I entered High School things began to shift. Hope and I dropped our native languages and also various customs and habits and thought of ourselves as only Canadians and really proud Canadians at that. I remember feeling totally integrated. Close friends included Joy Piper, Martha and Nancy Cairns, Myrtle Richmond and Thelma Richards, all affiliated with the Public and High schools.

Our world really opened up when Mother, my sister and I spent one summer visiting distant cousins Margit and Joe Csuka and little Margie who moved to Ottawa street in Hamilton, Ontario from Smooth Rock. Margit-nene, Mother's second cousin came to Smooth Rock as a young woman of eighteen to marry Joe when we lived in Hollywood. They married in Cochrane and a small wedding reception was held in our home after the ceremony. After a short time they purchased a little home in Mooreville where little Margie (my parents' godchild) was born. We stayed with them and spent the summer picking fruit in Stoney Creek which paid for our train fare and keep. In Hamilton I remember being intrigued by the busy city streets and the lovely huge trees, elms and maples which did not grow in the North. It was in Hamilton that I received my first kiss. The Kurpe's who owned the house Margit-nene rented lived in the downstairs section with their young teenage son Joey. We were pals and one evening on the verandah he suddenly kissed me on the lips without warning. I was stunned but also delighted until he went into a soliloquy not unlike a Clarke Gable movie – now you might be the right girl for me or maybe not, only time will tell – and I thought – all this after just one innocent kiss? Our paths never crossed again but I learned many years later that he married and formed his own electrical business so he obviously set off a spark somewhere.

Mother always enjoyed working, particularly outdoors picking fruit. I think it reminded her of happy times working in her vineyards in Szakasz. The second summer in Smooth Rock and for many years after we would go berry picking wild strawberries and raspberries which she would preserve for winter. On one of these occasions as she stood up to move to a more prolific patch she saw a long green garter snake on a reed, panicked, dropped her berries and we both scurried away fast. We also made an excursion to Nellie Lake with friends to pick blueberries. This time we encountered a real threat when she spotted a big black bear several feet away gazing at us lazily. She quickly grabbed my hand and her basket of blueberries as we made a quick exit. Obviously the bear was well fed and disinterested in feasting on us. We never again returned to Nellie Lake for blueberries!

The next year Margit-nene and Joe, a very hard working and ambitious couple purchased a tobacco farm in Tillsonburg, Ontario and again invited us to come and help harvest tobacco. On this trip we happily discovered an extension of the Tarcza family who also had a tobacco farm in Vanessa, Ontario. It was exciting to meet Emma and Charlie and their childrenJohn, Joe and Margaret and watch the family circle widen. Mother and I were tiers and handlers in the tobacco industry. It was hard work entailing long hours. At the end of the day our hands would be covered with a thick, sticky residue from the tobacco leaves and required a special solution to remove.

I found the Hungarians here warm and welcoming but a tightly knit group who maintained their culture which centred around their church and the Hungarian Hall where social events like weddings and other celebrations took place. There was no real need for the older generation to master or speak English so they didn't. Many of the younger generation, however, maintained their language and customs, but also spoke fluent English, attained university degrees and had professions reflecting this. Others chose to continue with the family tradition of tobacco farming purchasing their own farms and through hard work accumulating considerable wealth. Margit-neni and Joe eventually owned three tobacco farms but sadly Joe died in his fifties of a massive stroke. Like so many immigrants hard work and striving for him was a mantra.

The following year Mother and Helen went South without me for I was fortunate enough to acquire a summer job, with the help of my good friend Joy Piper, at the local Mercantile store in the grocery department. I had just completed grade eleven plus two grade twelve subjects successfully, still jitterbugging, bowling and playing tennis and my guitar for recreation. Hope was still my best friend and she talked about becoming a nurse one day. I, on the other hand, had no set plans except to complete grade twelve and decide my future then. It turned out that I didn't need to as Father came home from work one evening and announced in a stern voice, "well my dear, I've decided that in September you are going with Thelma Richards to attend Shaw's Business School in Toronto. Chief Richards will drive you both and you will live at the Stokal's (a former neighbour who moved to Toronto where their son Dan was to attend University and where they bought a large rooming house on Madison Ave.). You will study bookkeeping and secretarial work and come back and get a good paying job at the Mill Office." I was shocked to say the least, shocked into silence as Mother was away and I had no one to discuss my feelings (mostly fear and trepidation) with. In those days it never occurred to me to be anything but compliant. Parents knew best and therefor were obeyed. Many years passed before I even questioned Father's authoritative behaviour for I knew he thought he was acting in my best interest. I reasoned my way out of panic by reminding myself that I already had visited Hamilton and knew and enjoyed the big city atmosphere. I would also be with Thelma whom I knew and liked. Lastly, we would be living at Mrs Stokal's who was a dear friend and former neighbour. The icing on the cake was that Hope who had already completed grade twelve said she had applied for a job in Toronto at The Home for Incurable Children on Bloor Street where she would work until she turned eighteen at which point she would start her nursing training. So we would continue our friendship in Toronto. With all these assurances I felt less fearful of what lay ahead. Now the only task remaining was to await the return of Mother and Helen and break the sad/happy news to them about my imminent departure away from my beloved family and home town at age seventeen.

Mother and Helen returned from their summer sojourn in the tobacco fields and I tearfully told them the story of Father's well planned itinerary for my future. Initially Mother was shocked and very upset but then agreed with Father that it was the right thing to do. It would provide me with training for a good-paying office job when I returned. We gathered together my limited wardrobe – three skirts, a couple of blouses and sweaters and my pride and joy, a green tweed suit which I had ordered from Simpson's Catalogue and paid for with my own money, also a pair of leather shoes, some running shoes, winter clothing and boots. It all fit into one large suitcase. Departure day Saturday in the first week of September, 1945, was memorable. Mother prepared enough food for a starving army. She said there would be ample for Thelma and her father also. We set off with Thelma and I in the back seat and her father, police Chief Richards, driving. I was seventeen, Thelma a year older and we felt both sad leaving our families but excited about the prospects of going to the large city. After tearful goodbyes we were on our way.

And what a journey it was! Five hundred miles give or take and Police Chief Richards' car was no Cadillac. For ten hours we bumped along with a couple of toilet stops along the way . . . and to stretch our legs and eat something. But we made it.

Mrs Stokal, a former neighbour back in Smooth Rock, now to be our landlady in Toronto, waited to greet us – covering me with kisses.

After a quick catch-up on local news came the grand tour of our new 'home' away from home. A spacious room on the second floor, to be shared, with twin beds, two dressers, two desks and two chairs – somewhat spartan but we'd soon change that. From a large bay window we looked down on a beautiful maple tree, just changing into its fall colour.

Mrs Stokal had made her basement into a welcoming kitchen cum dining area, to be shared by all tenants. A large refrigerator, sink, ample dishes, utensils, pots and pans made sure we could eat well. A dining table and chairs completed the suite. For all this we each paid $3 a week – in advance!

Police Chief Richards liked what he saw for Thelma and me and happily motored the five hundred miles back to Smooth Rock Falls the following day.

Thelma and I soon settled in and eagerly prepared for the start of our new life, to begin with a year at Shaw's Business School on Charles Street.

CHAPTER 9

I was soon entrenched in my secretary/book-keeping class which included penmanship taught by the Principal, Mr Eccles, and rapid calculation, to sharpen our brains. I found the workload easy and it wasn't long before I excelled in short-hand and typing.

At the end of the month my cheque arrived covering my allowance for tuition, room and board. Thelma and I decided to go downtown to Eaton's to celebrate our first month in the big city. As we stopped at the candy counter we agreed the fudge looked too good to resist. So I pulled out my eighty dollars in twenty dollar bills and handed the cashier a twenty and after enjoying our first mouthful of fudge realized I had only one twenty dollar bill in my hand, the rest was gone. We panicked, looked behind and beside us but the money was gone. We later told our two friends Flo Allen and Helen Swartz, who shared a room next to ours. They were city girls and seemed more worldly than we small town girls. They quickly gave me good counsel. "Don't tell your parents, it'll only worry them. Come with us to the Barker Biscuit Company on Davenport, where we worked every week-night to make extra money. We will make sure the Supervisor hires you and you will soon make up the money you lost. One could not ask for better friends, they were so supportive and helpful. So each evening I returned from School at 4pm, cooked and ate my dinner and by 6pm were at our jobs at the biscuit company. I was placed on the assembly line beside a moving conveyor where various cookies would come down and quickly grab enough to fill a box, usually twelve, then place them back on the conveyor. Then the next group of girls would seal, label and stack them. On the second night cookies were replaced by lemon and apple pies. The girls quietly whispered to me that each night one of us would accidentally dint the meringue or crust so they could have it for coffee break. Only perfect pies were packed and sent away.

I found myself quite adept at packaging the cookies and later dinting the occasional pie when necessary. There were many shared giggles so night-work became fun and enjoyable. I saved the money I lost in two weeks but continued to work there until almost graduation time. I also opened a bank account at Royal Bank of Canada.

Thelma didn't fare as well and one day in typing class she broke down with frustration, banged the keys of her typewriter and announced she hated Shaw's Business School and particularly hated typing. Some years later she returned to Toronto and trained as a nurse at Toronto General Hospital. I was now alone in my little room on Madison Avenue where I often cried myself to sleep because I missed my family so much. Thanks to dear Mrs Stokal my rent remained at $3 a week and Mother never found out about the money I lost until many years later. It taught a very important lesson as I've been careful with money ever since.

One weekend just before Christmas I received a telephone call from Boris, a classmate from Smooth Rock Falls, who moved with his parents to Toronto, inviting me to go to a movie with him. Having no social life I eagerly agreed. After the movie and a cup of coffee at the Varsity Restaurant he walked me home and as he said goodnight suddenly embraced me and gave me a serious kiss on the lips. Being an inexperienced dater I suddenly broke into laughter as I always thought of him as a brother because our mothers were close friends. Boris never called me again and I had pangs of guilt for my lack of social graces – but life goes on.

On registration day at Shaw's I met a delightful young man, Jim Morrison, and we became fast friends taking several classes together. One day in typing class he told me that there was a young man who used to live in Cochrane, forty miles from my home town, and that if I agreed he would introduce us. Excited by the news I agreed to the meeting. The next day he approached me with his friend sheepishly behind him. I was astounded to see that it was the 'older looking' moustached, though handsome, man who had been winking flirtatiously at me for weeks when we passed in the hallways. I never responded, only thought to myself, why is that older moustached man winking at me? Then there he was wanting an introduction to me. Jim dutifully introduced us as two northerners which was about the only thing we had in common. Before long Joe Hawkins, ex Flying Officer RCAF, who had just returned from active duty in Europe was walking me home to Madison Avenue after school each day. Never did I dream that the moustached Cassanova would in the near future become my husband.

About two months before graduation I decided to stop work at the Barker Biscuit factory and answered an ad for a part-time job typing and book-keeping for Simlovitch Furriers on Bloor Street. It would be an asset in my cv when I applied for a full-time job after graduation. I was hired after the interview and worked there every weekday afternoon from four to six and all day Saturday. I brought their books up to date, typed required correspondence and answered the telephone. On Saturday's Mr Simlovitch had me model fur coats and mink stoles for prospective customers. If they purchased the fur I found a bonus in my weekly pay check. It was after this experience that I decided to take a modelling course at Central Tech, not with any intention of becoming a model but to improve my posture, appearance and grooming. It was considered a self-improvement course. For weeks we would walk with books on our head, eventually turning our heads from side to side, walking down staircases gracefully and even learn to enter and leave automobiles in a graceful fashion. It was great fun when the books flew off our head at the first attempt. It was after the modelling that I decided to take swimming lessons, that I failed miserably, then substituted sewing lessons that proved to be most prudent and beneficial.

Hope arrived in Toronto late October excited about beginning her training as a caregiver at the Home for Incurable Children at 152 Bloor Street East, an institution created for the care of chronically ill or physically disabled children.

First established in 1907 the growth and evolution of

this renowned institution is nothing short of remarkable. In 1899 twenty-two women calling themselves the Women's Committee, headed by their president Mrs C S Gzowski, decided there's a great need for such a facility. Interestingly, eighteen of the twenty-two women were also the founding members of the Hospital for Sick Children on University Avenue They opened their first home for incurable children at 138 Avenue Road thanks to the generosity of sponsors Mr & Mrs G A Cox. That residence housed fifteen children.

The Bloor Street residence, where Hope worked, housed twenty-six children and in 1921 services were increased in conjunction with the school board to full-day classes for the residents. In 1930 the nurses residence, previously on Jarvis Street, was added where Hope lived.

In the 1950's, through the generosity of Mrs Emma Vincent Campbell, expansion included a move to 350 Rumsey Road where the Ontario Crippled Children's Centre was built, housing forty residents with a major increase in services including rehabilitation, counselling and internships for the professional training of personnel through affiliation with the University of Toronto.

From 1959 to 1975 names of the institution included Bloorview Hospital, Home and School and Bloorview Children's Hospital. In the mid-1980's the Crippled Children's Centre was renamed the Hugh MacMillan Medical Centre, named after its highly revered administrator Dr Hugh MacMillan. With the participation of charities such as the Easter Seal Society, Variety Children's Charity and Christie Street Hospital by the 1980's the final and present location was at 150 Gilgour Road and named Holland Bloorview Kid's Rehabilitation Hospital. Services now included respite care for parents of disabled children and life-skills and independence training programs to prepare young adults to live independently in their communities.

Besides having dear friend Hope as one of the early staff members there's yet another connection with this amazing organization that I have.

In 1966 my sister-in-law's young niece, Myrna Blair, age five, of Packenham, Ontario had a most tragic accident. Living on a working farm she lay in the tall grass, arms outstretched waiting for her beloved uncle running a threshing machine to approach so she could jump up and surprise him. Sadly little Myrna was still lying down with arms outstretched when the machine ran over her severing both arms at the elbow. It was a horrifying and heartbreaking time for Myrna, her family and extended family. Indeed for the community.

The next ten years were spent trying to rehabilitate her and normalize her life. It was during one of these period that she stayed at our home in Thornhill and attended the rehab services at the Ontario facility on Rumsey Road.

A sweet bright child full of life and love, Myrna was fitted with prosthetic arms, not nearly as sophisticated as the are now. With every movement it would make a whirring sound and as she played with our pet kitten it sprang from her arms when it heard the whirring. Little Myrna immediately removed the artificial arms and continued to play with the kitten. After a week of rehab, assured she would adjust with time to wearing the prostheses, she returned to her home in Packenham.

Myrna did adjust miraculously well but never wore the prosthesis again as children at school would make fun of her. She learned to write in her own special way, with pencil wedged between the side of her cheek and stump of her arm becoming an accomplished writer. In her late teens she was living independently with a few hours of essential daily services from a care-giver, in her own home, a gift from a sympathetic sponsor in Western Canada who read about her plight and willed her estate to her. Another example of the generosity of the Canadian heart in times of need.

I marvel at Myrna's courage and determination not to be defeated. At one point she was even Drawing cartoons for the TV series 'The Racoons'. She is presently living in a Senior's Residence, not idly but answering telephones and helping seniors in other ways – a noble spirit and a tender heart! She could have wallowed in self-pity but chose instead to greet the world and embrace it.

CHAPTER 10

In my usual fashion, I worked diligently, excelled at shorthand and typing and passed all other required subjects to graduate with a diploma from Shaw's Business College. Many students decided to leave as soon as they passed shorthand and typing but Father insisted I stay until graduation with the diploma in hand, which I did after a year's attendance. Joe and I continued to date but the relationship remained platonic with a movie and dinner dates on the weekend. I scoured the ads in the newspapers for employment and finally was successful in getting an interview with the T H McDonald Machine Company on Bay Street. Mr McDonald, the owner, was an elderly man, somewhat gruff and serious. I thought the interview went very well but failed to get the job of secretary/bookkeeper. However, present at the interview was a tall handsome gentleman who kept smiling at me encouragingly to counteract the gruffness of the Owner. He was Paul R Scott.

Disappointed to hear I didn't get the job I continued my search through the ads. Two days later I received a telephone call from Paul Scott who reminded me he was present at the interview and impressed with my qualifications. He stated he was in the process of forming his own company for the sale of new and used machinery, with offices at 159 Bay Street. Would I be interested in working for him? If so we could set up an appointment and meet at a restaurant on Bay Street. I agreed to meet as we set the date, place and time – the following Saturday. Since

it was a rather unconventional appointment I told my good friend Myrtle, from Smooth Rock days, recently discharged from the WRENS, and asked if she would accompany me to the appointment. However, we would enter and sit separately. We had signals arranged whereby if the meeting was legitimate she would finish her coffee and leave meeting later at the streetcar stop on Bay. If on the other hand there were difficulties I would signal and she would come to our table and say it was time to go. Of course, the appointment was legit, Mr Scott was who he said he was and happily I got the job as secretary/bookkeeper and office manager. Mr Scott would be absent frequently buying and selling machinery. My starting salary was $22 a week with a 20% bonus at Christmas – an incentive to stay on no doubt. I was to start in a week's time.

Very excited at having a permanent job with good pay I felt uplifted and Myrtle and I went shopping to find suitable office clothes. My main purchase was a grey wool two-piece suit and black platform shoes with high heels.

I was now living on Dalton Street, north of Bloor, where I had a larger room with an attached kitchenette on the main floor. I immediately sent a letter home to my parents that I would soon be independent with a wonderful job to go to five days a week. Apart from being disappointed that I was not to return to Smooth Rock Falls they were happy for me. A week later, early Monday morning, dressed in my businesslike suit and high heels I set off on the Bloor then Bay St streetcars, arrived a half hour early, eager to start work. We were situated on the tenth floor in a suite of three offices facing east. Mine was the outer office, quite spacious where I would work and greet customers. The large inner office, occupied by Mr Scott, had large windows facing east. I recall taking dictation watching the Gooderham & Worts neon sign flashing in the twilight. The third room was for prospective salesmen in the near future.

As I reflect about my first full-time job I think how fortunate I was to get it. The average salary for a position of this type was between $16 and $18 weekly, with no bonus attached. The position was a responsible one especially with Mr Scott being away so much, which put me in charge. It consisted of diverse duties from shorthand typing and accounting to dealing with customers in a courteous and efficient manner, which meant acquiring a basic knowledge of machinery, its uses and its availability. Being only eighteen I never-the-less embraced it with great confidence. I felt I could do it and, with hard work and preparation, do it well. This, by the way, would become a consistent pattern in my life whether it was fund raising for my church, taking art lessons or studying for my under-graduate and graduate degrees. Yet I was a complete failure when it came to learning to swim – well not quite, as I did learn eventuality to float on my back.

I soon developed a routine and rhythm that made working a great pleasure. Before the end of the year I had memorized over two hundred telephone numbers that made life easier. Since he had no need of extra salesmen yet, Mr Scott rented the extra office to Formosa Breweries Ltd headed by Mr C C Craig. I was responsible for his correspondence and answered incoming phone-calls in his absence. I was generously rewarded for this extra work. I got $15 a week from him – that made my grand total for the week – $37, plus 20% bonus at Christmas! I was over the moon.

Occasionally my secretarial duties included taking Mr Scott's shirts to the laundry during my lunch break and retrieving them when ready. The women's liberation movement was far into the future so I felt no resentment as secretaries would today. It made Mr Scott's busy life a bit easier. In that era it was what secretaries did. Within a year or two salesmen were hired as business was successful and lucrative with tons of post-war and new machinery available and in demand. I remained with Paul R Scott Ltd until May 1949. No pregnancy leave programs existed at that time.

CHAPTER 11

In my personal life, my relationship with Joe Hawkins became more serious, so much so that he decided to introduce me to his married sister Alma who resided with her husband in a spacious apartment near High Park. I was rather amused to hear her calling him Preston (his second name) instead of Joe. Apparently the pro-Hawkins half of the family called him Joe and the other half called him Preston. This pattern of divisiveness was quite prevalent in his family as I was to find out later.

Dating in the forties included a movie, dining out or on special occasions dancing to the big band sounds. Favourite dance venues included the renowned Masonic Hall at the corner of Davenport and Yonge where both men and women would attend alone with hopes of meeting a dancing companion, or perhaps even a life-companion. I was never daring enough to go alone for the lineup of 'girls' waiting to be asked to dance, as the boys looked them over (often passing them by completely), seems too intimidating to me. Other favourite dance places included the Palaise Pier, near Sunnyside, and the Embassy Club on Bloor street.

I abstained from drinking as the legal age for drinking was twenty-one and I was only eighteen and strictly adhered to the law. It wasn't until 1971 that the drinking age was lowered to eighteen. Prohibition, in existence since 1916, ended in 1927 when the Liquor Control Board of Ontario (LCBO) was formed and a permit was required to purchase alcoholic beverages. The Ontario government kept a report of each purchaser's name, address and quantity consumed. In 1934 hotels were allowed to sell beer and wine with meals. It wasn't until 1969 that LCBO became self-served and the permits were scrapped. By 1981 drinking on one's patio became legal. I often questioned whether the regulations deterred excessive drinking or rather served as a control mechanism by officialdom.

In July 1946 I said a tearful goodbye to Hope who was now eighteen and leaving to begin her training as a Registered Nurse (R.N.) at Peterborough Civic Hospital. I missed her terribly but didn't seem to have difficulty meeting and developing new friendships, with women especially. One of these close friendships was with Dorothy Graham, of Shaw days, who lived with her widowed mother and young brother on Walmer Road in a large three story home, which sometimes became my home away from home. She became my closest friend particularly when Joe, dissatisfied with his job in Toronto after graduation (his salary was less than mine!), decided to accept a position as Chief Accountant with Toledo Scales in Windsor, Ontario. Although we corresponded regularly I often felt lonely and missed our weekend outings. Never-the-less I was overly cautious about casual pick-ups that occurred more on streets than in bars in those days.

One of these chance encounters happened when a handsome young man, Bert Drexler, started a conversation with me at our local library. After a few weeks he asked if I was interested in dating and I quickly replied I was already in a relationship but I had a girlfriend who might be interested. After checking with Dorothy she gave me permission to pass on her telephone number to Bert. Before long they were dating and eventuality married.

Christmas of 1946 I spent a week's vacation with my family in Smooth Rock. The overnight train ride brought back memories of the first long journey with my Mother in 1933. I was excited about my recent purchase, the first significant gift I would give to Mother and Father. A forty-four piece set of Johnson Brothers porcelain china dinnerware, cream coloured with a border of light green covered with a beautiful floral pattern. A final touch, a delicate gold trim on each piece. The only dishes my parents had all these years was a set of white Ironstone included with the purchase of a used dining room table and hutch purchased on our arrival in Canada. My parents were now living in a larger, four bedroom house located in an area called the 'Town Site', more centrally and conveniently located to all amenities.

As I disembarked from the famous Mattagami Railway coach just before noon, suitcase in hand I was pleasantly surprised to see two taxi cabs waiting to drive passengers to their destinations (signs of progress in the old town); but Mother was there with our close friend, Mary Purvis, who drove us the short distance home. Mary (Dubas) our former neighbour in Frenchtown was a few years older than me and had also attended Shaw's Business College in Toronto, stayed at Mrs Stokal's but after graduating chose to return to Smooth Rock and work at the Mill office. That is where she met and married John Purvis and settled in Smooth Rock until retirement many years later.

How exciting it was to visit with my parents as an independent 'almost adult' daughter, laden with gifts for all purchased with my 20% bonus at Christmas. Many surprises awaited me as we entered their new house. One was a new GE refrigerator in the spacious kitchen with an attached pantry. Also a new dining-room suite in dark oak with a large table, eight chairs with black leather seats and a lovely long matching buffet with ample room for the new set of dinnerware they were about to receive. The cosy living room had a lovely maroon velour sofa with two easy chairs. A large new Axminster carpet covered the floor.

The only familiar pieces were two wooden semi-circled end tables, a floor lamp and the reliable old floor model Stewart Warner radio which kept us in touch with the outside world.

After the excitement of our reunion and tour of the new house I could sense from Mother's demeanour that all was not well in their home. The next day she confided in me that Father had taken to serious gambling, a favourite pastime with men in the north country and had lost considerable sums of money that she had saved in hopes of buying their retirement home. He was also staying out until two and three in the morning and could be at risk of losing his job. The stress was playing havoc with Mom's ulcer which undoubtedly added to her misery. I tried to comfort her and said I would talk to Father. I wondered at the time, "how did these two dear souls end up together? They are so different." I would find the answer to my elusive question some twenty years later.

A brighter side of this saga was that Mother was at last fully integrated into her little community, was an active member of the Women's Catholic League, attended church regularly and even bowled in a mixed ten-pin bowling league with Father once a week. She had many new friends, French and English, to socialize with. Her warm personality and her determination seemingly helped her overcome the many hurdles in her life. Despite the stressful periods I thoroughly enjoyed being with my family and seeing my little sister again. The dishes and other gifts were greatly appreciated and we had a wonderful Christmas celebration.

Prior to my departure to Toronto, being eighteen, I was now officially allowed to date Ken, a High School friend whom I admired secretly from afar. After a pleasant and most enjoyable evening visiting mutual friends he drove me home and kissed me good-night (and good-bye) under the bright porch light that Mother (always a step ahead of us) kept burning when I, and later my sister, Helen, were dating. Competing with the porch light and totally outshining and obliterating it the magnificent Northern Lights created a wonderful spectacle of dancing waves of bright green light across the night sky. The high white snow banks were magically transformed into glistening banks of emeralds. A perfect setting for falling in love – but I didn't because my heart was elsewhere. Many years later studying art in Belleville and recalling this incident I produced a canvas depicting Northern Lights on a winter night. It was chosen a prize winner. Fond memories don't always fade away but often return to haunt us or please us in most unexpected ways.

Before my departure I also found an opportunity to have a quiet talk with Father explaining to him the effect his excessive gambling and loss of money was having on Mother's health. Typically, he immediately became defensive and denied there was any problem. He also assured me everything was under control and I shouldn't worry. However, his destructive behaviour continued and stopped only when he brought the family to the brink of tragic disaster a few years later.

I spent the remainder of the holiday using Mother's Singer sewing machine to make a pink chiffon formal gown, with sequinned trim around the neck and sleeves, to wear to a New Year's Eve celebration with Joe at Toronto's Club Kingsway – never suspecting it would become a very special and memorable occasion in my life!

The week long visit flew by quickly and we said our tearful goodbyes. Mother packed the customary bagged lunch for the return trip which unfortunately still remained in her hand as the train pulled away on its three mile journey. At the Junction I boarded the Ontario Northland railway to Toronto. Riding the Northland was never boring. This time it was packed with children, students and adults of diverse nationalities, French, English and immigrants. Since the trip was overnight people would often break into song to be joined by others forming a spontaneous choir. There was a jumble of languages to be heard, much laughter and frivolity, even a tipple or two, making the twelve hour trip seem shorter than it was.

CHAPTER 12

The Ontario Northland Railway has a colourful history beginning in 1902 when the Temiskaming and Northern Ontario Railway Commission (TNORC), an agency of the Ontario government, was mandated to oversee the construction and operation of the Temiskaming and Northern Ontario Railway (T&NO). The 253 mile line stretched from North Bay to Cochrane and was built to encourage development and settlement of this region of the province. As a result massive silver deposits at Cobalt and gold at Timmins and Kirkland Lake were discovered.

By 1921 the TNORC extended the railway north from Cochrane to the shores of James Bay and Moosanee where the last spike was driven in 1932. It eventuality extended service into western Quebec's gold and copper deposits in Rouyn and Noranda. In 1937 the mandate of TNORC was amended to also include buses, trucks and aircraft for transportation. To encourage further development Ontario Hydro built power plants in Island Falls and Frazerdale.

In 1946 the railway's name was changed to Ontario Northland Railway and subsequently to Northland Transportation. Under its new mandate the Commission included boats, hotels, tourist resorts and restaurants in its holdings. By 1960 they added bus service and a regional airline called NorOntair serving the North Bay-Timmins-Hearst region. The airline folded in 1996.

On March 23, 2012 the Ontario government announced the beginning of the end of ONTC due to decreased ridership, replacing the railway service with additional buses. Assets of the Corporation will eventually be sold off. Thus the end of the golden age of northern railways and its illustrious history of contribution to the development, settlement and ensuing wealth of the Province will come to an end. I think I speak for all northerners when I say memories of Ontario Northland Railways will always have a special place in our hearts.

Despite my nostalgic and fond memories of growing up in Smooth Rock I realized after my Christmas visit that I made the right decision not to return to live there. After enjoying the freedom, openness and stimulation of city life I found Smooth Rock Falls very confining, although most enjoyable to visit.

Furthermore the city was full of promise and

opportunity in terms of realizing my long-term goal of continuing my education.

I returned to Toronto to welcome in the New Year with Joe at Club Kingsway dancing to the music of bandleader Ozzie Williams, renowned for his two songs, 'Sunday in Toronto' and 'The Subway Song' with lyrics by Betty Carr and Charles Baldour. dressed in my home made pink chiffon sequinned dress with silver platform shoes and silver bag to match we danced the night away and celebrated with the usual hoof rah as the clock struck twelve. After the midnight kiss and Auld Lang Syne Joe thoroughly surprised me by pulling a velvet box from his pocket and presenting me with a diamond sparkler. Of course I accepted it and the proposal as we danced the last dance to the romantic strains of 'I love you for sentimental reasons'. Joe's plan was to return to Toronto by June having then spent a year working in Windsor.

Elated by my new status 'engaged to be married' I

immediately spread the good news to family and friends and of course to Mr Scott my employer. Congratulations and good wishes were gratefully received with a stern warning from my parents that I should not marry immediately but wait until I was at least twenty – good advice most thankfully received. I also shared the good news with my beloved Nagymama, writing to her in Hungarian and sending her pictures of Joe and me and other family members. Mother also excitedly informed her family in Brazil. We kept in close touch with each other the only way we could, through correspondence.

By mid-year Paul R Scott Ltd hired its first salesman increasing my workload substantially as business was booming. Joe returned to Toronto and accepted a position as Chief Accountant with a roofing company in Weston and shared an apartment in the Yonge/College area with a friend from Shaw days.

I also moved to new accommodation. Contacted by two friends from Smooth Rock Falls inviting me to share a house rental on Fern Avenue in the Parkdale district. I owned no furniture so only personal effects needed to be packed. Myrtle Richmond, Martha Cairns and I renewed our friendship during a wonderful year together. By the end of our lease Myrtle married Ronald Paige in a lovely intimate wedding ceremony in which I served as her maid of honour. Martha, also engaged to be married, moved into her fiancé's home with wedding plans set for late fall. Left 'out in the cold' so to speak I looked for new accommodation and found a spacious second floor furnished flat with living-room, bedroom and kitchenette on McPherson Avenue near Yonge Street. I spent two happy years there buoyed by the friendship of a lovely elderly couple, the Cundales and their married daughter, Flossie, who lived in the lower apartment.

During this period Toronto often was referred to as 'Toronto the Good' because it was a bastion of, so called, Victorian age morality. The Lord's Day Act, promoted by various religious organizations and prohibitionists, was passed by Prime Minister Wilfred Laurier in March 1907. It restricted trade, labour and recreation on Sundays. A large segment of the population felt oppressed and confined by this law, consequently Aussie William's single 'Sundays in Toronto', a comedic criticism of 'Toronto the Good' was a huge hit. The first public bar in Toronto was the Silver Rail on Yonge Street, opened in April 1947 and the jazz greats played Massey Hall in 1954.

In 1960 the Lord's Day Act was amended to permit cultural and recreational activity, trade shows and horse racing. Toronto was gradually shedding its limited image and on its way to becoming a world class city. The Lord's Day Act was finally voided by the Supreme Court of Canada in 1985.

1947 was the year that Britain nationalized its coal mines and introduced Universal Health Care (NHS) and Mahatma Gandhi's first March for Peace began. In the United States the Truman Doctrine was introduced to fight and contain Communism, the Marshall Plan introduced to help Europe recover from World War Two. In 1947 B. F. Goodrich produced the first tubeless car tire and the microwave oven and transistor radios were invented in the U.S. 1947 was also the genesis of NBC's program 'Meet the Press' and the International Monetary Fund (IMF) was conceived to oversee the international monetary system after the Great Depression of the Thirties.

In Canada, Canadian citizenship, separate from British nationality was created in 1947, which I proudly applied for and received next year. Whipper Billy Watson defeated Longpon to become champion wrestler in 1947 and the Maple Leafs defeated Montreal for the Stanley Cup.

A year flew by quickly as I was introduced to Joe's parents and extended family so wedding plans could be announced and discussed.

It was indeed an eventful year for many of us for Joe and I set our wedding date to be Friday, November 19th, 1948. We would be married in the Church of the Redeemer at Bloor and Avenue Road, with a small reception to follow at the The Hearthstone Inn a few doors away, also on Bloor Street.

Joe, Bessie, Alma, Currie, Robert

Since most of Joe's extended family were abstainers there would be no alcoholic beverages (only fruit punch) served at the reception – rather an awkward and embarrassing situation for my side of the family. Given my Hungarian ancestry, eating, drinking and dancing were an essential part of any celebration, especially weddings. However, being so young and in love I was pliable and willingly deferred to Joe's wishes setting the stage for numerous deferrals in the future which did not bode well for a happy marriage. I went a step further. Despite being baptized a Roman Catholic as an infant in Szakasz, due to the harsh environment in the Roman Catholic church in Smooth Rock Falls I eventually became a non-practicing Roman Catholic often attending the United Church. Therefor, it seemed natural and common sensical to officially become an Anglican, Joe's religion, for our future children's sake. I attended the necessary preparatory sessions given by the Reverend Sproule at the Church of the Messiah at Avenue Road and Davenport where I was confirmed an Anglican. Mother was quite upset but reassured by dear Father

Forget, "Matilda, don't worry, because Roman Catholics and Anglicans are very similar in their beliefs." Father Forget, a great humanitarian was ecumenical before it became a buzzword in religion.

CHAPTER 13

The first meeting took place at the home of Joe's aunt, Bertha Hawkins, who had a beautiful home on Brook Avenue in the outskirts of Toronto on what was once the O'Keefe estate. During the Depression, the dirty 30's, her brother Albert, who was a builder in Edmonton, Alberta, found himself without work so she hired him to come to Toronto to build her a house, which he did. It was to be a two storey stone and brick building with three bedrooms, bathroom, living room, dining room and kitchen. He added lovely touches with African mahogany plate rails in the dining room, in the living room, a beautiful stone fireplace flanked by glassed-in book case filled with first edition books. On the mantle stood a magnificent collection of Royal Doulton Dickens characters. Centred above the mantle hung a beautiful painting of Anne Hathaway's cottage. On each side of the fireplace stood two lovely antique Chippendale fireside chairs, the floors carpeted with genuine Persian rugs.

In the dining room a lovely curved front, china cabinet was filled with a treasure trove of collectibles. Porcelain figurines such as the Blue Boy, The Dolly Sisters (Dresden china), Moorecraft china, Irish Belleek china and real old Willow dinnerware. A collector's paradise, to be sure.

The family welcomed us warmly and showered us with congratulations and good wishes. They were especially pleased I was confirmed an Anglican, as they were a religious family attending church regularly. We discussed the wedding plans and after a lovely evening including dinner, prepared by Aunt Bertha, we departed happy and content that our wedding plans were so well received.

Joe with his Father & Aunt Bertha

I was very taken with Aunts Bertha and Elizabeth, two high spirited, intelligent and very likeable women. They were both spinsters, strong minded but very approachable and fun loving.

Aunt Bertha, now age 55, and her sister, 70, grew up on the family farm on the 9th Line Carleton Place, two of nine siblings, including Joe's father Wellington. In 1911, following the death of father, Bertha age 19 and Elizabeth age 34, attended Willis Business College in Ottawa and after graduation worked for the Canadian Parliament. After WW1 Aunt Elizabeth ventured by rail to the west coast and for several years settled in British Columbia where she started a business buying households of furniture and reselling it at a profit. When the east beckoned a few years later, she moved back to Toronto where she rented a large three storey house at 574 Sherborne Street and operated a very successful rooming house until she retired in her seventies. Sadly, Aunt Elizabeth died in 1956, age 80, and is buried beside her twin sister Martha in Carelton Place Cemetery.

Aunt Bertha, enjoying her work as a secretary with a Toronto legal firm, decided she would like to advance further and become a lawyer. Her first attempt was futile as she was told women were not considered persons under the BNA Act of 1867 and therefor could not become lawyers or serve in the Senate. This judgement, that women were not considered persons, was contested by the 'Famous Five', sometimes known as the 'Valiant Five' who fought so courageously for women's rights and whose commemorative statue stands on Parliament Hill, Ottawa. The judgement was finally overturned by the Privy Council on October 18th, 1929 and is referred to as "The Person's Case"! The radical change engendered by the Privy Council in its approach to the Canadian Constitution is also referred to as the "Living Tree Doctrine". Clarissa Brett Martin was called to the Ontario Bar in 1897, while Annie MacDonald Langstaff, the first woman graduate at McGill, was excluded from the

Québec Bar until 1941, performed legal administrative work during her long wait.

Aunt Bertha prevailed, applied again to Osgoode Hall, successfully graduated and was called to the Bar November 18th., 1926. She joined the law firm of Malone, Malone and Montgomery of which she became a full partner in 1943 and where she worked until retirement in her mid-seventies. She was awarded a QC in the latter part of her career, a propitious journey from a one room school house in rural Ontario to the Halls of Justice in our great country. But Aunt Bertha's largesse encompassed more than her profession as you will discover in coming chapters.

CHAPTER 14

————

I excitedly telephoned Mother to discuss our wedding plans and despite her effort to sound happy I detected an underlying sadness in her voice. Due to the close bond between us (we spent the first five years of my life together), we had an uncanny ability to detect the real emotion beyond the façade with each other. As I prodded further she confessed she was very worried about father's continued gambling, which was now an addiction and he spent increasingly less time at home. Consequently she was now working as a janitor in the public school to supplement their income and to help save for their retirement. I commiserated with her and was deeply saddened by the news. She assured me they would attend the wedding and pay all costs incurred. She also informed me she had bought a cedar lined 'Hope Chest' and was slowly filling it with sheets, blankets, embroidered table clothes etc., a tradition in those days. I thanked her for being so thoughtful especially given her personal problems. Mother was the most thoughtful and giving person I've ever known, not only with family but with friends and neighbours also.

By September I had chosen my wedding gown – white satin with panels of rose-point lace, with matching white satin shoes. Also a full length veil with a crown of orange blossom to be attached. Mr. Scott offered to drive me to his home one evening after work where he said Hilda (Mrs. Scott) would help with the veil attachment, which she did. Hilda was a few years older than Mr Scott and had recently given birth to their only son, Robin, a beautiful blonde, blue-eyed baby. She had a very lucrative job as Executive Secretary to the CEO of Gooderham Worts. They had a lovely home in South Kingsway, Toronto.

Dorothy Graham, a friend from Shaw days, would be my only attendant, wearing a dark turquoise taffeta gown and a glamorous pink feathered head-dress. Joe's brother Currie would be his Best Man and younger brother, Robert, an usher. We would have fifty guests at our simple but well planned wedding.

A week before the wedding Mr & Mrs Scott had kindly offered to host a prenuptial party, including all the attendants, at The Old Mill. Dinner and dancing were included. Excitement was mounting – until the day before the party when the first shoe fell. It was Thursday 9th, November, 1948. Will I ever erase it from my memory?

Unlikely!. I was at work and at 1pm I received a telephone call from the prospective bridegroom. He sounded very nervous and said he couldn't go through with it, the wedding that is. I asked why? He replied he had the jitters. I said that we had to meet that evening to discuss this appropriately which I couldn't do at work and he agreed.

When I hung up the phone, Mr Scott, overhearing some of my replies, asked, "is everything OK Miss Tarcza?"

"Not really, Mr. Scott," I replied, "Joe wants to back out of the wedding because he feels jittery."

Mr Scott looked very perturbed, hugged me and said I would always have a job there. He would never fire me. Then he asked me an interesting question.

"Miss Tarcza are you really deeply in love with Joe?"

"What do you mean by that?" I asked.

"Do you feel like you would die without him?" He replied.

"Yes I do" I replied, tears welling up in my eyes.

On many occasions during our sixty-six year marriage I recalled Mr. Scott's penetrating query wondering whether I gave the right answer. I know I cared about Joe, enjoyed our social activities together, admired him for his service to his country, found his maturity comforting. He was nine and a half years older than me, a substitute father figure perhaps? But what did I really know about "love"? Not too much I think.

Mr. Scott suggested he rent a room at the King Edward Hotel and I should get Joe up there immediately to talk things out. He was also willing to join us as mediator, if we wished. I graciously declined the offer and said we would work it out that evening when we met. When Joe arrived at my apartment he apologized profusely for his behaviour, said he loved me, wanted to get married but got the pre-wedding jitters and was worried about my 'Mother's accent' – how his family would react to it! I could feel a terrible anger of indignation rising in me, ready to explode but I contained it and explained the hardship my Mother went through studying the English Reader each night, writing out words and getting help from me and my father in pronunciation. I also made clear to him how much I loved my Mother and admired her courage and hard work to make life better for my sister and me. I must have hit one of his few soft chords as he apologized again and again and asked me to tell Mr Scott we would be at the party the next night. In retrospect I feel now that had I been more mature I would have happily walked away with my head held high. But I was young and foolish and supposedly in love but what a price I paid for my immaturity!

The prenuptial celebration was a great success with a lovely dinner and dance at the Old Mill. Originally called the Old Mill Tea Garden, was opened by Robert Home Smith in 1914 on the first day of WW1. In 1921 the Old Mill Tea Garden introduced live music in the Print Room with violinist Sec Ryder and pianist Nelson Hatch. In 1929 the duo expanded to a nine-piece orchestra when a dance floor was added. That is where we danced the night away thanks to the generosity of Mr & Mrs Scott who suggested we end the evening with coffee at the Royal York Hotel in downtown Toronto.

Preparations at the Church of the Redeemer were finalized including church decorations and rehearsals etc. Cannon Armstrong, a most lovable man with a great sense of humour, was to officiate and after our wedding there would be another wedding after which he would officially retire! We congratulated him for his lengthy and valuable service and said how much he would be missed. He gave us a short 'sermon' about the importance of the wedding vows and the need to work together in harmony and how helpful prayer could be in achieving this. We agreed and hoped being devout Anglicans would be a positive thing in our marriage. Then he had a rather mischievous look on his face and directed this more to Joe than me.

"As for the honeymoon, a bit of foreplay always helps", giggling as he said it, as did Joe. Not being knowledgeable in that area, quite green in fact, I thought it meant that Joe would joke with me or tell me jokes before the 'big event'. How naive I and many like me were in those days. Not so now it seems! Cannon Armstrong then asked me to telephone a young lady called Anna regarding decorations for the church because there was a wedding following ours. Anna informed me that the church decorating was all resolved, flowers and beribboned pews and she hoped I would be pleased by what was done. I thanked her and offered to pay half the costs which she generously declined. The church music was selected, Trumpet Voluntary for the processional instead of the traditional "Here comes the the Bride." Jenny Swerk, a friend from Smooth Rock days who had an angelic voice kindly agreed to be the soloist.

I then contacted the Hearthstone to finalize the menu and details of the reception. It amazes me how at the age of twenty I had the organizational skills to successfully plan such an important event by myself. No doubt my work experience was an important factor and a valuable asset in that regard.

Mother and Father arrived by CNR railway from Smooth Rock Falls. I met them at Union Station and on our bus ride home to my apartment Mother recounted the sad tale of Father's gambling addiction. He had been out the whole night previous to coming and slept on the train the whole trip. I kissed and hugged them both and asked them to try to be happy for me while they were here. They agreed. I shed silent tears for them when I was alone but was overjoyed to see them again nevertheless. My beloved little sister Helen was not able to come as she was writing exams.

I cooked them a lovely dinner – chicken paprikas, with homemade noodles (a favourite Hungarian dish) and had Father's first choice of all desserts – lemon pie. The plan was that we would all go to Dorothy Graham's house on Walmer Road early the next morning to get dressed and leave for church together. Joe's out of town relatives stayed with Aunt Bertha, Aunt Elizabeth and his sister Alma. November 18th was filled with great excitement and anticipation. What would tomorrow bring I wondered as I spotted the moon through my window? Suddenly uncontrollable sobs shook my body as I thought of my darling Nagymama who would not be there for the celebration. I finally calmed down as I said my nightly prayers. Of course she would be there every minute in spirit! Good-nite Moon.

We arrived at Dorothy's early via limousine after an early breakfast of cereal, toast and tea. Mrs. Graham welcomed us with open arms, covering us with kisses. Dorothy was in her bathrobe, ready to don her beautiful gown and headdress. Mother and Father were assigned a bedroom to change in. Dorothy and I occupied her bedroom to do the same. Little brother couldn't quite figure out what was happening but was obviously excited. Dorothy's room had a full length mirror which was very convenient as we started our dress up. My wedding gown was a size 9 and I weighed approximately 115 pounds. It fit perfectly! Dorothy kindly assisted me with the veil and I then helped with her head Dress. We laughed and cried and giggled when all was done and proceeded down to the living room where the Photographer and the Florist's delivery of all the flowers arrived simultaneously.

The photographer we chose was Robert McMichael who had a wedding photography business in Toronto. He and wife Signe years later donated their home and art collection in Kleinburg to the Ontario Government, now the famous Group of Seven Gallery, a favourite of Art lovers far and wide. Mr. McMichael patiently followed us to church and the reception and recorded our special day superbly for which we were grateful.

The driver delivered us to the Church of the Redeemer where we were greeted by Cannon Armstrong and before long Trumpet Voluntary signalled us to begin the wedding procession. I nervously took Father's arm as he kissed my cheek lightly. Dorothy, looking beautiful and almost regal led the procession down the aisle as we followed. The Church was beautifully and most tastefully decorated. I remember seeing Joe, handsome and well groomed waiting near the altar, with his two brothers Currie and Robert by his side. The rest seemed like an ecstatic blur until I heard Jenny's' beautiful voice singing 'Because' while we were signing the register. The last few words "and pray His Love may make our love divine" remained with me for a long time as our union went through both good times and despair. Jenny also sang 'The Lord's Prayer', especially for Mother as she was so devout. Fond memories still remain of smiling faces in the pews as we happily marched out of that beautiful renown church. Cannon Armstrong, although he was invited to join us for our reception could not as he had another wedding to perform following ours.

We, together with both sets of parents and our attendants formed the receiving line, greeted our guests cordially and graciously accepted congratulations and good wishes. Father really surprised me with his superb toast to the bride and groom. It was very well thought out and presented in a heart-felt way. I will never forget his last words "may your happiness be as endless as a circle!" In other words, may it go on forever. What a lovely thought but not always easily achieved. Mr. Scott toasted the bride, very sweet and moving and the attendants did their bit. After a tasty lunch served with non-alcoholic drinks and tea and coffee, the wedding cake cutting ceremony, saving the top layer for the christening ceremony of the first child, lightened the atmosphere somewhat. Mrs. Scott then kindly came with me to help me get into my 'going away' outfit, a cranberry coloured suit, a saucy black hat and black suede high heels. She looked at me, kissed me and said, "there is something missing". She smartly removed her black leather gloves and made me put them on. At that moment

I felt my sister was at my wedding. Joe and I said our thank you's and goodbyes and escaped into our rented car to drive to Buffalo where we would spend our honeymoon. It was raining when we left and by the time we reached the West end of the city the windshield wipers stopped working. We spent the next hour in a car garage where they were replaced. I reminded Joe of Shakespeare's warning "the course of true love never doth run smooth" and we drove on trouble-free the rest of the way.

As an aside, I learned later that Father took all his Hungarian relatives and friends to a restaurant for dinner and drinks – the alcoholic kind! They had a second celebration and enjoyed the reunion thoroughly.

We arrived at the Statler Hotel worn out from the exciting day and dined royally on hamburgers and fries. The next evening we attended a Dinner Theatre where the evening's entertainment included a Hypnotist showing off his skills using the audience as "Guinea pigs". Twelve people, including Joe and I were chosen to be a part of the act! Out of the twelve only four succumbed to the hypnosis. The remaining eight non-co-operators were told to hold out their arms, pretend they were still hypnotized and return to their table. The hypnotist then proceeded to order the four remaining to do various acts that made the audience ooo and ahhh and laugh. He then snapped his fingers before each and they came back to the present and returned to their seats oblivious of their act on stage. I was glad I remained bloody minded and wouldn't let myself be hypnotized. We toured the city, visited museums, shopped and before we knew it, it was time to head home.

CHAPTER 15

My present day recollection of our honeymoon is not pleasant. I was a virgin, knew very little about sex while Joe admitted to me during our courtship that he had several affairs while in the RCAF, par for the course for someone going off to war with the possibility of never coming back. I remember bedtimes being filled with tension and sunrise being a great relief. When we finally returned to Toronto, with work, friends and new marital duties as distractions, tensions eased somewhat as we established our daily routine. Preparations for Christmas kept us busy and the new bridegroom was overwhelmed with the culinary skills coming from the kitchen, so much so that he gained ten pounds the first month we were married! We spent our first Christmas with friends who, having been married for a year or so, were more settled. We also celebrated New Year's Eve with them at the Club Kingsway and had a wonderful time. Returning to work after the holidays I was quite perplexed that each morning on my way to work I experienced a severe nauseous feeling, often having to get off the streetcar for relief. After a week or so I mentioned my nausea to Flossie, my landlady's daughter, telling her I thought I had the flu.

"I don't think it's the flu," she said laughing uncontrollably, "I think you might be pregnant!".

Flossie referred me to the physician she worked for, Dr. J. J. Johnson on Avenue Rd. and made an appointment for me. A week later Dr. Johnson confirmed that I was pregnant and became my gynaecologist.

I received the news with mixed feelings – first, utter surprise, because of my naiveté, then a panicky feeling, what now? and finally an ecstatic feeling – I'm going to be a mama with my own little baby, recollecting the feeling of the joy I had when my baby sister was born.

When Joe returned from work I gave him the good news.

He reacted similarly, first with surprise bordering on shock, then with joyous laughter.

"I'm going to be a daddy!" he cried. We celebrated by eating out.

After Joe, one of the first family members I wanted to share the exciting news with was Aunt Bertha. Her office was located at King and Bay St, while mine was at Front and Bay St. So we often met for lunch, usually at the food counter of Raleigh's pharmacy nearby. I telephoned to set up the lunch date stating I had some exciting news for her.

We met at noon, always happy to see each other, when with a sly smile she asked, "is your exciting news that Bessie, Joe's sister, is having a baby soon?"

I expressed surprise and delight at the news, then went on to say, "there's another bit of exciting news to share. I'm also going to have a baby in September."

At this point Aunt Bertha and I had a warm relationship and affection for each other. Tears welled in her eyes and she hugged me and said how happy she was to hear my good news. She then posed an unexpected question.

"Do you think I would have made a good Mother?"

"You would have been an excellent mother, Aunt Bertha. You have all the required qualities," I replied.

She gave me a mixed happy, sad, smile and I realized that her adamant choice, early in her career, "I'm married to my profession" excluded marriage and children. Yet, I sensed an element of regret in her reaction which saddened me. Fortunately women now have many more options and can have both.

I continued working having to get off the streetcar with nausea, that lasted about three months. By the fifth month my pregnancy was visible and I searched for a new wardrobe, smocks and dresses which were loose and gathered and tended to hide the little bundle. So unlike what young women wear now, body fitting dresses that show off their pregnancy – and why not!

It was time to tell Mr Scott the good news – bad for him – and help find and hire my replacement. We were successful in finding a suitable person, Miss Sleighthomme, who was well trained and competent before I left. Mr and Mrs Scott and I said our tearful farewells with a promise to let them know when the baby arrived.

The next few months were spent sewing and knitting baby clothes, sweaters and hats, buying baby toys and enjoying the prospect of motherhood. Both families were overjoyed with the news and Mother who was a great knitter and could crochet, got to work making baby blankets and little outfits.

In mid-summer I suddenly felt homesick for my family in Smooth Rocks Falls so Joe and I drove there for our summer holidays. My sister, Helen, was fifteen and thoroughly excited at becoming an aunt. A most joyful and restful vacation.

Following our return to Toronto we realized we needed more space than we had on MacPherson Avenue, so went apartment hunting. We finally settled on a house rental on Rogers Road in the Weston area, a semi-detached house with three bedrooms, bathroom, living room, dining room and kitchen. But, it came with a hitch. The owner, Elsie Jones, a senior citizen, was to remain in one of the bedrooms but would be away all day and only use the room for sleeping. We signed the lease for a year and moved into our new home. Fully furnished, we had very little to buy in the way of furnishings.

115

CHAPTER 16

Our new neighbours were a widowed Mother, Mrs Pringle, her daughter and son-in-law, all friendly and compatible. We became fast friends and enjoyed their company. During the latter part of my pregnancy I developed a fetish for ice-cream and when we went for our daily walk Joe would jokingly say, "there goes the fat lady with her ice cream cone!" Of course, he had one too but wasn't pregnant.

On August 30th, 1949, early morning I was awakened with severe pains, alerted Joe and we quickly dressed and drove to Toronto General Hospital, Burnside Division, where he left me in the care of the nurses and went off to work at Frigidaire. Dr. Johnston checked in on me and said it would be a while and asked me if I wanted an epidural to alleviate the pain.

I said, "no thank you, I can tolerate a lot of pain."

During labour I had a surprise visitor – Thelma Richards of Shaw days, who was in training as an RN. It was comforting to see her and she kept popping in throughout the day and evening. Finally my darling little daughter was born at 12:15am September 1st, 1949. Seven pounds and fifteen ounces, healthy with a good head of dark brown hair and a sweet, chubby little face. Despite the long ordeal I was overjoyed to hold and cuddle her. I thanked God for his blessing. Joe was notified but didn't appear until 6:30pm after work that night! He was, apparently, too devoted to his work

We named our little angel Nancy Elizabeth and were discharged from hospital after five days. How different life became, thoroughly child-centred. After a few months I had frequent crying spells for no apparent reason, which I now suspect could have been postpartum depression. Joe slowly became attached to Nancy and delighted in her little antics. Our neighbours, the Pringles, were very fond of her and really served as parent substitutes, for which I was grateful.

It was then we connected with Dr. Isabel Grimshaw with offices on Vaughan Road who became our family physician for many years to come. At six months Nancy Elizabeth was baptized in the Church of the

Messiah where I had become an Anglican before my marriage.

We purchased a baby bed, with sides, a carriage, high chair, mostly gifts from family and friends. And had enough clothes for baby Nancy for at least a year. Our camera was clicking a lot as we had to send pictures and updates to relatives far and wide. I spent considerable time reading, singing and talking to Nancy to which she responded enthusiastically.

At age one we had the pleasure of looking after Alma's (Joe's sister) first born, Paul, age two while she was in hospital giving birth to brother David. Both Nancy and Paul were gentle children so got on well and enjoyed each other's company.

At age two Nancy, who was very fond of Mrs Pringle, would invite her over with her special invitation, "come Mingle sedee." (come Mrs. Pringle and sit with me) – pointing to the chair beside her. Of course Mrs. Pringle never refused for she loved Nancy.

All was not a bed of roses however. It turned out that Elsie Jones, our landlady, had a problem with more than a 'wee Dram' and consequently often missed the toilet bowl. We shared the same bathroom! Further more, she was accompanied frequently by her male friend who also missed the toilet bowl too often. Finally it became intolerable so we decided to look for another home.

After searching for weeks we found number 30 Bonnie Brae Boulevard, located in East York near the General

Hospital. It was a lovely little semi-detached two story house with living room, with stone fireplace, dining room with mahogany plate rails and beautifully papered walls, large kitchen with cupboards, stove and ice box. It also had an attached heated room (porch), off the kitchen. In the back, garage and a fenced in back yard, a wonderful play area for children. Across the front of the house a roomy veranda, also a potential play area. There were three bedrooms and a bathroom on the second floor. It was built by the Cairns Brothers, reputable builders and we decided it would be perfect for us, especially as I was pregnant with our second child.

We discussed our potential purchase of the house with Aunt Bertha, who would do the legal work and she agreed it would be a good buy. It was listed at $10,900 and we had $1,500 cash saved so Aunt Bertha offered to lend us $2,000, with no interest, so we could put $3,500 down and mortgage the rest. We were very moved by her generous offer and accepted.

Aunt Bertha said we should be joint owners and that she would forgo legal fees. Much to my chagrin Joe objected profusely and said that the house should be in his name only. Aunt Bertha became very indignant and said, "You are wrong Joseph. It is imperative that you protect your beautiful wife and child, with another one on the way. If you do not agree to put Margaret's name with yours you must find another lawyer because I will not do it.

At that moment I felt Aunt Bertha was not only my

protector but also my hero, standing up for the rights of all women which didn't happen until 1973 in Murdoch v. Murdoch in the Alberta Supreme Court. Joe coloured, obviously embarrassed but succumbed and the deal went through.

CHAPTER 17

We informed Elsie Jones that we were planning to move to our new house and gave her the mandatory three months notice. She tried to sell us her good china dinner set but we declined as we didn't have extra cash to throw around. Margaret, her daughter, and her husband had also moved to their new home and she was alone in the house. We promised to keep in touch and did so.

Our move to 30 Bonnie Brae Blvd opened a new, exciting and memorable chapter in our lives. We moved in mid-summer 1951 after doing some re-decorating in the kitchen, halls, bedrooms and bathroom. We also decided that we would rent the up-stairs for a year so we could quickly pay back Aunt Bertha the money she loaned us.

The move went smoothly. By putting curtains on the glass doors we turned the living room into our bedroom, including Nancy's little crib. The dining room held a pull-out studio couch and two easy chairs. We bought a new kitchen table and chairs. My sewing machine, a Christmas gift from Joe, was well used for the next few weeks making Drapes, curtains, table clothes and new clothes.

We rented our up-stairs easily to a young couple, the Cross's, who turned out to be wonderful tenants and friends. Our immediate neighbours were the Williams in the attached half, with no children. Next door lived the Clarke's, also a middle aged couple with no children. However, the rest of the street were young people like us with children, most renting their up-stairs. We made such good and lasting friends on Bonnie Brae, many of them became life-long friends.

What a street! What an adventure!

We soon got into a daily rhythm in our child-centred life. Joe was much closer to his work-place at Frigidaire so could spend more time at home with us. We were happy and pleased with our new home and gradually met every resident on the street – it was a short street. I've never had such a large array of friends who shared so much in common. We were all about the same age, all had at least one child, were outgoing and friendly and rented the upstairs for extra income. The children immediately took to each other and became good friends right up to school time and beyond.

Joe and I immediately joined the Anglican Church of the Nativity where I became a member of the women's auxiliary and later taught the junior group every Sunday.

Joe also volunteered his services as an accountant. We really missed church and were happy to be back.

In late October I had an appointment with my ophthalmologist downtown on King St, so I telephoned Mr Scott who had already been informed about Nancy's arrival, to ask whether he would like to see her.

The answer was an excited, "absolutely!"

Nancy was rather advanced in her language skills, picking up words easily and walking and exploring constantly. I dressed her in a cute bright yellow hooded snow-suit – a material resembling curly sheepskin. She was wide eyed and looked adorable with curly hair and bangs. We popped on the street car, stroller and all, ending up on the Bay St. car down to Front St. We arrived to be warmly greeted by Mr Scott and the rest of the staff. The hugs were flying around. I prompted Nancy to say "Hi" to Mr Scott and with a big smile she exclaimed, "Hi Scotty" a character in one of her many books I read to her. Mr Scott roared with laughter and excitement as did the rest of the staff. We spent some time catching up on each other's lives – including my second pregnancy. It felt so good to be back in my old rendezvous where I spent so much productive and enjoyable time. Mr Scott, grey at the temples, was still extremely handsome and fun.

As time for my appointment was Drawing near I announced that we should be going when Mr Scott impulsively blurted out – "Miss Tarcza would you please leave little Nancy with us and come back after your appointment so we can spend time with her?" Surprised but pleased I answered, "of course if that is what you wish." And off I went to King St. pleased as punch.

When I returned with the prescription for new glasses Nancy was *sans* snow-suit looking cheerful and quite at home and not particularly anxious to be interrupted. She was happy with all the special attention. I finally dressed her. We said our good-byes reluctantly as Mr Scott accompanied us until we boarded the Bay St car homeward bound. What nostalgia!

For the rest of the day until bedtime Nancy kept asking,"Where's Scotty?". I recounted our adventure to Joe when he returned from work. He remarked, "no friends like old friends".

On Bonnie Brae our closest friends became Kay and Walter Cole (3 children) Irene and Gord Green (2 children), Bette and Don Schafer (2 children). I was also fond of Jo Sheluk (2 children) with a much older husband, Nick and Lolly and Denis Edminson with one child.

The men all worked while we women stayed at home, mothers/housewives. Staying at home didn't mean we were idle, I spent considerable time sewing my own clothes plus household items, Nancy's little dresses and sun-suits, crib sheets etc. During this time I also taught Irene to sew which she undertook with great passion. This ultimately led to our Saturday escapes to Eaton's and Simpson's department stores downtown looking for bargain material and Vogue patterns for our next fashionable outfit. We eventually progressed to making summer hats after frequent visits to dress Makers Supplies. We both had (and still do) active imaginations and came up with some dandies. Our excursions resulted in a very close friendship which exists to this day when we are both nano-generations and the only two of the Bonnie Brae gang to survive.

The other pastime consisted of get togethers on Saturday night, bring your own Mickey, beer, ginger ale etc. and we would end up dancing to the latest tunes blasting out of our gramophones. We would each take turns hosting this athletic evening. With plenty of work and play and shopping I can't say life was boring. Social interaction on Bonnie Brae was frequent and memorable.

Shortly after Christmas my dear Mother came to our new home so she could look after Nancy while I was in hospital delivering our second child. She loved our humble little house and the fact that we owned it. Her lifelong dream in Canada was to own her own home again as she did in Europe and every penny she could save went toward that goal.

On January 29th, 1952 the familiar stabbing pains reoccured during the night. We quickly dressed and Joe drove me to the Wellesley Hospital. Again he kissed me and went off into the night.

Peter, 18m with Nancy

Dr. Isabel Grimshaw and her brother Dr. William Grimshaw attended me and our darling little boy was was born 1:30pm January 30th, 1952. Dr. Isabel telephoned Joe promptly telling him he now had a beautiful baby boy and all was well. As per his obnoxious habit he didn't appear until 7:00pm that evening. Need I say More?

Joseph Peter weighed in at 8lbs 10oz with blonde hair, dark eyes and a big appetite. He was a gentle little boy, cried very little and smiled a lot as he grew. A disturbing incident occurred the second day. The nurse brought a little baby to me – feeding time – with black hair (baby's didn't wear little hats in those day) and a thinnish little face and I knew immediately it wasn't my child (he was blonde with a chubby face). I asked the nurse to check the toe for the name tag. Sure enough it was my room-mate's baby. She apologized, corrected the mistake. We all laughed about the incident after it was all over.

Baby Peter was dressed in his Sunday best for the trip home to Bonnie Brae. Mother had crocheted him a lovely little blue hat and sweater and a blue and white wool shawl to bundle him in. We arrived home to an immaculately clean house and lovely dinner, thanks to dear Mother. Nancy was overjoyed with her baby brother and couldn't stop hugging and kissing him. Mother wept and held little Peter, probably recalling memories of little Feri who died shortly after birth. I embraced her and thanked her profusely for taking such good care of Nancy and Joe.

She stayed another week and then departed, worrying about Father being alone for so long. Joe drove her to Union Station with a tasty lunch for the trip. She got hugs and good wishes from some of our neighbours and I realized how blessed we are to have loving Mothers – and Fathers. They're always there for you.

CHAPTER 18

We moved Nancy's crib into the back room attached to the kitchen, while Peter was happy in his little baby basket with us. It was during this period that Joe decided to upgrade his qualifications and enrolled in a correspondence course for his RIA (Registered Industrial Accountant) and was preoccupied with his studies for the next two years. I admired his tenacity and determination to improve himself. Little did I know this was just the beginning, there was more to come!

No postpartum depression this time – I was too busy. I went to Dr. William Grimshaw for a checkup and he quietly suggested several forms of birth control. I quickly agreed and chose a diaphragm which he fitted me with. Dr. Isabel continued looking after the children's health as well as ours.

Peter was baptized in the Church of the Nativity at

Easter 1952 and shortly after I resumed my volunteer work at the church. Irene and I continued our Saturday escapes to Simpson's and Eaton's. They added another member to their family with David's birth. He was born prematurely at seven months but thrived and eventually became a good friend of Peter, Johnny Cole and David Muldoon. Back yards were fenced off, as were verandahs, so there were plenty of play areas.

Hope, my dear childhood friend from Smooth Rock Falls, visited us to meet Nancy and Peter. She had obtained her R.N. in Peterborough General Hospital and undertook extra studies which qualified her to teach nursing at the same hospital, where she spent her working years until retirement. She came bearing exciting news, her upcoming marriage in August and asked me to be her Maid of Honour. Talking it over with Joe he agreed he would look after the children so that I could be away for the weekend. I made my own gown – coordinated with the two bridesmaids gowns – which was soft blue taffeta with full skirt, cap sleeves and covered buttons down to the waist. I also made floral head-dresses for myself and the two bridesmaids.

Hope was marrying a Veteran Naval Officer, Kenneth Hotston whose parents owned a corner grocery store well known to people in Peterborough. We visited Hope a month later to meet Ken and coordinate the wedding plans. She was pleased with my home made gown and the pretty floral head-pieces. Our first visit out of town with our two little ones went well and we enjoyed it thoroughly.

A few weeks later I boarded the Greyhound bus, suitcase and gift in hand, to attend dear Hope and Ken's wedding. It took place in All Saints' Anglican Church, which they attended, followed by a reception with approximately sixty guests. The groom's parents honoured them with a lovely bungalow next door as their wedding gift, which we all applauded. The Bride and Groom left happily for their honeymoon at the end of the evening, after the bouquet throw and shower of rice. I often look at the wedding photograph and wonder how did I not know.

Joe welcomed me back affectionately more than usual. He experienced what a Mother's day entailed and was happy to see me back. Then came the exciting but unexpected shock of our lives. After the wedding I began to have episodes of nausea that were 'vaguely familiar'. But, I thought, it can't be with my contraception in place, And I'm still nursing Peter. There existed a myth in those bygone days that women could not get pregnant while nursing a child. Ha ha! Not true.

I made an appointment with Dr. Isabel who gave me the confirmation. Her explanation was that sometimes the diaphragm is installed too soon after the birth of a child.

So in time it might not be as reliable as it needs to be to prevent pregnancy. My explanation was quite different. God wanted this birth to happen, so it will! Dr. Isabel referred me to her brother's care for the rest of the pregnancy.

Dear little Peter was put on formula and pablum – he had a voracious appetite and life went on as usual. Joe stopped night studies for a short period, probably worrying about the coming changes in our lives.

During all my pregnancies I always continued to practice the golden rule of housewives, cooking hearty and nutritious meals, preserving fruit for the winter, peaches, pears and cherries, making zucchini relish and dill pickles. Keeping the house clean and attractive, washing and ironing Joe's shirts for work and also – through necessity – sewing all the clothes for myself and the children. Proudly following in my Mother's footsteps. I worked on a budget of $40.00 a week – for food and everything else. Being blessed with good health, physically and mentally, my usual weight hovered between 115lbs and 120lbs. I noticed that during the current pregnancy I looked quite hefty and did gain more weight than usual. I went to Dr. Grimshaw for regular checkups and voiced my concern about the weight gain and the fact that I had been sleeping with my head propped up against several pillows, as it was too uncomfortable laying stretched out the normal way.

He began the usual examination, walked around me

carefully checking both sides, suddenly he exclaimed, "Oh, oh." and I caught him signalling to the Nurse with two fingers on his right hand – similar to a "V" for victory sign. She gasped, "Oh NO!".

He then said to me, "Margaret, I think your discomfort sleeping is because you're carrying two babies. Are there twins in your, or your husband's family?"

I giggled and replied, "yes, twins on both sides and triplets on my husband's side."

"Well, I'm going to order an Xray to confirm."

As Joe and I got into the car for the trip home I relayed the exciting news. We both laughed hilariously, after the shock, and went out to a movie to celebrate.

One thing Dr. Grimshaw said during the examination, to distract me I think, "did you know that Eaton's and Simpson's have a wonderful policy?" "If you have twins and it's a surprise they will give you everything you bought in their store, including baby furniture and carriages, free of charge for the second child." I made a mental note of that.

The next day the Xray confirmed I was carrying twins and soon the whole street got the good news. We also informed our lovely tenants, the Cross's, that they should start looking for another place to live as we would soon require the extra space. They congratulated us and complied, moving out shortly after.

In the next few weeks Joe successfully transformed the house, painting all the upstairs, moving our bedroom furniture to the second floor three bedrooms. Then reorganizing the downstairs into living room, dining room and kitchen. We purchased a new living room suite with side-tables, an easy chair beside the fireplace and new lamps. A new dining room suite was added and of course new drapes and curtains and pictures. The new look was cheerful and welcoming and really lifted our sprits. What really was uplifting was the fact that we paid back dear Aunt Bertha the $2,000 she loaned us. She was reluctant to take it but we insisted.

Eventually Joe resumed his night studies with more urgency and helped a little more around the house. Mother and Father couldn't believe the news, she cried then laughed and said she would be in Toronto early April to look after Nancy and Peter. Such comforting news!

When Bette Schafer, another close Bonnie Brae friend heard about Eaton's and Simpson's policy she insisted we go there Saturday and spend the day shopping. And we did.

CHAPTER 19

Mother arrived in the middle of April and we gave her the grand tour around the recently decorated house. She was overjoyed and praised Joe for his hard work and the wonderful result. Nancy and Peter both responded to her lovingly, almost as if they knew her. Due to the long periods of separation from the grand-parents I developed a clever little habit with the children. After story-time, reading to them, I would often hold up photographs of the four grandparents and say, "this is grandma, this is nana," etc. After practicing this ritual a few times I would hold up the photographs and ask, "who is this?" Nancy at a very early age, two and a half, correctly identified each one. Peter, being younger, possibly stored it in his long term memory for he didn't shy away or make strange with either of the grand-parents, Joe's or mine.

I cooked Chicken Paprikas to welcome my dear Mother

and cherry pie and ice cream for dessert. Remember the preserved fruits stored in the basement? It felt so good to have her here. Joe and I occupied the master bedroom. The middle bedroom, with twin beds, was assigned to Nancy, and now her Granny and the third bedroom, with a good size crib, was for Peter. A little aside about Peter, he was miraculously walking at nine months. Wondering how he got out of his crib we watched with amazement as he grabbed crib rungs with both hands, flung himself over the side and slid to the floor. Wasting no time he lifted himself up and walked away. We were stunned at his ingenuity at such an early age.

"Necessity is the Mother of invention" – since I couldn't lift him, he found a way himself.

Mother came with bags full of crocheted hats, sweaters as well as a dozen nighties, bibs and other essentials. We were well prepared for the big day. On the morning of April 20th I dressed and fed the children, had breakfast with Mother and Joe and the familiar pangs of pain started. I alerted Mother and told Joe he would have to drive me to the Wellesley Hospital pronto. After loving good-byes with the family Joe got me there in record time. Adhering to his usual custom, he kissed me goodbye and left for work. This time it brought tears to my eyes – too many 'unknowns ahead'.

The nurses attended to me and Dr. Isabel checked me over and cheerfully said, "see you soon". But after eight long hours of labour the pain subsided and Dr. William

Grimshaw said, "it won't happen today." So I was discharged and Joe picked me up after work with the admonishment, "and don't you have a false alarm again." I replied, "and don't you be such an idiot."

The tension between us was palpable for I had never talked to him this way before. We made it home, Mother had everything under control. Dinner was ready but I chose to go straight to bed. After a stressful night propped against my multi-pillows I awakened cheerful and optimistic that the day would go well. Joe went to work, the children were happy and playful and Mother and I spent a lovely day together reminiscing. She decided to make stuffed peppers for dinner and they were delicious. After dinner the children were read to by Joe and put to bed.

Early in the evening i decided to shower and go to bed early. As I began dressing for bed my water suddenly broke with a gush. It's finally going to happen, I thought. I alerted Joe, informed Mother and within a few minutes we were on our way again to Wellesley Hospital. Having been prepped by the nurses the day before there wasn't much to do. We called the two Grimshaw doctors from home so they were already there for me when we arrived. The greatest irony of all – Joe couldn't escape to work. He stayed for the whole procedure for the first time. My darling little 'twinners' were born April 21st at approximately 8:30 pm with Dr. Isabel and Dr. William attending me. Janice Emily was born first weighing in at

6lb 10oz and Judith Marie (breach birth) a few minutes later weighing 5lbs 15 oz. Overjoyed that it was over I said goodnight to Joe and slept well that night. However, peace and contentment were short lived.

Early, very early, the next morning Dr. Grimshaw informed me that Janice was perfectly healthy but Judith had developed jaundice due to the Rhesus (Rh Neg) factor – difference between the baby and Mother's blood type. She was Type O Positive and I Type O Negative so she would be transferred to the Hospital for Sick Children(HSC), where she would be treated with a blood transfusion to correct the condition.

Still another factor made their birth unique. They were Dizygotic (Fraternal) twins with different blood types sharing one amniotic sac which happens in one of five million births. Therefore baby Janice accompanied her twin sister, Judith, and numerous doctors and researchers were invited to witness and study this phenomenon. I was heartbroken to be separated from my babies so suddenly but realized how imperative it was for Judith's survival. In the meantime I had to pump my breasts three times a day and have the milk delivered to the HSC for the new-borns.

Bonnie Barnes, a close friend of ours, through Frigidaire where her husband worked, volunteered to be the blood donor which we were so grateful for. The generosity of friends in time of need is almost overwhelming. A year or so later Joe was able to repay the favour when Bonnie, delivering her first child, ran into problems. Joe, having the same blood type was able to repay the favour and Mother and baby thrived.

I was discharged in three days and immediately headed for HSC to see my little darlings. They shared a room, with two little cribs and were sleeping peacefully when we arrived. Judith was no longer yellow but a beautiful pinkish colour like her twin sister. I sat quietly thanking God for the love and gift he bestowed on us – the culmination of my opinion that God wanted the birth to happen and so it did, successfully.

We thanked the doctors and nurses for looking after our little ones and convinced they were in good hands left for home, returning daily with pumped breast-milk for them. Janice was discharged after a few days healthy and active. When we arrived back at the house Nancy and Peter were at play on the gated veranda with Mother sitting in a lounge chair watching over them. Excitement was mounting as we approached.

"Baby," Nancy, three and half, shouted, "Baby sister."

Peter, fourteen months old, ran to Mother and she held him. We and the welcoming committee were crying, overwrought yet overjoyed.

Whenever I tried to hold Peter to kiss and hug him he would put his little arms around Mother's neck and hold on. Obviously receiving good and loving care from Grandma. Can we ever adequately thank or repay parents for such love and devotion.

CHAPTER 20

The next two weeks were hectic. The hospital informed us Judith was now on formula, with additional nutrition added to it, so they would not need breast-milk any longer. Joe thought a new refrigerator was a must as ice boxes were not always reliable and a nuisance. So, he purchased a new Frigidaire and we proudly installed it in the kitchen. The freezer was very handy in our busy new life.

The neighbours were very generous with visits, baking and little gifts for the babies. When Judith arrived home on a very sunny day in early May, Nancy gave a repeat performance. This time she placed her hands on each side of her head and exclaimed, "More babies, more babies." Mr Williamson, our immediate neighbour roared with laughter at her antics.

We kept the camera clicking to record the events and beautiful little faces, thinking of all the relatives far and wide. We placed two little cribs in the room attached to the kitchen, as well two baby baskets in our master bedroom where the twins stayed until they were over a year old. Night feedings, were particularly difficult. I would feed Judith her bottle, after which she would sleep soundly and I'd creep back to bed, only to hear Janice wailing for her bottle. Thankfully night feeding ceased after they were put on pablum.

Mother decided to leave shortly after my twenty-fifth birthday on May 12th. She made a beautiful cake for the occasion, candles and all and presented me with a generous gift for some new clothes. Joe gave me a bouquet of roses and babies breath which I also received every anniversary.

After Mother's departure I got into a daily routine of bathing, feeding, playing, nap time, dinner, play time, reading (story time), bath time and bedtime. Joe insisted on washing the diapers for the three little ones – Peter wasn't quite trained yet. No automatic machines so he used a special wooden paddle to lift the diapers from the hot water and feed them through the wringer. No easy task! Then he would hang them on the clothes line in the backyard. He and Walter Cole would socialize and laugh about their chores. Easy for Walter to laugh, they only had one on diapers, Johnny. We had them for three! We soon adapted to the hard work but gave up a lot of our social time with friends on the street until things got easier.

Late summer Joe successfully obtained his RIA in

accounting and received a raise at work. Always looking for new opportunities he had an interview for a position as Controller with Schlegel Industries in Oakville, an auto parts and trim manufacturer, with a substantial increase in salary but turned it down. He thought the distance commuting was too great and would interfere with helping me at home.

In mid-summer my sister Helen, nineteen, came to Toronto to start her studies at St Michael's Hospital to obtain a Registered Nurse (RN) designation. Consequently she spent many weekends with us for the next three years. The children loved their Auntie Helen for she was always fun to be with. She often looked after them so that Irene and I could resume our hunt for material in the downtown stores. During one of her weekend visits I informed her that Nancy was able to read her little story books at age three and a half. She could hardly believe it so took out the Toronto Star and asked Nancy if she would read the headline. Nancy did so, stunning her Aunt in the process.

Helen graduated with honours and a scholarship for post-graduate studies at University of Toronto, 1956-1958, when she lived with us full time. After graduation she taught nursing at St Michael's for several years. We were all very proud of her achievements.

Our beautiful twin daughters were baptized in the Church of the Nativity in September. Needless to say I had to give up all my volunteer work at church but we still attended as much as possible separately.

We purchased a double carriage for the babies and I placed Janice and Judith in the carriage while Nancy held on to one side and Peter the other and off we'd go for a walk or shopping on the Danforth. I can't count the times I had people stop and ask me, "are they all yours?"

"Of course they are and I love them all", I replied. I suppose having four children in three and a half years could seem incredible and somewhat of a feat.

The veranda now held a large play pen, two chairs and four children. Nancy and Peter were free to roam around with toys, bikes etc., while Judith and Janice were confined to the play pen. Trouble, trouble – when they got into little scraps over toys Judith would bite Janice and Janice would pull Judith's hair by the handful. Not wanting a bald baby or arms with scars we invested in another play pen and placed them just far enough apart so they could touch hands but not pull hair or bite. It worked beautifully.

Joe was closely bonded with Nancy when she was the only child but when Peter turned two he suddenly started taking him on trips to the grocery store and the park, leaving the girls behind. On one trip Peter somehow wandered away up an aisle and was lost. Someone took him to the office while Joe scurried around looking for him. When they finally met a tearful little Peter exclaimed to his Father, "you old 'de'il' Daddy, you lost me," and jumped into Joe's arms. Children can be so humorous without meaning to be. This Father son attachment was the beginning of sibling rivalry between Nancy and Peter which lasted into their early teens. Nancy was the little favourite until little brother came along and changed everything. Of course we didn't recognize or even know about sibling rivalry then, or we would have taken measures to correct it, i.e. divide Daddy's time with the children more equitably.

Our social life on Bonnie Brae resumed with Saturday night get together's and we purchased our first black and white TV which opened a new world of entertainment for us. Prior to that we only had radio and the gramophone with our favourite records.

In late Fall we received a surprise visit from Flora and Wellington, Joe's parents, who were anxious to meet the two new arrivals. I cooked a lovely roast beef dinner, homemade cherry pie, which received great compliments. We had a wonderful visit after which they left to spend time with dear Aunt Bertha and their daughter Alma. Joe's parents owned and operated the family farm on the 9th Line, Carelton Place which he inherited from his father, an emigrant from Ireland, who had died at an early age. Wellington spent an arduous life working the farm with his helpmate, Flora – who also cooked for years for harvest gangs. So, shortly after their son Robert married Isabel, they decided to retire and move into a house in Carelton Place owned by Mom Hawkins that she had inherited from her family. We visited them with Nancy and Peter to celebrate their retirement and after a happy weekend with them were ready to leave. Dad Hawkins came to the car put his hand on my shoulder and seriously counselled Joe, "you take good care of this little lady. She's a wonderful Mother and also takes good care of you."

I was very moved by his compliment as it was the first sign of an emotional exchange coming from him and changed my previous opinion of him – that he was cool and unemotional. Sadly we didn't have him for too long for he passed away in hospital, November 1956, with a massive heart attack just after they visited us. He is buried in the Hawkins family plot in St James cemetery in Carleton Place.

After Dad Hawkins' death Aunt Bertha decided her ageing sister Elizabeth should move in with her on Brooke Avenue. She hired a lovely caregiver named Miss Donahue to look after her while she worked. During this period we were often invited to Aunt Bertha's for Sunday dinner so Aunt Elizabeth could spend time with us. Bertha was a fabulous cook and we thoroughly enjoyed our visits despite having to lug playpen and high chairs with us. Nancy and Peter, being older, were introduced to stamp and coin collections by Aunt Bertha. The children each received a silver dollars dated the year of their birth. Sadly, Aunt Elizabeth died shortly after her brother, 1958, and was buried beside her twin sister, Martha, in St James Cemetery, Carleton Place.

The following summer, for Joe's vacation, we drove to Smooth Rock Falls for two weeks where Joe had a wonderful time fishing with my Father. Mother enjoyed having the children with her. So began a yearly habit where Joe would drive me and the children to Smooth Rock Falls for the month of July, then pick us up at which time he would enjoy a week of his vacation.

This really was a 'life saver' for it gave both of us time to relax and recuperate from our busy stress-ridden life.

The time soon came for Nancy and her little friends to start kindergarten at MacGregor Public School located near the East General Hospital. The history of this area is rather interesting. It all began in 1921 with an eccentric pig farmer named Billy McKay. Billy, then in his fifties, owned valuable land in Blocks A to C of the newly established East York Township. He offered plots for a dollar to build a hospital, new municipal offices and at the corner of Coxwell and Mortimer a large school. Unfortunately the school was named after a local politician, Robert MacGregor, not Billy. All was not lost for years later some thoughtful politician named McKay Road for Billy. What a great example of one person's generosity greatly benefitting a community for years to come.

Nancy loved school from day one, always enthusiastic about learning and eventually became an Ontario Scholar, the last year they had the award.

The 'old gang' on Bonnie Brae began to disperse in the late '50s. The Schaefer's with their kids Judy and David started the exodus moving to North York. The Green's with Robbie, Kathy and David – Julie later – moved to Don Mills. The Muldoons with David and Effie settled on O'Connor drive in East York. The Cole's with Linda, Ted and John, Catherine later, moved to Pharmacy Avenue in Scarborough. Finally, the Edminson's with Janet and Judy, a little son later, settled north of Hwy #7 in Markham.

Joe accepted a position as Chief Account with Sankeys Furniture, a British company in Smiths Falls, Ontario. We tearfully said goodbye to all our dear friends and parted in the Spring of '58. We rented our house to a young couple because the market was slow and rented a house in Smiths

Falls on Brockville Avenue for ourselves. It was a large two story semi-detached brick house where we spent some happy and memorable times.

I will never forget our time on Bonnie Brae Blvd. We lucked out to find our lovely little house on a street with so many compatible couples who were interesting, creative and fun loving. Our social life was a perfect antidote to the stress of parenting and resulted in lifelong friendships. Further more, we found ourselves among a group of like minded couples with young families eager to succeed, convinced a bright future lay ahead. Bonnie Brae certainly was a springboard toward that dream, for Don Schaefer rose to great heights in Nesbitt Thomson, a leading broker, Gord Green formed his own company Rosewood Furniture Finishing, a very successful and renowned company in Toronto. Trevor Muldoon went from managing the Fruit and Vegetable Department of Loblaws to become a very successful Agent with a Life Insurance Company. Denis Edminson in the retail diamond business, became an executive in his company. Finally Joe worked his way from Controller to Vice-President of DuBois Chemicals in Weston. All in all a wonderful experience with so many good memories.

CHAPTER 21

The next chapter of our life was spent in Smiths Falls
– originally called Smyth's Falls in 1784 after Thomas
Smyth, a United Empire Loyalist, who was awarded two
lots (four hunDred acres) forty-five miles south of Ottawa.
He died in 1831. Construction of the Rideau Canal began
in 1826, that included four locks harnessing a thirty feet
Drop in the Rideau River near what became Smiths Falls.
The canal was completed by 1832. Smiths Falls as a village
was incorporated finally in 1954!

Our move to Smiths Falls went smoothly. Jim Martin,
Joe's boss at Sankey Furniture, was an affable gentleman
whose wife Margaret was originally from England. Once a
year they would hold a board meeting with Mr. Rothesay,
Chairman of the Board, attending from England. After
the meeting he would take the four of us and his wife for
a delightful dinner at the Chateau Laurier in Ottawa. Joe

seemed to enjoy his work at the company and watched it grow significantly.

Our new neighbours were Judy and Ken Ain, whose sister, Pearl, owned the half of the semi-detached we rented. They had a lovely family of four – Richard, Ali, Marilyn and Suzi. On the other side were the Cowley's – Jessie and Bill with John, Jill, Jane and Danny. Bill had played for the Boston Bruins and the St Louis Eagles from 1934 to 1947. After retirement he settled in Smiths Falls where he owned and operated the Russel Hotel plus he also owned the Elmdale Hotel and Pub in Ottawa.

Jessie, Judy and I became instant friends and were like three sisters by the end of our stay in Smiths Falls. Jessie was a happy-go-lucky, vivacious and energetic young woman with a loveable personality who cared about people more than about housework. Consequently she would frequently entertain with a sink full of dishes or the living room un-vacuumed but remained a delightful cook and hostess.

Judy, on the other hand, was very tidy and orderly, had a serious but also fun side. She worried a lot about Ken and the children. Ken operated a local men's wear store, was a jovial good natured young man, loved cracking jokes and was a beautiful pianist entertaining us often. They took us into their homes and hearts immediately and the children became the best of friends. It wasn't long before we became members of St John's Anglican Church which we attended every Sunday. I also joined the Women's

Auxiliary and enjoyed meeting a new group of friends. As a fund raiser I spotted an ad by Raleigh's showing how their bottled vanilla and ground black pepper can be used as fund raisers for organizations. I talked the committee into trying it so we purchased twenty bottles of vanilla and twenty tins of black pepper. Despite numerous sceptics in the group the vanilla and pepper were all sold within a month.The group asked for more innovative ideas.

Due to Smiths Falls proximity to Carleton Place, approximately sixteen miles, we often paid weekend visits to the family. Mom Hawkins was now a widow living alone in her two storey house so she always looked forward to our visits. We would also call on Joe's sister Bessie and Art Fee. Art was a veteran who served in the army in WW2 and on one of his leaves he and Bessie married. After the war they purchased a farm, stocked it with cows, horses, pigs and poultry and earned their living farming. Peter particularly loved the farm especially animals and on one of our visits Uncle Art gave him a Rhode Island Red hen as a pet, which he kept for a year. When the hen became too difficult to handle we reluctantly returned it to Uncle Art who promised Peter he would take good care of it. The hen and our current kitten became good friends and used to nuzzle each other. We all have happy memories of Aunt Bessie and Uncle Art in Appleton. Their two lovely daughters, Barbara and Lainey, still reside in the area.

Robert, Joe's younger brother, inherited and operated the family farm successfully and some years later purchased another farm, the 'Cram Farm' situated beside a lake nearby. An avid business man he also purchased a shoe store, the leading one in Carleton Place and gave up farming altogether to work in the shoe store until he retired and son Douglas took over the operation. Robert and Isabel had two wonderful children, Douglas and sister Karen who presently works for Guelph University in Ontario.

Currie, the eldest brother, married Thelma Maynard of Stratford, Ontario and they had one beautiful little daughter Linda. Currie also served in the Navy during the war, then was employed in Ottawa as an engineer with the Federal Government.

Our short period in the eastern part of Ontario gave our children a wonderful opportunity to get to know and love their Grandma, Aunts and Uncles and all their cousins. They spent special time with their cousins growing up and the friendships continued into adulthood.

These frequent visits also gave me the opportunity to get to know Mom Hawkins better. I was always very fond of her but distance between Toronto and Carleton Place made it difficult to visit frequently. That all changed now with weekly visits which we all looked forward to and enjoyed thoroughly.

Mom Hawkins was one of seven children of the McNaughton family whose predecessors came from Scotland to start a new life in Canada. Her father, Robert McNaughton, was a portrait artist who in 1892 decided to move his family from Carleton Place to Alberta where he hoped there would be more opportunity for his profession. Mom Hawkins recounted sadly how they decided to leave her behind, at age nine, with an Aunt who could not have chilDren. She tearfully said goodbye to her parents and siblings not ever knowing why she was 'the chosen one'. She went on to explain that her Auntie was very kind and loving but she always missed her birth family and didn't see them again until she took a trip out west in her forties. There was an additional sister born in Alberta in 1895 making a total of eight siblings.

Her story moved me deeply and more than a few tears were shed for I was aware of other stories whereby she was 'short changed'. Joe recounted to me that when they were childrenDad Hawkins had an odd habit of turning his chair with the back facing Mom Hawkins. He sat at the head of the table and she beside him to one side. The children- probably unaware of the significance of such an act – would turn the chair to the proper position giggling in the process when Dad Hawkins left the table. When he returned he was not amused and quickly turned the chair with the back facing Mom Hawkins. Dear Mom Hawkins didn't have many options in life, like many other women in those times, so she just tolerated these indignities and carried on. Like my Mother and Aunt Bertha she became one of my heroes.

The children were growing fast so I had to keep up with new dresses, coats and clothes for them and myself. Peter's clothes were more complex – windbreakers and jackets – so they were always purchased. Janice and Judith started kindergarten in Smiths Falls, Peter Grade One and Nancy in Grade Four. It was in Smiths Falls that Nancy skipped a Grade as she was advanced in all her subjects.

On weekends and holidays we took advantage of opportunities to visit Ottawa, the Parliament buildings and often took the cousins along. We also took time to explore the Gatineau Region of Québec and Montréal, both extremely interesting. Our life seemed full and satisfying.

Joe, always restless to improve his qualifications, studied and wrote exams to attain membership in ACIS (Association of the Chartered Institute of Secretaries). It was December and the second Board celebration, with dinner at the Chateau Laurier. Joe asked what fur piece I preferred in coat form and presented me with an early Christmas gift, a beautiful Persian Lamb jacket to wear for the occasion. Margaret Martin and Mrs Rothesay both wore luxurious Mink jackets. I was the "black lamb" of the group with my new jacket.

While in Smiths Falls we had the good fortune to meet another couple that we became close to, Blythe originally from Toronto and Warren Hunt were a charming, outgoing couple with a young son, Bradley, born in 1956. They built a beautiful home on the riverside in the outskirts of Smiths Falls. Through our visits the children became very friendly. One of the fun times was watching the frog population in the reeds behind their house leaping around and making croaking sounds. On March 20th, 1962 an unimaginable tragedy struck. Little Bradley got permission to stay at his friend's house, also on the riverside, and the two little boys were allowed to walk on the deeply frozen river. Unbeknownst to the family a deep narrow crevice had formed in the middle of the river. Apparently while the little boys were playing Bradley accidentally slipped and fell, face first, into the crevice which contained about a foot of water. Unable to lift his head from the water he drowned by the time help came. Our hearts were broken for Blythe and Warren and the whole town was in mourning, including our children. Dear little Bradley's funeral was held in St John's Anglican Church. Terrible years of sadness followed for Blythe and Warren but they did adopt a little boy eventually which helped to heal their broken hearts.

In the summer of 1960 Joe got word that Sankey Furniture would be moving to Guelph, Ontario and amalgamating with Royal Furniture. They wanted him to move with them, offering a raise to stay with the new company. He spent a few sleepless nights pondering and in the end decided he did not want to move to Guelph. Always very successful in finding employment he was offered a position as Comptroller with Stuart Warner Corp. of Canada, manufacturers of radios, televisions etc., located in Belleville, Ontario. He graciously declined the move to Guelph and we prepared ourselves with great anticipation for our move to Belleville.

It was difficult saying goodbye to our dear friends the Ains, the Cowleys and the Hunts, and also our family members in Carleton Place and Ottawa. Several days before the move I was at my usual hairdressers when I inadvertently turned my head towards the entrance and was sure I saw Mom Hawkins go by. I excused myself and ran outside and sure enough there she was. I called to her, we embraced and she informed me she came by bus to say a last goodbye before we departed. A substantial walk from the bus station to our house on Brockville Avenue! I took her into the shop and we left together to surprise Joe and the children. She was such a loving Mother-in-law/Mother/Grandmother. In a few days all our furniture, bikes etc were loaded and taken away by transport and we packed our car with our pet cat, Stripes, a recently acquired puppy, a black spaniel we called Inky, and four excited children waving goodbye to friends. Our time in Smiths Falls was short but filled with both happy memories of family and friends and tears for little Bradley. We waved goodby with promises to keep in touch.

CHAPTER 22

Belleville, located at the mouth of the Moira River on the Bay of Quinte, was incorporated as a city with a population of 17,000 in 1877. It is in the County of Hastings and has the usual colourful history of Loyalists and Grist Mills. Our family laughingly look at it as 'Belle Ville' the pretty city where everything happened.

After a short drive of approximately two hours we arrived in Belleville at our new rented house on Catherine Street. Mayflower Movers were already there waiting for us. They filled the house with our furniture and other belongings while the children enjoyed a picnic lunch in the yard. So did Stripes and Inky, our pets.

The house, a two story brick with a wraparound veranda, was on a corner lot with a concrete sidewalk at the front and the back, plenty of grass to cut. There was also a detached garage in the backyard.

The neighbours, the Vaders across the street and the Teackelas' beside us, welcomed us to the neighbourhood. At the beginning of the week the children registered in their various Grades and Joe went off to his new job with Stuart Warner Corp. I tackled the unpacking of boxes and organized the various rooms. I felt like an old pro with all the moving experience behind me.

Before the week was over we looked into the housing market and decided to have a house custom built. We promptly placed an order with De Mille Construction to build a two storey, four bedroom house in Plaza Square, with lots in an old apple orchard off Bridge Street. There is also a large shopping plaza within walking distance. It was a unique experience choosing details ranging from the colour of the walls to choice of kitchen counter tops and window styles. The centre piece of the large living room was a beautiful Angel Stone, floor to ceiling fireplace, with a raised six foot hearth around it. The house would be ready for occupancy in five months, convenient for the children starting in new schools.

At the top of the hill from us was an interesting house at 114 Bridge Street West called the 'Moodie Cottage'. Once the home of Susanna Moodie, author of children books, short stories, articles and novels. She was an English woman who, with her husband, first settled in the countryside. Her first book "Roughing it in the Bush" (1952) described that experience. She was also involved in the anti-slavery movement in 1840, writing many articles denouncing slavery. They had seven children one of whom tragically drowned in the Moira River, (a seven year old son).

By a strange coincidence one of the couples we met and became good friends with were renting the Moodie Cottage. Bernice and Bill Andrews were a very friendly, exuberant couple, she originally from the East coast, he from Ontario. Bill served in the RCAF during the war and remained in the Service. At the time we met they had three children, Liz, Stuart and Ronnie and much later in life, little Patrick. As a couple we had so much in common and the children became good friends.

Before long we started a social habit which we thoroughly enjoyed for years. Since Joe was a WW2 RCAF veteran he could attend the Officer's Mess in Trenton Military Base. So Saturday nights we would go there for dinner and dancing. It soon became a ritual we looked forward to so much and usually spent New Year's Eve celebrations there as well.

All was not fun and games, however, we also experienced a lot of heartbreak. Inky, our little black spaniel, didn't adjust to the move too well. If let loose he would immediately chase after people on the street, barking. So we had to buy a long leash and confine him when the children were at school. One day he wiggled out of confinement and chased a little old lady down the street frightening her badly. We apologized and made sure she regained her composure. Then family circle – what are we ever going to do about Inky? He easily breaks out of his shackles and we can't have him chasing vulnerable people. Sadly the conclusion was we took him to a farmer nearby who wanted a dog. He loved Inky and we tearfully said goodbye. Mr John, the farmer, said we could visit any time. On our fourth visit Inky was nowhere to be seen. Mr John recounted how he started chasing cars and trucks on the road and finally got hit. He was as upset as we were but assured us Inky loved the farm and they loved him. To us he will always be a happy memory.

Up to now I would call our marriage an extremely 'child centred' one, how can it be anything else having four children in three and a half years! Now the children were older and more self sufficient so we had a little more time to spend enjoying friends and social events.

The children liked their school and teachers and made friends easily. Extra curricula events included hockey for Peter, baseball in the summer, the girls enjoyed tap-dancing lessons and kept me busy making endless costumes for their recitals. All the children took piano lessons and at one point Joe and I joined them. Mrs Scobie, a wonderful teacher, came to the house Saturday mornings and spent almost five hours giving Joe and I and the children piano lessons. When Mrs Scobie retired the girls continued with Sister Polycarp who used to gently tap them on the knuckles with a pencil if they hit the wrong note. Peter switched to guitar for which he developed a lifelong passion. He could play the guitar without having taken a lesson. He would listen to a Beatles song and repeat it perfectly on his guitar, plus words and song which was fantastic! Nancy continued, writing her exams in the Conservatory of Music, Toronto and remains quite accomplished. It was obvious to us at this point that our darling daughter Nancy was a 'gifted child', excelling in everything she tried. She proved us right time and again in the years that followed to adulthood. What a loveable little gem.

The children also joined the "Y" and learned to swim. I never could master it so I made sure they all learned to swim as children.

Shortly after our move we got word that Mom Hawkins had suffered a heart attack. We immediately moved Peter to our bedroom and painted and furnished the room. When we went to see her after her hospital stay and invited her to live with us until she was fully recuperated, she graciously declined stating she would get more peace and quiet in her own home. Robert and Isabel would be near by if she needed them. We understood her point of view but were, never-the-less, disappointed. Peter was happy to get his bedroom back.

We also received some good news which helped to lift our spirits at this time. My sister Helen announced she was engaged to Gerald Flaherty, a young man who was studying law at Osgoode Hall, Toronto, about to graduate in the near future. Helen was teaching nursing at St Michaels Hospital and sharing a house with her friend

Diane, also a nurse. The wedding would take place June 30th., 1962 at Holy Name Catholic Church at Pape and Danforth with the reception following at the King Edward Hotel in downtown Toronto. Helen also asked that Nancy be her Bridesmaid with Diane as Maid of Honour. Also Alex McDonald who introduced Helen to Gerry and Gerry's brother Paul would be Ushers. his brother Michael, the Best Man.

I arranged a week in Toronto to meet with Helen and Diane discussing colours of gowns, flowers, details of the reception, etc. Also I was delighted to meet the prospective bridegroom, a handsome, affable young man with dark wavy hair. I also took the opportunity to look for my outfit for the big occasion. I chose a Dior ribbed silk beige dress which I was fortunate to find in 'The Room' at Simpsons at a greatly reduced price, size 10, with fancy handbag and fancy beige high-heels to match. Remembering my millinery skills I also visited dressmakers Supplies to buy materials for two glamorous hats, one for Mother, one for me. Diane and Nancy would wear identical dark turquoise satin gowns with matching head-dresses and satin shoes. (Nancy's first bought dress by the way).

About this time we started the tradition of "Family Reunions", (Joe's family that is), while we lived on Catherine Street, where I had the first one during mid-summer. I cooked and baked and prepared for days. We happily hosted twelve adults and eleven children to a sit-down dinner. The adults were seated in the dining-room and the children in the adjoining vestibule area. It was there Aunt Bertha started her 'sweet tradition'. Being a devout Christian she was constantly contributing to various charities and this was a new one. The Kiwanis Club sold tins of maple syrup as a fund raiser and Aunt Bertha decided what better gift for adults and children than maple syrup. Each summer thereafter she would stock up and present a large tin to each family or individual. She kept this up to the end, she died at age ninety-eight. After a lovely evening of fun, laughter and reminiscing Mom Hawkins stayed overnight with us and the others with Aunt Bertha and Alma in Toronto. It turned out that my sister-in-law, Isabel and I each took turns having the reunions for many years to come. She usually had close to forty people as she invited all the cousins and their families in the Carleton Place and Ottawa Regions.

I valued these annual reunions for it kept the family in touch with each other physically as well as emotionally, keeping us connected. It also taught the next generation of the importance of family and respect and love for them.

How fortunate that we had that wonderful reunion, for sadly, Mom Hawkins passed away April 2nd, 1962 in her seventy-ninth year. A dear, loving, generous soul who always put her family first. The family gathered together for her funeral at St James Anglican Church and she was buried in the family plot next to her husband in St James cemetery, Carleton Place. We cried a river for her, she was so loved. Sadly the only inheritance she received in Dad Hawkin's will was the rental money for twelve acres of land. The final insult after the 'back of the chair' and 'no buggy ride' to church incidents. (Oh for Murdoch v. Murdoch.)

When we visited Mom Hawkins the last few times she brought up the subject 'when I'm gone' . . . which we dreaded hearing. However, she insisted. Their living room furniture consisted of a wicker settee with matching rocking chair and armchair with velvet seats. I almost always sat in the rocking chair, usually with one of the four on my knee when they were little. She then started to tell me I was always her favourite daughter-in-law. Very moved by her statement my curiosity prompted me to ask, "why is that so?" She replied, "because you are so much like me – a hard worker, sewing for yourself and the children and the house. You're a dedicated mother and wife cooking good meals, baking, preserving fruit and you never complain." She apparently saw herself in me, nose to the grindstone, always putting family first and not complaining. I embraced her and thanked her for the wonderful compliment. Her touching tribute is one I'll never forget. She continued by saying, "when I'm gone I want you to have the wicker settee and chairs." Then she brought out pieces of glassware and china that Joe had given her over the years. "Please take these too, they're special to me." The bond between us was strong to the end.

On many occasions in the years ahead I'd ask myself, "why, if we were both so dedicated and hard working why were we so undervalued by our husbands?".

CHAPTER 23

The school year was ending successfully for the children and they were happily looking forward to Aunty's wedding and summer holidays. I completed the two wedding hats which turned out better than I expected. Peter was outfitted with a snazzy new jacket, shirt, tie and trousers, even new shoes – and a short haircut. Jani and Judy would wear their beautiful full skirted sleeveless organza dresses covered with pink and blue roses which I made for a dance recital. New beribboned white straw hats and white shoes completed the outfit. Joe would wear his Sunday best with a new tie.

On Friday the 29th. we drove to Toronto to Aunt Bertha's house where we would stay two nights thanks to her kind invitation. She welcomed us warmly as always, prepared a lovely dinner and after catching up on all the news we retired for the night.

Early to bed early to . . . . and we did excited, about Helen and Gerry's wedding day. All decked out in our wedding outfits we descended on Helen and Diane and Mother and Father who had arrived earlier. I asked Mother to try on her new hat, a cloche covered with beige tulle and flowers to match her beige silk dress. She loved it so I took Mother, Dad and Helen to the back yard and snapped several pictures, as did the photographer. The limo then took the wedding party to church, Joe took the rest of us.

It was lovely seeing so many familiar faces of friends at church. With strains of "Here Comes the Bride", Helen, looking radiant and beautiful in her exquisite gown entered on Father's arm following Diane and Nancy. Nancy looked so grown up in her gown and high heels. It brought tears to my eyes.

The ceremony was memorable especially Ave Maria and the choir renditions. After the ceremony the wedding party and both sets of parents formed a receiving line down the steps of the church to greet and welcome the guests.

The reception was held at the King Edward Hotel downtown with cocktails then lunch, very tastefully done. Both sides of the family met and enjoyed each other's company and at approximately 5pm the bride and groom departed through a hailstorm of confetti. My baby sister was now Mrs Gerald Ambrose Flaherty, smiling happily and waving goodbye to us all. A memorable day.

Mother and Father went on to Tillsonburg with relatives where they would spend a week or so. We spent some time with Aunt Bertha then departed for Belleville not wanting to tire her out by staying another night. A wonderful weekend we'll always remember.

Our new home on Plaza Square was ready for us in July and we happily prepared for the big move. The house came with new 'fridge and stove and had plenty of cupboard space. Nancy and Peter had their own bedrooms while Jan and Judy shared one. The master bedroom was spacious with an adjoining bathroom. I could see my work was cut out for me decorating the whole house, making drapes, curtains and bedspread!

The children met neighbourhood friends and before the week was up picked their favourites. Our immediate neighbours were the Hales on one side, a rather quiet couple who chose not to mix with the neighbours and on the other the Wrights, Janet and Jim, young and gregarious expecting their first child. The Prestons, Browns, Wards, Aleyas and Foys, all with children, comprised the rest of our neighbours.

Plaza Square was a large semi-circle with an outer and inner row of houses. Ours, in the outer row, had a backyard with two apple trees that bloomed every spring, producing apples in the fall. In the inner row across from us lived Sylvia and Leo Logue with little daughter Diane. The other side of the semi-circle was developed mostly by Lambert Construction, successful brothers one of whom lived on Plaza Square. Bobby Lambert had a married sister next door, Ruby and Hank Williams, who had three children, Chrissie, Craig and Robbie. We became very close friends, partied together and played bridge every Sunday afternoon. It almost felt like a repeat of Bonnie Brae but with a distinctly diverse group. We were all different but got along well socially.

We found the Anglican Church nearest to us, St Margarets on the Hill, with Reverend Dunlop in charge. We joined the church, Joe volunteering to be their accountant, I teaching juniors and joining the women's Altar Guild. We attended church every Sunday that we were home.

Nancy, age thirteen, was entering Grade 9 at Moira Secondary School, Peter Grade 5 and Jani and Judy Grade 4 In Harry J Public School. It was here that Nancy and Anne-Marie Knudsen became close friends, a friendship that was destined to last far into the future.

The piano lessons, dancing lessons, baton twirling for the girls, hockey and baseball for Peter continued but with something new added. I decided to take art lessons at Moira Secondary Night School with Mr Ritchie our instructor. I always think of this phase of my life as the 'Mind Opening Phase'. Imagination is a crucial component in art so it was an exciting addition to the mother/housewife part of my life. A t the end of the season we displayed our work in the Belleville Library where my contribution won first prize – an oil painting named "Northern Lights" based on one of my favourite memories growing up in Northern Ontario. Mr Ritchie urged me to continue painting which I did for several years.

During summer holidays Joe drove us to Smooth Rock Falls in July and left us there for a month. It was such a good experience for the children as half the population was French Canadian with a good number of immigrants and English Canadians making up the rest. The children made good friends, spoke some French and learned about other cultures. After several summers of this our children eagerly looked forward to spending time with their new friends in Smooth Rock Falls. Shortly after our arrival Peter's little pals, a diverse group of French, English and immigrants would rush over and welcome each other with hugs and laughter and have a great summer of fun – the girl's friends would do the same. I always liked to photograph these touching events for an album "Memories of Childhood" which they loved looking at when they got older. When I did the same, though extremely pleased about the friendships I'd ask myself, "why wasn't I welcomed and befriended this way at age five when I arrived at Smooth Rock Falls"? All immigrant children got 'sticks and stones and nasty name calling'! There was obviously a definite shift in attitude toward newcomers which was heart warming to see.

On weekends Father would take us all on his motorboat to his cottage at 'Cat's Ar..'' so named by sporty fisherman and spend the weekend fishing, steeping in nature and eating delightful fish fry by Father. Mother prepared the veggies and desserts. Children loved these weekends in the northern woods and were fascinated watching Gramps clean and filet the fish. When Joe arrived for his holidays he enjoyed the cottage, fishing, bowling and time at the Legion, a customary meeting place for the men. We all looked forward to the interesting sights on the journey there and back, always commencing at 6am! When Father retired at sixty-five these holidays up north ended and we had a new venue to visit, Brantford.

Grandparents play a very important role in children's lives. Traditions, customs and family values – thoughtfulness, kindness, generosity and respect are often taught in subtle ways. We are indeed blessed when we have loving grandparents.

CHAPTER 24

The children always excelled in school with Nancy leading the pack. They did their homework diligently and enjoyed reading and art. Everything seemed to be going so smoothly, both at school and the home front, almost too good to be true. Then Mr. Moore, Judy and Jani's teacher, decided to separate them placing them in different classrooms. There is no explanation as to why this was necessary. Naturally, it caused the girls a bit of trauma. Their grades went down a bit but they both maintained a high eighties average.

About the same time Peter asked if he could get a black leather jacket which the boys were getting into at school. We being narrowed minded said he could get a new brown leather jacket but not a black one (black jackets were associated with motorcycle gangs!). In retrospect we were too rigid about dress codes and should have given Peter more options as he was a more creative thinker, dresser, guitar player and should have been supported more by us. Parents do make mistakes unintentionally which they live to regret later.

Another trauma we suffered around that time was finding our pet cat, Stripes, dead beside a pile of broken branches in the back yard. We buried her and put wild flowers on her grave as a marker. Judy found a solution by bringing a lovely homeless black cat into their bedroom and hiding it in the closet. In a few days the cat had four little kittens and the secret was out. We kept Mama Kitty and one kitten and gave the rest to a pet shop. It was at this point that Judy threatened, "when I grow up and have my own house I'm going to have several kittens." She did.

In 1964 Joe decided instead of going to Smooth Rock for the summer we would take the children to the New York World's Fair and visit the Boston area on the east coast where the pilgrims landed. I agreed it would be a wonderful experience for us all. Before we departed Joe went to his doctor complaining about a cold. Dr. Pierce examined him and said he had a slight touch of pneumonia. He prescribed an anti-biotic and said it would be OK to proceed to New York.

We departed on a warm sunny morning in late July and drove straight to Long Island where we would stay. Joe and I in a double bed, the girls in the other double bed and Peter in a cot they set up. I made new outfits for the girls and myself and Peter had a few new outfits plus a new wind-breaker. Joe seemed to be fully recovered after about four days.

The children thoroughly enjoyed the spectacle of New York's World Fair especially the model space ship we climbed up into. We also took car trips to areas bordering Long Island. Then back north to Boston around Plymouth Rock we boarded the Pilgrim ship which the children thoroughly enjoyed. All in all it was a super adventure and fun trip getting there and back.

In the Fall I resumed my art lessons, this time with renowned artist Philippa Burrows Faulkner. Born in Belleville in 1917 she was a painter, sculptor and graphic artist specializing in cubist water colours and abstract works in acrylics and oils. She attended Bishop Strachan School in Toronto, Parsons School of Design in New York and received a Master of Fine Arts Degree in Mexico. She was married to Dr. George V Faulkner who died in 1955 at the age of forty-seven and had two children Anne and George. She resided in what is known today as Glanmore Museum which was originally built in 1882. It was here she conducted her art classes.

I attended classes one night a week and found Philippa a most interesting and stimulating teacher. After teaching us about different genres of art and materials we could use our first assignment was to produce a collage. This involved using various materials, colour, balance and layout to produce an art piece of your liking. No rules only imagination applied. The next morning after the children had left for school I sat eating my soft-boiled egg in an egg cup wondering what sort of collage I should produce. As I started to clear away the empty egg shell my eyes landed on some bright apple-green serviettes in a holder and BINGO! Two materials were chosen right at the breakfast table. In the living room I had an antique white pitcher filled with flowers on a table in front of the picture window. Excitement was mounting. I rushed to the basement where I kept a section for my art supplies and pulled out a 15" x 18" canvas board to start my collage.

I covered the canvas with light glue and started the background material – crunched apple-green serviettes with empty space in the centre for my white antique pitcher. Then I boiled twelve eggs, next day's lunch and carefully shelled the eggs and placed them on my work table, crushing them into mosaic like pieces. Using a pencil I traced the shape and size of the pitcher in the centre, covered it with glue and proceeded to make my white egg-shell mosaic pitcher. Now what, I asked myself? Being an avid knitter I added white yarn to form the stems of a mystery bouquet. So far so good! What kind of flowers? In a flash I thought about the lovely buttercup bouquets I used to pick in Smooth Rock Falls and take to my Mother. Out came the Bell Yellow Pages with a shiny yellow cover. With perforator in hand I created a little mountain of yellow petals for my Buttercup Bouquet. After hours of carefully formed buttercups at the end of the yarn stems the collage was completed – almost. I hurried down to the basement to my collection of frames and lo and behold the perfect antique white and gold frame. Joe helped me assemble it, wire and all. Now, what would I name it? Breakfast Collage of course.

Needless to say Philippa was enthralled, told me I picked the perfect frame because of the antique pitcher, made me enter in the Art Contest in Belleville's Library where it won first prize. I value it highly to this day.

Another assignment consisted of any art style, using any medium we wished and this was near the end of our year with Philippa. This time I thought about the woods at sunset, late Fall. I used acrylic burnt umber over the whole canvas. Then instead of the traditional brush I decided to use the flat end of a clothes peg to form my woods by pressing and drawing the peg through the thick acrylic which, luckily, gave the trees the perfect texture. A brush was used to add paths though the woods and the golden sunset. I placed the canvas in a modern beige ribbed wooden frame with an inner white edge and it looked wonderful. Philippa when told about the technique marvelled and continued her praise. It also won first prize at the Belleville display of amateur artists.

Philippa's reactions during my time with her did so much for me. It certainly opened my mind to other possibilities – success breeds success, as they say – I will always remember her not only as an outstanding artist and teacher but the person who opened many doors for me in the years to come. She died in 2001. God bless her beautiful soul.

CHAPTER 25

My sister, Helen, with her husband Gerry, now graduated as a lawyer and working with CBC Ottawa, had their first child, John, born April 1st, 1963. Helen followed him to Ottawa where Jamie was born in 1965. I took the train to Ottawa to meet my beautiful little nephews. At the time they were renting a house on Alta Vista Drive but planning to soon buy a house in Ottawa.

It was during this visit that Mother had a gall bladder operation in Smooth Rock Falls hospital. However, we were not informed by my Father that she nearly died after it. Much to everyone's surprise in the hospital she recovered and lived to fight more battles. We were so grateful her life was spared.

After a wonderful visit with my sister and her family I returned to Belleville, welcomed with hugs and kisses. The children apparently missed me.

During the return train trip I had the opportunity to reflect on our life and marriage. I think we were good, devoted parents who gave their children every advantage we could afford. Our marriage was another thing. I believed Joe was too rigid in his behaviour with the children and myself. For instance, we never shared a joint bank account, all money was controlled by him with my housekeeping allowance at forty dollars a week for food and other essentials, until 1968 when he raised it to fifty dollars a week! The house was jointly owned thanks to dear Aunt Bertha. I take full responsibility for not bringing up issues of excessive control but I loved my children intensely and would never start any action that would affect their security. What would I do if Joe left me, how would I raise the children alone? Having very few or no options I chose to tolerate these abuses. However, always in the back of my mind was, "I have to make myself independent, both financially and emotionally, raise the children the best I could and not stir up trouble." I felt at this point that emotion was lacking in our marriage and that art lessons and further education at a later time would help to fill that void.

Another factor that helped fill the void was, we made friends easily. Ruby and Hank were close friends and we had weekly social gatherings usually playing bridge or partying. Bernice and Bill Andrews were also an important part of our life making the less enjoyable times more tolerable.

At the end of the 1967 school year Nancy graduated with top marks and was awarded an Ontario Scholarship for university. She applied and was accepted at the University of Toronto. We drove to Toronto to look over university residences and she chose Victoria College, the residence located on Charles Street close to University Avenue. She would commence university in September to study political science. Anne-Marie, her closest friend, chose Western University to study art. I had a lump in my throat at our dearest, eldest child leaving home but swallowed hard and carried on.

When we returned Joe wanted to take the children and me to Montréal Expo. Nancy had a summer job so did not join us. We drove to Montréal, checked into our motel and turned in early to prepare for the next full day. We had an early breakfast and set off to enter the world of Montréal Expo. Not as spectacular as New York Expo but interesting never the less.

One of the exhibits we visited was, again, a model space ship which we explored and marvelled at. There was a room you could enter that caused weightlessness but nobody volunteered to try it. On exiting the space ship, Joe and Peter leading the way, a strange feeling came over me. The height on the way down suddenly made me feel faint. A new feeling, I stopped my descent and called for Joe to help me. He laughed and stood his ground. Jani and Judy immediately then took my arm, one on each side, and helped me safely down to ground level. Joe laughed off the event in his usually insensitive manner. He then proceeded to drive up Mount Royal, another height that panicked me (and him) so he quietly turned around and descended. Looking back on these incidents I think it was a case of 'bad nerves' over Nancy's upcoming departure plus the insecurity I felt in our marriage.

We spent considerable time shopping for Nancy's new clothes for university, buying her luggage and other essentials. We then drove her to Toronto and had lunch in Chinatown to celebrate her new life and left her in her residence on Charles Street with tears, kisses and good wishes. I thought about how different my leaving home was with Chief Richard's and Thelma when I moved to Toronto many years ago.

I found life at Plaza Square quite empty after Nancy's departure. Nothing I did alleviated the feeling so I had a sudden whim. Why don't I apply at Queens to start my BA? I hadn't completed Grade 13 and only had Grade 11 plus three Grade 12 subjects completed in the same period. My marks were first class and my record at Shaw's Business School was excellent. I sent the application in hoping for a miracle. It came in two weeks – I was accepted, ready to commence studies in September!

Unbeknown to me, Joe had been answering ads for positions in Toronto and finally was offered one. Nancy's departure probably was a trigger. He accepted a position with Dubois Chemicals, an American company producing dishwasher and car-wash products. Quite new to Canada and opening a branch in Weston. Joe would be Office Manager and Comptroller with Mr Robinson, an American, as the CEO.

He would leave in a week, we would put our house on the market and hope for a quick sale, then relocate in our beloved Toronto. I immediately got in touch with Queens, thanked them and cancelled my application as I would have no means of transportation. Joe would have the car and was planning to live at Aunt Bertha's until we were able to all move, coming home every weekend. We informed all our close friends of our plans and they were all happy for us.

The Real Estate market was sluggish and we had very few couples looking at the house. In the middle of the year Joe decided we should order a custom built house in Thornhill, a northern suburb of Toronto off Bayview, north of Steeles. We looked at several models of Wimpy homes between Young and Bayview Avenue and finally picked a two storey, four bedroom, three bathrooms, living room, dining room, kitchen and a large family room. We chose brown rug brick for the exterior, bay windows in the living room and dining room, a spacious entrance with a clothes closet and a washroom. Our bedroom would have an ensuite and large clothes closet. There would be a large bathroom with tub shower and sink. Everyone seemed happy with the choice. We also changed the plan and placed the stone fireplace and mantle in the living room instead of the family room. There was also an attached garage and paved driveway. The back and front yards were spacious enough for flower beds, trees and shrubs.

Since the house didn't sell in Belleville we rented to a young couple with one child. She was a Registered Nurse, he worked for a Book Company selling books to schools. The Eisners seemed like a decent couple so we gave them a two year's lease.

We moved to our Thornhill home in August 1968 after several trips back and forth during its construction. The price shocked us, $29,900, but we soon got used to it. The children, as usual, passed into the next Grade with high marks and good reports. They said goodbye to their many friends and teachers and were looking forward to the move. Nancy was doing well in university and looking forward to our move (so I could help type her essays). We moved in the middle of August with Mama Kitty and Blackie in tow. We had them in a cage in the car which I think they didn't appreciate too much but we couldn't bear to part with them.

CHAPTER 26

New home, new life, new beginnings. My feeling was that up to now much of my life was spent looking after, giving to and thinking of others – mostly my family and extended family. There seemed very little or no time or even desire for exploration of 'self', which was buried under a mound of obligations. This upcoming phase of my life is one of self-examination, growth and achievement bringing me great satisfaction and happiness. But happiness never rules alone for long, there's also sadness and unexpected tragedies that come with living one's life.

Tears turned to smiles when the children saw their new home. By this time we collected a piano, and organ purchased from Uncle Art Fee and Peter's numerous guitars. The piano and organ were placed in the basement to which we added a new pool-table to complete the play area.

The rest of the furniture seemed to fit in well. We decided to buy a new sofa and chairs for the family room. We also had a permanent table (semi-circle) built against the wall of the family room with beige oak round-back chairs around it.

The house came equipped with new 'fridge and stove so we placed our old 'fridge in the basement for an extra. Having learned about Picasso from dear Philippa I purchased a new Picasso print for the living room – 'guitar and violin' to keep the art phase alive and well. Peter chose the bedroom closest to the bathroom which was rather secluded from the others. Jani and Judy chose the large bedroom next to ours and preferred staying together. So we had a guest bedroom which Nancy used on her infrequent visits home.

Next door we had lovely neighbours, Olive and Wilf Neil and daughter Judy. Wilf owned Neil Sales Ltd., manufacturing steel products. On the other side Jean and John Collins and little Sandra. John was a high school teacher at Thornhill Secondary. Jean also was a teacher. Across from us the Cranes, Muriel and Al with two daughters, Linda and Barbara. Al was also a veteran of WW2.

After a brief time commuting to Woodbridge High the children finally attended Thornlea Secondary, a somewhat untraditional high school located on Bayview across from our sub-division. I was asked by the Neils to join them as an Office Assistant working half days each week. I also enrolled in an evening course to complete my Grade 12 English with Mr Truscello who after successful completion urged me to apply for studies at York University. With his reassurance ringing in my ears I wrote the admission test for studies in Atkinson College, York University and was accepted!

I began studies in the Fall of 1971 with Professor Michael Herren and his team. The course was in the genre of humanities and at some point we studied the Epic of Gilgamesh. Enjoying the studies of the ancient Sumerians thoroughly I stood up in class and asked, "who would the present-day descendants of the ancient Sumerians be"? Professor Herren smiled and replied, "In all my years of teaching I've never been asked that questions before. The answer is the Turks and the Hungarians." "I'm glad I asked, because I'm of Hungarian descent." What a delightful coincidence, Ancient Sumerians had apparently devised an alphabet even before the Egyptians. My first mark in University was A+ and my lowest a B+. I started by choosing Sociology as a major and Psychology as a minor. After taking a course in social work with Doctor Wilson Head I decided that would become my profession.

I met many like minded friends during my studies in Atkinson College – Mary Benedetto, Pauline Lower, Angela Conte and June Campbell. At the beginning of my studies Joe surprised me by buying me a new Ford Escort which I appreciated greatly. Peter, when he turned sixteen and the girls similarly, took lessons and received their driver's licence so we shared the car.

After the Eisner's lease expired we successfully sold Plaza Square at a good price, so ending the chapter in Belleville.

In 1971 after my annual medical, my family doctor, Dr. Gary Magee, said the ultra sound indicated a large tumour in my uterus, so sent me to a gynaecologist. Dr. Bateman recommended surgical removal of the tumour. He went on to say it wasn't malignant but there was the danger of it tearing away if it got much larger and I could haemorrhage to death. I booked a date for surgery in July and the tumour was removed successfully. As usual Joe went to work and didn't appear at the hospital until 7:30pm with newspaper in hand. I told him he could go home and read his paper. In the meantime Peter, Jani and Judy were huddled together worrying about my condition. Finally our neighbour and good friend, Olive, arrived at the hospital in the afternoon and reported back that their

Mom was well after the operation. I was discharged after a few days, now weighing about 115lbs and slowly recovered with no ill effects.

Nancy had graduated from UoT with honours in Political Science and was away on a European holiday during my surgery. When she returned she was hired to serve on the Commission on Newspaper Publishing which lasted almost a year. She then worked for CBC Radio and later for the CBC TV program Market Place. Seemingly her professional career would be in the Media.

Since age sixteen Peter continued to fill the house with wonderful music with his best friend Bill Barrow. They played Beatle music and sang to it, even made a recording. Bill developed a mole on the back of his leg and his doctor at the time said, "we can wait until school is out to check it and remove it if necessary." What a tragic decision! The mole was a melanoma and had metastasized. Bill died from it by the time summer arrived. He was an only child and his parents suffered terribly. Peter and other friends of Bill served as Pall Bearers and he was buried in Thornhill. Our dear son had constant nightmares and seemed depressed so we sent him to York Central for help. After a few sessions the experts declared he was OK but I think it impacted him negatively for some years as he lost his motivation and sort of withdrew from life for a few years.

The children always had summer jobs – Peter at the Ladies Golf Course in Thornhill, Judy at York Central Emergency Dept and Jani at Uplands Golf Course and

Dairy Queen. As for Joe, it seemed he couldn't be idle for too long so at 6am one Saturday morning he announced that he needed exercise, dressed for the occasion with a bottle of water in each jacket pocket but didn't say where he was going. Approximately twelve hours later he reappeared looking quite bedraggled and told us he had just completed the walk of his life – from Thornhill down Yonge Street to the Toronto waterfront – 21 miles. He very prudently took the subway and bus home though. He showered quickly and found the bottoms of his feet a mass of blisters. He confessed he kept the 'walk of his life' a secret because he didn't want us dissuading him. After a few day's application of Penaten cream he stopped limping and seemed almost normal again. I suppose a fella needs something to talk about!

His other strange escapade occurred the following winter when – again not telling anyone – he threw his ice skates in the car and drove to the pond turned skating rink on Centre Street in Thornhill. There was one other family, man, wife and child, skating there who probably saved his life. He enjoyed his skate for about an hour then hit a piece of twig sticking out of the ice and had a bad fall. To make things more complicated he couldn't get up. His shoulder was dislocated and in terrible pain. The friendly couple kindly helped him into their car and drove him to York Region Hospital further along Centre Street. Joe called me from Hospital saying he had a broken elbow and dislocated shoulder and could I please come to get him.

Our car was still at the pond skating rink. Joe spent a week at home recuperating then decided it was time to return to work. So each morning I had to literally shower him, dress him and drive him to work in Weston. Being used to stress and able to handle it I managed to get through the whole ordeal successfully but warned him, "no more athletic feats, PLEASE." These were replaced by 'dream travels'. Away alone and ten trips before they were over. The countries included Hungary, Romania, France, Spain, Brazil, Cuba (twice), Mexico (twice), Venezuela and Argentina. I was the ultimate 'grass widow'.

CHAPTER 27

Mother and Father had a great retirement and farewell party in Smooth Rock Falls. Father had a ribbon with three hundred and fifty names saying, 'Goodbye and Good Luck". And Mother had her lady friends, about twenty, throw a farewell party with gifts of luggage and other mementos. I think they were both sad and happy to be leaving. Sad to be leaving lifelong friends in Smooth Rock but happy to be coming closer to us and the grandchildren, plus countless relatives in the tobacco region around Tillsonburg. They finally decided to rent a house in Tillsonburg close to Mother's cousin Margaret. They stayed a year and then were anxious to buy a home.

They finally decided on Brantford, Ontario, an attractive, busy little town and ordered a bungalow in a Court with very large back yards – for a future vegetable garden and fruit trees. In the meantime I helped them look for and purchase new living room and dining room furniture plus Drapes and curtains for the whole house. They moved into their lovely new three bedroom bungalow in August. The neighbours were all friendly in the Court and also in the Church they joined almost immediately.

They spent the next few years happily gardening, planting three fruit trees – peaches, pears and apples – and a lovely vegetable garden for their new freezer. Father also built a 10' arbour to grow grapes. The side and front of the house was planted with Mother's favourite flowers – roses, peonies and hydrangeas.

They were extremely happy and content there for many years with bi-weekly visits from our family and occasionally Helen and her family. I spent considerable time in the coming years helping my parents as they did not drive and was happy to do so. They were a couple who spent their life giving and doing for family and community and so deserved the love they received in return.

Joe's work was going well, so well they added a substantial Christmas bonus annually as the Company was prospering – an incentive to stay perhaps? He seemed restless and fidgety and decided to sign up for Hungarian and Spanish lessons at night school at Jarvis Collegiate. He explained to me that he intended to do some travelling at holiday time and wanted to master these two languages. I agreed it was a good idea, the more languages the better.

After several months I began to get strange 'phone calls

on lesson night. The voice said, "This is Joe's Spanish teacher, would you tell him to stop at my apartment before he goes to class tonight."

I didn't think much about it at first and gave Joe the message. When it started occurring every study night I asked the voice, "Do you know who you are speaking to?"

The answer, "I don't give a damn who I'm speaking to."

I replied, "I'll tell you anyway, I'm Joe's wife."

The reply, "I don't give a damn who's wife you are, give him the message."

I confronted Joe about these messages and he laughed it off with, "She just wants a ride to school."

After two years of study Joe mastered the two languages, speaking, reading and writing them. I congratulated him on the good work and we attended the end of studies party at the school. Joe was to present a bouquet to the Hungarian teacher, Ada, with words of thanks in Hungarian ending with, "eza virag a viragnak." This flower for the flower. Great laughs and clapping followed. I met Ada and his class mates but no sign of the Spanish teacher. So I lived on with an unsolved mystery – but not for long.

Peter decided to look for full-time work as he seemed disinterested in finishing Grade 13. He applied for and got a job at the Thornhill Post Office sorting mail. The girls continued with high school and part-time jobs in the summer. Joe restless without extra-curricula events to absorb him applied and was accepted at York University to begin studies for a BA majoring in political science. Never a dull moment in our family!

At York University I had completed the required courses, one being Natural Science at Glendon, then Psychology courses on "Death and Dying" and the mourning process, Abnormal Behaviour, which included the study of mental illness. All valuable toward my goal of becoming a Social Worker. I graduated with an Honours BA in Sociology and Psychology in September 1975. Aunt Bertha and all our family attended the graduation, what a feeling of elation.

Now our social calendar was filled with various events. First we attended the last family reunion held by Isobel and Bob at the family farm. It was a joyful occasion as we met several cousins of the Hawkins family I had not met before. The photo taken of the happy group showed forty people present in front of the farmstead including dear Aunt Bertha with her gifts of maple syrup for each family. It was particularly touching for her because she hadn't seen some of her relatives for years. These Family Reunions were replaced by a Thanksgiving weekend ritual for the next decade. Isobel, Bob and family would visit us in Thornhill and spend Thanksgiving with us, turkey dinner and all the trimmings. On Sunday, Aunt Bertha would join us to drive around the area to marvel at the Fall colours everywhere and then sit down for dinner. On Monday afternoon, after a delightful visit, they would drive home to Carleton Place.

Excitement was mounting on the home front with the announcement that our beloved eldest daughter Nancy was about to be married to Ernest Louis Balmer in the summer of 1974. After weeks of preparation the wedding took place on Bigwin Island in Muskoka. Ernest was one of the several owners of the island, a vacation resort and also owned a summer home there, a spacious two bedroom condo. It was a fully equipped summer resort with tennis courts, golf course and a beautiful large restaurant where the reception would be held. Since it was an Island, guests had to be transported there by boat, so they were!

The ceremony took place outdoors on a beautiful sunny day in an attractive venue. Nancy, age 25, was a beautiful radiant bride, with Anne-Marie her best friend as matron of honour. Ernest's close friend from California served as Best Man. The reception was held later inside the restaurant complete with music and dancing. It was a joyful occasion for all.

That winter, at Ernest's urging, I accompanied him and Nancy and his Mother Laura, who became a close friend, on a holiday to Zhiuatenejo, Mexico for two weeks. We rented a bungalow, cooked our own breakfast but ate other meals out. My first aeroplane ride was exciting with nothing to fear and I enjoyed it thoroughly. We had a wonderful time and flew back home together. No more fear of aeroplane rides.

July 17th, 1975, we just had enough time to catch our breath before wedding number two was announced. Our beloved twin-daughter, Judy, who had just successfully completed her second year at York University, was marrying Bruce Smith, an accountant with BP Oil. Twin sister Jani was her Matron of Honour with bridesmaids Judy Thomas and Elaine Eisner. Bruce's best friend John Eisner served as Best Man, brother Wayne and Judy's brother Peter served as Ushers. They were married in St. George's Anglican Church on Yonge Street with a reception held at Heinzman House in Thornhill. Again music and dancing followed the reception. Judy looked petit and exquisite in her wedding gown

The next social event occurred in November when we celebrated Mother and Father's fiftieth wedding anniversary. We chose the Best Western Motel in Brantford and invited all their close friends to dinner, with ribbons, balloons and flowers to make it festive. They loved the gifts, good wishes, hugs and kisses. Also special greetings from the Prime Minister, the Premier and the Pope!

A few weeks after the anniversary celebration some sad and shocking news. Mother and Father's neighbour's on one side were Mr & Mrs Osborne and their two young boys. Mrs Osborne, Gerry, came over to Mother crying and in shock, she said her husband had just died of a massive heart attack and she was beside herself. Mother immediately tried to console her, gave her a cup of tea and let her talk. Gerry had to make funeral arrangements so Mother offered to go home with her and help in any way she could.

They arrived next door, the house very disrupted as Gerry couldn't do a thing after the bad news. Mother took over and completely cleaned the house, the dishes and helped Gerry put the little boys to bed. She stayed with Gerry until the next day so that she could complete the funeral arrangements while Mother stayed with the little boys. Mother and Father were there for the next month baby sitting, cleaning and whatever was necessary to help her through the sad time.

Gerry never forgot Mother's kindness. For years, on Mother's Day, she would come over with a large basket of fruit, a cake or a gift for Mother. I happened to be there on one occasion and she explained to me that she looked at Mother as her Mother too because she was so kind to the family during their crisis. She continued this ritual until our beloved Mother passed away with cancer.

CHAPTER 28

————

After Judy's wedding Joe decided to start his first dream travels to see as much of the world as possible. His first trip was to Europe alone, as were many others that followed. Destinations included France, Hungary and Romania, where he would visit all my relatives and communicate with them in Hungarian. They were thrilled to meet him and astounded when they heard him speak Hungarian. The visit included a trip to the wine cellar for a drink and sing-song.

While Joe was away Father developed serious health problems to the point where he couldn't keep food down. I took him to a specialist in Brantford who, after an MRI, came out with Father and announced to me, before a waiting room full of patients, "your Father has cancer of the pyloric cavity and there's nothing I can do for him." A death sentence, so to speak.

"Why do you think that, doctor," I asked

"Because my Father died of the same thing," he replied.

I was shocked and incensed at such a callous reply and answered, "thank you doctor. I'm taking my Father to Toronto immediately, where he will get help."

"Suit yourself," he replied, with a cold glare.

I immediately telephoned Dr. Fader, the Head of Emergency at North York General Hospital, explained the situation and he replied, 'Bring your Father here as soon as possible. I will have a bed ready for him and the surgeon Dr. Ross and I will look after him."

I drove Father and Mother to Toronto the same afternoon, checked him in and left him in the good hands of two wonderful doctors. They pumped his stomach and the next morning successfully removed the cancer in his pyloric cavity. Because it was localized they were sure they removed it all so no chemo-therapy was necessary. Those two wonderful doctors saved his life and he lived sixteen years longer! My motto, always get a second opinion.

By the time Joe returned from Europe, Father was recuperating at home in Brantford. We immediately Drove there to show him the pictures and videos of his family which certainly cheered him up.

I immediately signed up for studies toward my BSW, Bachelor of Social Work. My professors included Dr. Wilson Head, Prof. Bill Lee and Prof Susan Watts, all excellent and highly regarded teachers.

One of the essays I wrote for Susan Watts was entitled,

"The Revolving Door Syndrome" about patients suffering mental illness, getting treatment, being released and the illness recurring. It discussed various ideas, one being community support to eliminate readmission to hospital, much of which is practised today. She gave me an A+ and was so impressed stating the paper should be published in Social Work magazines.

At the end of the university studies Social Work students had to complete a Practicum under the supervision of an MSW who would guide you and eventually grade you.

I chose to do my Practicum with MPP Ross McLellan, MSW of Bellwoods Riding in Toronto. I studied and worked with him for a year assisting clients with claims at Workman's Compensation, Unemployment Insurance, Rental Tribunals etc. However, the highlight of my Practicum was preparing for and attending the first ever Public Forum held by the Ontario Advisory Council on the Physically Handicapped, dealing with their needs, held November 16th 1978 in council chambers, City Hall. We worked for weeks visiting buildings housing the disabled – there were very few – finding ways and means to make their lives easier. The Disabled and Institutions working with them were also invited to attend and take part in the process. We had wonderful coverage by the Press which helped raise public awareness.

The agenda for the day's proceedings contained eight categories relating to the problems and needs of the physically handicapped – Accommodation, Income Maintenance, Extra Ordinary Costs, Transportation, Accessibility, Wheelchair Sports, Public Awareness and Human Rights.

A total of twenty-three briefs were presented by the aforesaid groups reflecting the multi-various problems and needs of the physically handicapped, with a discussion period ensuing after each category. This forum initiated many positive changes in all the categories listed. I felt it an honour and privilege to be a part of this movement.

I admired Ross McLellan's sense of social justice and during Bob Rae's tenure as Premier of Ontario he was able to effect changes that definitely improved the lives of the Disabled – a true Social Worker/Politician. I graduated with an Honours BSW in 1978 and became a founding member of the Ontario Certified Social Workers Association formed in 1980. I was offered a position as Tutorial Assistant by Dr. Wilson Head which I graciously declined for I was anxious to start my career helping clients directly.

In the Spring of 1979 I joined the Salvation Army's twelve step program for young offenders, a rehabilitation program to raise awareness and solve problems – addiction and lack of motivation, etc. – so the person could get help and eventually return to his community. Maurice Bloch headed up the program and I would assist him. It provided excellent hands on experience until I got a full time job in Social Work. I eventually convinced Maurice, a very bright and compassionate person, to apply for studies for his BSW, which he did successfully in the next few years.

About the middle of my Practicum Joe and I were driving home on Hwy 401 from a friend's cottage in Port Perry. Just as we approached Oshawa a station wagon full of teenagers, four in the back and three in the front, drove by us in the passing lane and for no sane reason cut into our lane at high speed hitting our front left fender, Their car flew over the middle divide and landed on the east bound lane upside down, resulting in several broken ribs and other injuries. Our car was hit hard, sent us swerving across the two lanes and landing in the newly sodded divide where the front of the car ended up buried in the soft sod, which probably saved our lives. The car was covered in mud and felt like a coffin, closed in. The police arrived quickly and the ambulance took us to Oshawa General Hospital to be checked out. Joe had a bad knee injury and I had a bad hip injury which they said might require a hip replacement. I continued treatment at York Central Hospital and physiotherapy for my neck and hips. I took time off from my Practicum but was able to return after two weeks, continuing therapy when I needed it. I thanked God that our lives were spared. I was awarded a generous settlement which didn't really compensate for the pain I would have to endure the next few years and then eventually a total hip replacement of my right hip.

In late 1979 I applied for a position as Probation Officer overseeing twelve young offenders conducted by St. Philips Anglican Church. I and four other applicants sat answering various questions, then were asked whether we had any health problems, at which time I mentioned my injured hip. Of course, I didn't get the job. A young woman of twenty-seven did, I was fifty-one at the time. However, in a few days I received a call from one of the interviewers at St Philip's. It was Mr Roy Hawkins, no relation, the regional head of the Ministry of Correctional Services. He told me he was very impressed with my qualifications and my interview and would I be interested in the first position opening for a Probation Officer in the York Region? I certainly would, I replied. He estimated I would receive a call within a week or two. I thanked him, very excited about the future.

In exactly two weeks the call came and I had an appointment with Mr Roy Hawkins in York Region, Richmond Hill. After a lengthy interview I was hired forming my own company, York Counselling Services, with an attractive salary plus bonus at Christmas to cover benefits. I was provided with an office and secretarial services and reported to Mr Porter, the Office Manager.

During my tenure with the Ministry of Correctional Services and with Mr Roy Hawkin's guidance, many positive changes were made to reduce recidivism and help the young offender return to his/her community successfully – employment, further education etc.

New programmes included seeking opportunities in the community (several companies were successfully recruited that would employ young offenders to help normalize their lives).

We also initiated parent groups where any parent of an offender who wished to attend to talk about positive parenting that would help keep the young person out of trouble and encourage continuing education etc. It also provided parents with a 'support group' where they could talk with each other openly and develop more positive attitudes. Mary, my Social Work friend, offered to oversee this new program after it was initiated and did a wonderful job directing it.

Volunteering was also introduced with a program inviting Social Work students at York University, who might be considering a career in Probation, to serve as volunteers, which proved very successful.

Also several visits were made to the Clarke Institute (Forensic Division) where important advice was received regarding more difficult cases which in the end helped both the Offender and the Probation Officer writing pre-sentence reports.

After several years working for the Ministry I decided to apply to the University of Toronto for an MSW, Master of Social Work degree. University of Toronto awarded me a Fellowship to continue my studies. I asked a good friend, Mary Benedetto, to complete my contract with the Ministry while I studied.

After informing the Provincial Judges that I dealt with of my plans it was most heartening to receive great commendation for my work and good wishes for my studies.

Mr Roy Hawkins, a visionary leader, and a great humanitarian achieved his goal of changing Probation Services from a punitive to a rehabilitative model. It was a great privilege and honour working and learning from him.

CHAPTER 29

Starting in the mid to the end of the 1970s Dubois Chemicals were making various changes in their company structure. The president, Mr Robinson, retired and was replaced by an American to lead the company. Some employees were let go, others hired. Then a shocking occurrence – the new president gave termination notice to Joe, who was Vice-President and Comptroller and also to another Canadian, the Plant Manager. In his whole career Joe had never been terminated by any company so he was obviously upset and shocked to the core of his being. So was the Plant Manager. Joe had been receiving bonuses annually based on performance so was utterly confused also. He retained a lawyer and after lengthy negotiations a mutually satisfactory agreement was reached by both parties. The company continued operating for a short time then closed completely with its American president moving back to the USA.

Joe completed his BA at York in 1980 and decided to work three days a week for a Translating Company. He also enrolled in Woodward College, UoT for an MA degree studying Russian for his first course.

I commenced my studies at UoT but found the commuting time consuming so moved into residence at Knox College. I had a neat little room on the ground floor, moved in my own bed and belongings, pictures etc. and was quite happy and comfortable there. The bathroom and showers were located down the hall and most classes within walking distance and libraries close by. The cafeteria where students gathered for their meals was a large room. The food seemed edible.

The first person I met in the cafeteria was a lovely lady, Dr. Catherine Chalin, who taught psychology in the Faculty of Medicine and also was a student working for her Master of Divinity degree. She came to my table, introduced herself and said, "rumour has it that you are a wealthy horsewoman from Newmarket and what would you be studying, may I ask?"

I was wearing knee-high leather boots with brown pants tucked in and a brown sporty jacket over a white sweater.

No whip though! I laughed at her remarks and introduced myself as a lowly mature student from Thornhill working for my MSW and had never, ever ridden a horse. We both laughed and were good friends from then on.

Catherine was a twin, with a twin sister in Ottawa. Somewhat younger then me, a very bright woman with a great sense of humour so I thoroughly enjoyed her company.

For my MSW I picked courses in Family and Marital Counselling with extra subjects in Ageing and Group Therapy. The workload was heavy for I was in the habit of reading all the recommended books and then my curiosity would compel me to read at least three extra books for each course. I was an avid student and usually the eldest one in my class.

In my second year I met a charming Korean student Carol Kim, an artist studying for a Master's degree in Fine Arts. She did some beautiful and interesting artwork. We got along famously and she chose to call me 'Mom' instead of Margaret because her Mom was in Korea. I considered it a compliment and we became close friends. She is presently a well known artist with showings in Vancouver galleries.

One morning I received an urgent call stating Joe had had a heart attack and was hospitalized in York Region Hospital, Thornhill. I quickly contacted the Head of the Department explaining the situation and they assured me

I could take as much time off as necessary, then return to complete my studies.

I spent several weeks in Thornhill helping Joe recuperate. Fortunately the heart attack didn't damage his heart at all, so recovery was complete with no side effects. Just before I was ready to return to my studies Joe told me he was considering applying for assignments with CESO (Canadian Executive Services Overseas), a highly successful Volunteer Development Organization founded in 1967 (our Centennial Year), under the auspices of CIDA. Many of the Volunteer Consultants are retired or semi-retired executives willing to share their skills in areas such as finance, marketing, resource management and manufacturing with various enterprises. These include forty-nine Third World countries. Also the indigenous population in Canada which is supported by the Department of Indian Affairs and lastly, fifty-eight Central and Eastern European Countries supported by External Affairs.

Under the leadership of its brilliant CEO, Mr Dan Haggerty, CESO has proved to be a great success expanding its central office in Toronto to eight regional offices countrywide. The projects vary from one to three months. Air fares are covered by CESO, while the host country covers Volunteers' living expenses. Volunteers are great ambassadors of goodwill for Canada, by stimulating local employment and improving economic stability they are promoting social justice and dignity for all with their services. An Organization dear to my heart as you will note.

Joe's first assignment was for a Canadian Native Indian business on a reservation near Brantford. He set up their accounting system on the computer which modernized and improved the business. He enjoyed the assignment and asked for another.

His second assignment was to the Dominican Republic. He would be working for a hardware company owned and operated by the Haché family in Santo Domingo, the capital. Again it was to modernize their system by computerizing it. He accepted the assignment and prepared for his departure.

In the meantime I returned to Knox College and my studies – Marital Counselling with Professor Marian Bogo which I enjoyed thoroughly. I could see myself as a Marital Counsellor.

One day I received an unexpected call from a dear friend, Susan Lower, who had just successfully completed studies for her CGA. She wanted to come over with a bottle of champagne to celebrate. I said yes, yes, yes! She was the daughter of close friends, Pauline and Doug Lower who were living on Fleance Drive, just behind us on Rothsay Road. Pauline and I met at York University and became good friends and neighbours. Sue had a little son, Nicky, aged three, and was having difficulties in her marriage so her parents asked if I could talk to her and perhaps help her, which I did. My first invitation to her was in the form of poetry entitled "Come into My Garden".

Come into my garden and leave your cares behind
While sweet bird songs wipe sadness from your mind
Tarry here awhile and with clarity of vision
Feel peace and unity with God's great creation
Then let beauty and harmony penetrate so deep
Form a wellspring of strength, some to give some to keep
Now colours seem brighter than ever before
And dew on the lily evokes wondrous joy
Savour exotic perfumes that draw you to new places
But always return to explore inner spaces
Ask who you are and where you are bound
For only in knowing can a true course be found
And while in my garden take time to reflect
On life's greatest blessings, your loved ones and friends
Then as you depart take peace and great pleasure
And know now my garden is more precious than ever

She liked the poem and accepted lunch in our backyard, filled with beautiful flowers and foliage, a continuation of a beautiful friendship which began when I held a bridal shower for her first wedding. Her grandmother, Ethel Lower, visiting from England and her Auntie Jean from Toronto also attended.

The shower was a great success and grandmother Ethel wrote me a thank you note and asked if she could have the recipe for the chicken liver paté I had served at the shower, which she enjoyed so much. I sent her the recipe and thus began a wonderful friendship via correspondence until her death in 1997, at age ninety-six. What a delightful, intelligent and interesting human-being with a history of marching in the E nglish suffragette m ovement a nd the Jarrow Death March in 1928, a practicing feminist before we knew the meaning of the word. That was Sue's beloved grandmother and my dear friend Ethel.

Sue arrived with champagne and we celebrated her wonderful achievement with a toast, fun and laughter.

My professors at UoT included Joyce Cohen, Doreen Winkler, Marian Bogo, Ben Schlesinger and Howard Irving. They're highly intellectual in their areas of expertise but also all possessed a humanitarian bent, respect for the person, protection of the child, social justice etc..

One of the assignments Professor Ben Schlesinger gave our class was most interesting. Each student could choose five b ooks o n v arious S ocial W ork t opics w hich they would read carefully then write a précis on each book. When completed the book titles and précis would form a compendia to be placed in the library so future social work students could use it as reference in their studies. We gained invaluable information by reading the books and completing the précis; likewise the future students would have available a comprehensive guide for their studies.

I felt extremely grateful and privileged to have such

exceptional teachers, studying for my MSW. Professor Schlesinger asked me if I would be interested in joining the faculty of Social Work. I thanked him profusely but explained I already had a contract with the Ministry of Correctional Services with my company York Counselling Services.

By the end of October I was feeling uneasy about Joe's absence given his history of a heart attack. What if he had another in Santo Domingo, who would look after him? I had one paper to write and then my Practicum to complete. So I discussed my problem with the Head of the Faculty of Social Work. He saw no problem in my taking a leave of absence for as long as I needed. I could finish my paper and my Practicum later. I thanked him and began to pack.

CESO was happy that I was joining Joe for a month and booked my ticket and return. I telephoned Joe and told him my plans and he was delighted by the upcoming visit. The girls and Peter would take care of the home front and off I went, unafraid of the upcoming plane ride.

The flight was uneventful. I disembarked in Santo Domingo where they kept my passport – to be returned when I left the country. Joe was there with a friend's car to meet me.

CHAPTER 30

The Dominican Republic, a Caribbean nation, is two thirds of the Island Hispaniola, the other third being Haiti and is the first permanent European settlement in the Americas. In 1492 Columbus stopped there on his journey searching for a route to India hoping, among other things, to initiate the spice trade with Europe. It had undergone centuries of take-overs by different countries including Spain and France and suffered under many dictatorships from Trujillo to Vasquez. But finally it won its independence as a nation.

Santo Domingo, the capital, is a beautiful city with many interesting ancient cathedrals the eldest Santa Maria de Menor built in 1512-40. Another interesting point, the humpback whales migrate there annually between December and March to breed, creating a spectacular sight – others are the pink flamingo and crocodiles. The

National Bird is the Palmchat, the national dance the Merengue. It is also a favourite vacation choice with wonderful resorts – Casa de Campo, Samana, Puerto Plata and Punta Cana.

As Christmas was approaching I was missing my children and grandchildren- we had four – so on one of our 'phone calls I suggested it would be wonderful to have Nancy and her little one Jessica, age two and a half, to visit for two weeks. She agreed it was a wonderful idea and arrived a few days before Christmas. We booked her in an adjoining room next to ours. I taught Jessica to say, "como seyamma?" and "miyamma Jessica." She made many friends before she left. So did her mother.

The official language in the Dominican Republic is Spanish so Joe quite comfortably fit in and made many friends before his departure. The population was approximately 6.2 million when we were there. After visiting points of interest while Nancy was there I found the time dragging but had the great fortune to meet an interesting woman, Mary Marranzini, who headed a group called the Dominican Rehabilitation Association (DRA), founded formally in 1963. She was one of the founding members. The DRA provides treatment and rehabilitation services for the disabled in the Republic. The service includes an Orthopaedic Workshop that manufactures approximately 29,000 prosthetic devices and 18,000 pairs of shoes for orthopaedic patients yearly.

Mary was kind enough to take me on a tour of the facility. I was very impressed with their programs for the disabled and their facility, a total of seven units country-wide. Mary mentioned that any help from Canada would be greatly appreciated so on my return I passed her information and request on to Mr Joe Cashen, Easter Seals Society Toronto and later to GEMS operated by the renowned Doreen Wicks. Both responded with help. It is very difficult for Social Workers or anyone in the helping professions to walk away when they see a need. So this was the beginning of my contribution, as a CESO spouse, to the urgent needs of Third World countries – which, needless to say, I found most fulfilling. What an eye opener!

On weekends we spent the time at various beaches visiting Samana, Puerto Plata and Punta Cana, so Nancy and Jessica could enjoy themselves with us. Christmas in the Dominican Republic is celebrated as a religious holiday. The gift giving part comes later on Three Kings

Day along with special dinners, cheerful music and dancing the Meringue. The Haché family, originally from Spain, were very kind and hospitable to us, including us in family celebrations. Also Indiana, the office manager at Hachè, invited Joe and I to meet her family, which we enjoyed very much.

Nancy and Jessica left for home after their two week visit, very pleased with their experience. Joe completed his assignment successfully and we made several friends, one of the couples visiting us in Canada a year later.

I left with an indelible impression of a nation of kind, hospitable people, many who are poor, yet despite hardships manage to find joy in life.

After our arrival home I returned to University of Toronto to complete my last paper on Marital Therapy successfully. I then applied at Sacred Heart Children's Centre located at St Clair and Warden, for Family Therapy practice. A highly regarded Institution they offered both Residential and Outpatient Treatment for children and families in need. I learned so much under my Supervisor, Vince, who was an excellent Therapist. It was from him I learned that Family Therapy was an 'Art' as well as a profession.

Upon completion of my practicum, which I enjoyed thoroughly and also learned so much, Vince informed me that if I was interested he would award me a scholarship to attend the Family Therapy Institute in Washington DC.

Again, I expressed my gratitude but explained my commitment with my contract with the Ministry.

I graduated in 1984 with my MSW degree, with congratulations from Mr George Ignatieff, Chancellor of UoT and Governor-General Jean Sauvé who were at the ceremony. Also my family and friends enjoyed a celebration which my eldest daughter, Nancy, hosted. Two of the guests included Catherine Chalin and Susan Lower. My student days were over at age fifty-six but the beginning of an exciting and most interesting phase of my life was just around the corner.

CHAPTER 31

Change is inevitable in families as time goes by and ours was no different. Our dear son, Peter, decided to leave the Post Office to pursue a career in music, his passion since his teens. The one thing I regret deeply as a parent was the lack of encouragement and support he received from both Joe and me. Joe did not think Peter could earn a living in music and kept pushing Accounting as a profession, absolutely willing to help Peter with advice and financially. But Peter was not interested. I, on the other hand, had tried to convince him to enrol in Atkinson as a mature student, which he did do for one semester, did well but his heart wasn't in it. He decided to move in with two friends living off the Danforth, both in music. Before long he formed a Band which included two guitarists, a keyboard, drums and a soloist, little Dave, his friend. They had regular gigs at the Gladstone Hotel which was recently renovated. One night Joe and I attended and were pleasantly surprised at how professional and enjoyable the band sounded. People were dancing to the music all night. We congratulated Peter and his band members and left happy and convinced that he would do well. He also had several gigs in the Midland area during the summer months.

Peter was dating a young woman teacher, named Jocelyn Turner. They eventually married but that saga is to come later.

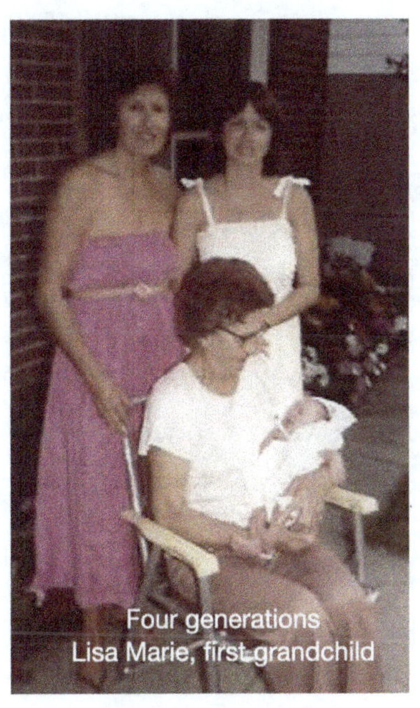

Jani, who had an unbelievably tragic life but is a brave survivor, was employed by York University Library, the Cancer Society, Wellesley Hospital and eventually a government job doing secretarial work. Despite a bizarre auto accident, which nearly killed her, she bounced back and is living a quiet and contented life most of the time. She loves her family and we love her dearly and are there for her when she needs us. One of our greatest strokes of luck after her accident was acquiring her new doctor, Dr. Alan Fink, who has given her excellent care for many years and thus enabled her to gradually overcome the trauma. Kindness is an important element in the healing process and Dr. Fink was consistently a kind, gentle and compassionate physician. We thank him for his devoted care of our beloved Janice

Judy and Bruce, happily married, have three beautiful children- Lisa Marie, our first precious grandchild born 1979. Then four years later in 1983, double delight, twin grandchildren, number three and four – Ashley Elizabeth and Shawn Michael. We feel blessed.

Nancy, who had a lucrative career as producer with TV Ontario, is happily living in her home in East York with beautiful little daughter, Jessica, our second beloved grand-daughter born in 1981. All's well that ends well, as the saying goes, but not for long!

After completion of my studies I had a decision to make, go back to Probation with my company York Counselling Services or join Joe in his assignments with CESO. To help reach a decision I asked him if we had enough money to sustain us in our retirement. His blunt reply shocked me.

"It's not your money, I earned it. It is for my trips and my Nursing Home."

Great-Grandpa and the kids

"What about my Nursing Home," I asked.

"The house is your Nursing Home, you can sell it."

Needless to say the sh*t hit the fan. I think it occurred to me that I shouldn't be controlled this way any longer. I discussed the issue with my parents and in unison they said, "divorce him".

They are Catholic and it is the last thing I expected to hear them say but they were adamant.

I consulted my son-in-law, Andy Knox, who stated their divorce specialist was onmaternity leave and referred me to another lawyer. A very painful period ensued.

Joe retained a female lawyer in Thornhill and when he submitted his household expense account showing I was receiving $50 a week raising four children she advised him to raise it to $100 a week as the Judge wouldn't look favourably at it, So he did.

Cam, my lawyer, said he'd have the papers served on Joe. I replied I'd do it myself.

"It could be very dangerous, you know," was his reply.

I did it successfully, thinking of his affairs helped. The details of the divorce were spelled out. I would buy his share of the house and retain ownership. My plan was turn the family room into an office and set up a Social Work practice to earn a living. Joe would have to find accommodation elsewhere and move out.

Amidst tears and anger, and sometimes laughter, we reached the end with signatures completed ready for the Court, when Joe broke down, put his head on my shoulder and cried like a baby.

"Don't leave me, baby, I still love you and I don't want to live without you."

He certainly knew how to play my heart-strings for I went to pieces and could feel the compassion rising in me. I thought of his age, he is ten years older than me, his brave service overseas in WW2 and the fact that he was the father of my four dearly loved children. I was like jelly. We tore up the divorce papers and called off the divorce. I told him he would have to sleep in his own room – that part of our lives was over and would remain so. He agreed to everything. I left one important element out – joint bank account, an omission that would come back to haunt me down the road. For some obscure reason I could never fight about money. While I was working for Probation I started a Savings Account and invested $3,500 for twelve years at 12.5%. That was my RIFF. Financially I became somewhat of a wizard to this day. I had to for Joe, despite several lucrative positions he held, never chose the option for my protection in the event that something might happen to him. When questioned ab

out this omission he callously replied, "it would cost me $100 a month and I needed to save that money for my trips to see the world."

What a great reward and thank you, after sixty-six years of marriage.

My life settled down. I continued to accompany Joe on CESO assignments which gave me great satisfaction, as you will see. It was during this period that we received a thrilling surprise. Indiana and her husband, from the Dominican Republic, decided to visit us in Toronto We spent a lovely week together showing them around.

CHAPTER 32

Joe's third CESO assignment was to San José, Costa Rica, working for Olympia, manufacturers of athletic footwear, revamping and modernizing their accounting system.

While on our flight to Costa Rica I smiled at a young woman across the aisle and we soon started to chat. She told me she was a student at UoT on her way to Sao Paulo, Brazil for a short vacation. I replied that I was a recent graduate of UoT with an MSW and that I had many relatives in Sao Paulo whom I have never met, except by correspondence. She excitedly asked me if I had their address. Out came my address book. She let out a shriek of delight and said, "they live just two blocks from me." She asked me to write them a note and she would deliver it and meet them. Which I did. On our return to Canada two months later a beautiful letter and pictures were awaiting me. What a small world after all.

Costa Rica is a beautiful little country situated in Central America with Nicaragua to the north and Panama to the south, the Caribbean on its east coast and the Pacific Ocean on the west coast. It was colonized by Spain in 1561, for two hundred and fifty years, gaining its independence as a democratic republic in 1821. About a fifth of the

country is covered with forests, the Monteverde Club Forest Reserve with two thousands species of trees and nine thousand flowering plants making it a popular tourist attraction. It also has two mountain ranges, the Cordillera Volcánica and

Cordillera Talamanca. The national flower is the orchid of which there are hundreds of species. The beauty of the Country is indisputable but this final fact is why Costa Rica and its beautiful people are so dear to my heart. In 1948 they abolished their army to finance a university and three hospitals.

Another interesting cultural event held in Costa Rica, the second Sunday in March, is the Ox Cart Festival – DRA del BOYERO del OX CART introduced in 1840 to honour the country's agricultural traditions. In early days

people hand pulled the carts loaded with agricultural products. As they progressed that changed to oxen pulling the cart.

For the Festival the carts are beautifully decorated and often carry family members. We are looking forward to attending it!

The general manager of Olympia, Judy Cohen, met us at the airport, welcomed us and drove us to our apartment, The "Lamb Apartments", in San José. She was a young American woman who met her husband at university and they eventually married and chose to live in his homeland, Costa Rica. Husband, Jorgé, was a handsome young orthopaedic surgeon and they had a beautiful young son aged seven. The five of us became bosom buddies during our two month stay.

Joe was impressed with the staff he had to work with

Joe with Dr Jorgé's family

and enthusiastic about the project. The apartment was fully equipped so I was able to cook most of our meals. Joe usually came home for lunch. Most weekends Judy and Jorgé took us for drives to the beach which we enjoyed thoroughly. One weekend Jorgé took us to his parent's home to meet the rest of his family and what an interesting and warm-hearted family it was! He had one sister, the eldest, and three younger brothers. Jorgé explained to us the system they used to educate the whole family. The sister became a teacher. When she started working she helped the next sibling, Jorgé, financially to achieve his goal. Scholarships all helped. Then Jorgé in turn helped the next brother who was a dentist, and so on. The children therefor all had professional careers. We were very impressed with the whole family and Mama and Papa also.

Another time some of the staff invited us to their home for a sing-song with guitars and banjos strumming. To our surprise and delight they played and sang 'Oh Canada" in English. It brought tears to my eyes.

Prior to our departure to Costa Rica my sister, Helen, informed me that their neighbour Millie's mother, Amelia Egerton, a well known sculptor resided there and could we please look her up. We agreed we would. When we 'phoned Amelia she immediately welcomed us and invited us to her home. What a beautiful, warm-hearted person and what an accomplished artist!

As we spent time getting acquainted she explained she was a widow. Her husband, an American pilot in WW2, died during the war. She has an adult, married daughter living in Canada. She then took us on a tour of her garden which was stunning and we stopped under a large mango tree filled with fruit. She picked three, one each, and preceded to show us how to eat a mango without spilling juice over our clothing. It's amazing how we learned something new almost every day. Amelia then took us to her club for lunch, where there was a beautiful display of her art. A memorable day with many photos to remember her by.

When I asked Judy Cohen where there would be a possibility of doing Volunteer work she suggested the University of Costa Rica. She introduced me to Dr. Herrara, a dentist who was the Head of the Social Work Department. We had an initial meeting during which he addressed me as Doctora Margherita. I quickly informed him I had a Masters degree not a Doctorate. He quietly replied that in Costa Rica anyone with a Masters Degree is addressed as Doctora. I learned something new.

He explained that he was teaching a new course on Comprehensive Rehabilitation and did I have any knowledge of the subject that I could pass on. What an incredible coincidence, they were topics I spent considerable time in doing my Practicum, Comprehensive Rehabilitation of the

Disabled and a program we set up in probation also. Our first meeting lasted four hours. The next meeting included two female and one male professors from the University who spoke perfect English and it became a two hour session on a weekly basis. I found these sessions very enjoyable and stimulating as I was learning as much from them, about their culture, as they were from me. It was mutually satisfying and beneficial.

I found out through the grape vine, my sister Helen in Ottawa, that Carleton University was hosting a conference on Comprehensive Rehabilitation the following year. I passed the information on to Dr. Herrara who was most interested in attending. My sister and brother-in-law kindly offered to host Dr. Herrara during his stay in Ottawa so air fare and incidentals would be his only expense. To make a long story short I found out too late, about a week before the conference, that Dr. Herrara was not able to raise the air fair to Canada, so cancelled his visit. Sadly, had I known early enough I could have approached CESO for help or even got together with my friends and gifted him the air fare. We were all disappointed in the missed opportunity; however I was delighted to be able to enhance their knowledge as Canada was somewhat advanced in the study and implementation of Comprehensive Rehabilitation for various needy populations.

Judy and Jorgé had a wedding to attend while we were there and kindly extended an invitation to us. They picked us up Saturday mid-morning and we drove to the church together. The ceremony and music were impressive with a lot of white handkerchiefs evident. The bride looked very solemn during the wedding but by the time we left the church, she looked radiant and happy.

The reception followed with a lovely dinner and toasts, then dancing like I'd never seen before. It didn't stop until shortly after midnight. Joe and I finally learned the Meringue and were tuckered out all day Sunday. It was great fun to experience a wedding in a different country and culture. The bride and groom left for their honeymoon in Florida.

Midway through Joe's project Judy Cohen received a visitor from Boston, a personal friend, Annie Lord, who drove to Costa Rica in her panel truck! Annie's mother had just retired from a career in the army, so Annie decided it was a good time to take off to visit her good friend, Judy. We had great conversations about life and then she left us to spend time exploring the Galapagos Islands 1,300km away by air. The islands are famous with Charles Darwin visiting in 1835 working on his Origin of Species. Later in the year Annie visited us in Canada for a week before taking off to Switzerland.

Our project was coming to a successful completion

when we had another important visitor, the CEO of CESO, Mr Dan Haggerty. After a long conversation with Joe about the project he asked if I could please call him when we return, to discuss some ideas I might be interested in regarding CESO. I replied I would be happy to do so.

We left Costa Rica feeling sad to leave the many friends we made, especially Judy and Jorgé and little junior. The owner of Olympia was totally satisfied with the changes Joe made to modernize his business and asked Joe if he could come again if he had any problems in the company. Joe replied, "just ask and I'll be here." Such wonderful memories of an extremely beautiful country and its warm-hearted people. We'll always remember our 'Tico' friends!

On our return journey we took a few days stopover to visit friends in Florida then flew home to Canada – home sweet home again.

CHAPTER 33

As per our custom upon return from holidays and volunteer projects we telephoned all family members to check in and see how everyone was. The children and grandchildren were all faring well. When we went to see Aunt Bertha we thought she had failed significantly. She let the cleaning woman, who came on a weekly basis, go and seemed to be suffering memory loss.

We spent the next two weeks cooking and eating with her. Joe would put her garbage out on garbage day. When we arrived the next day the garbage would be inside her hallway, lined up neatly. Joe and I quickly discussed what should be done. I suggested we call Doctor Fader as soon as possible to give us an assessment of her condition.

Dear Doctor Fader arrived the next day. He asked her name, age, birthdate etc which she answered automatically – she had them memorized. He didn't seem to think she was ready for the nursing home. What should our next step be? She gave us the answer by saying she couldn't climb the stairs any more and was sleeping on the chesterfield. I sponge bathed her every day as best I could and dressed her in clean clothes. The garbage was still being brought back in. She was also showing signs of incontinence which worried me.

Since we need authorities to guide us I telephoned my Member of Parliament for advice. Great move! He informed me they had a special team at Sunnybrook Hospital – a psychiatrist, a nurse, a doctor and a social worker who will go to the person's home to complete an assessment. He assured us they were very reliable. We telephoned immediately. They were there the next day. After examining her thoroughly the doctor asked Aunt Bertha her name, a good answer.

He asked her birthdate, another good answer.

Then he asked, "Miss Hawkins, what season is it?"

"Why it's winter, isn't it?" she replied. Wrong answer.

The team had a conference in the other room and returned to us.

The doctor said, "given her age, ninety-three, her memory loss, her other personal problems and stairs being a challenge," he recommended that she be placed in a nursing home with full care as soon as possible. He suggested Cummer House in Thornhill and said he could recommend her as an urgent case. Needless to say we were so relieved as we were too elderly ourselves to undertake her care.

Since Aunt Bertha's memory loss we had other serious problems to contend with. As I mentioned earlier she was an avid collector of rare stamps and coins all neatly packaged in albums and beautiful pieces of valuable china like Royal Doulton figurines across her fireplace mantle. To our shock and dismay, on one of our weekly visits, the Royal Doulton figurines were gone, nowhere to be found. When we searched for her coin and stamp collection they also were missing. Joe questioned her about them and her reply was, "an old timer borrowed them. He will bring them back." She didn't approve of reporting her loss to the police so our hands were tied.

We had a fairly good idea who the thief was. While she was still working downtown she was standing on King Street, in the rain, waiting for the bus when man came out of a Funeral Home and asked her to come in out of the rain. They became friends eventually and she jokingly referred to him as B.F. – boyfriend. BF used to come with large shopping bags with dusters and pretend to be cleaning – we actually caught him in the act. Our suspicion was that he would fill the bag with valuables each time he came. She, of course, would believe he was borrowing them to show to his family and return them.

"He's an old timer," she said, meaning friend, "and will return them."

After the disappearance of the stamp and coin

collection and the twenty-four Doulton figurines we never saw BF (Bruce) again. Sadly we couldn't

even alert the police so they could investigate as they would have to involve Aunt Bertha too. Theft of seniors, a disgusting occurrence, unfortunately has become more prevalent in our society and we must all be more vigilant to try to curb it. It's not unlike battering a child.

In two days we received the call that Aunt Berths'a room was ready. We packed her suitcase, got her ready and drove to Cummer House. She went quite willingly, no questions asked. We stayed until she was settled in her semi-private room and then kissed her and hugged and left.

In the car going home sobs shook my body and I could not regain my composure for quite a while. Aunt Bertha was like a mother to me. She was my hero since that day long ago when she insisted my name must be on the deed for our first house purchase. She was a very kind and gentle woman but also a very strong one who experienced the bias against women lawyers and finally became one of the first few in Ontario. Her hard work and dedication earned her a partnership in her law firm and she spent many long years there. During the depression she fed the hungry on her doorstep with a sandwich and glass of milk and one to go as well. She joined fund raising events at her church, St. Timothy's Anglican in north Toronto. She and

I also attended Old Testament lectures together at UoT. What an incredibly talented, kind and loving human being. Her strength, as I thought of her, seemed to seep into me. I stopped crying and thanked God for her life. When I regained my equilibrium I told myself she is in a good, safe, caring place and will be happy there. And she was. We or a family member visited her on a weekly basis until she passed away at age ninety-eight.

We visited Mother and Father in Brantford and found them fairly well. Father occupied his time gardening and making his delicious homemade wine. Mother kept busy with her annual ritual preserving jars of fruit for the winter and freezing produce from the garden. I did their investing and their income tax returns annually.

It was during this period that the family and friends gathered in Brantford to celebrate Mom and Dad's 60th Wedding Anniversary. A joyous event full of music, singsong and reminiscing. Having the grandchildren present made it very special for them.

CHAPTER 34

Nancy had a successful career with TV Ontario as producer of a program on Canadian authors. She was living a happy and contented life in East York with lovely neighbours Dorothy and Art Rennick next door. She suddenly announced that she and Andy Knox, a young lawyer, were to marry. We were booked to go on another CESO assignment in about a month's time, in January, so they rushed around preparing to have the wedding before our departure.

After many meetings and 'phone calls they decided the wedding was to take place at St. Andrew's Presbyterian

Church with Rev Ian Clark (Catherine Chalin's husband) officiating. Anne-Marie would be her Maid of Honour, David Crozier, Andy's Best Man; the reception at an up-scale restaurant with about forty guests. The wedding took place as planned, a very beautiful ceremony with the joyful reception following. Two touching events at the reception will stay with me forever.

One was Andy's uncle, his mother's brother, who became an ordained minister later in life, held Jessica in his arms and declared, "we will all love this little girl like our own."

The second event was Father spontaneously getting up during the reception to say, "Andy, you are now part of our family, we love you and welcome you to our family."

Catherine & Ian's shower

It was fortunate that Mother and Father were able to attend. Mr & Mrs Andrew Knox tied the knot and lived happily ever since producing a beautiful little son, Jeffrey Kenneth, our fifth precious grandson, a brother for dear little Jessica. She was delighted. Never a dull moment in our family!

While I was packing for our next CESO project a

documentary was aired on CBC TV about an exceptional woman named Doreen Wicks. She came from a poor family of ten children in Bristol, England. She eventually married a fellow Brit, Ben Wicks and they emigrated to Canada in 1957. Parents of three children, two daughters and a son, Doreen was an RN working at Sunnybrook Hospital, Toronto, Ben a renowned cartoonist. I was one of his great admirers. I couldn't draw myself away from this fascinating documentary as I listened on. In 1982 while visiting her daughter, Susan, who was in Haiti working with deaf and blind children, Doreen was very moved by poor children infested by worms which affected their health profoundly. She returned to Canada, resigned her position with Sunnybrook Hospital and created GEMS (Global ED-Med Supplies) to help Third World countries battling malnutrition, disease, poverty and illiteracy. Wherever there is a need Doreen either goes to the country to assess it and help, or responds to the need immediately.

GEMS expanded from just sending medication to needy people to distributing hospital supplies including beds and equipment. She collected used beds from hospitals who were upgrading. One sent her 15,000 bedsheets. CIDA helps GEMS by funding projects. What a fascinating woman! What an incredible life. I must meet this woman I thought to myself as I hurried back to my packing.

Joe's next project (1985) was in Panama, Central America

in a city called Chitré, the capital of the Province of Herrera with a population of approximately nine thousand. We arrived at Panama City Airport where we connected with another smaller flight to Chitré, the plane a small commuter holding fifteen passengers and two pilots. The flight was very short, about 45 minutes and very scenic. The CESO representative, Enrique Williams, met us at the airport and took us to our hotel in Chitré.

Early the next morning after breakfast, starting with fresh pineapple, Joe was eager to start his project at one of the three hospitals serving Chitré. There we discovered a fellow CESO volunteer, Stan Renton, a retired Hospital Administrator in the Etobicoke Hospital, a suburb of Toronto. Our interpreter (Joe didn't need one as he spoke and wrote Spanish but Stan did) was Rosa Chitreana Rojas, a friendly outgoing twenty-five year old woman. I especially appreciated her friendship, as time went by, as English wasn't as prevalent in Chitré as other parts of Central America.

It was through Rosa that I learned about Spanish lessons offered by the local university with classes three afternoons a week. Three of us, all women, attended together. We were given a printed manuscript, a copy of the whole course, which comprised two hundred pages which we would follow (like a text book) during our studies. After approximately three weeks there was rumour that Jean Kirkpatrick, the US delegate to the United Nations was about to pay a visit to Panama.

Panamanian citizens started to protest her upcoming visit with large gatherings around the university so it was quickly closed down as a precaution. That was the end of our Spanish lessons with a class of fifteen students. I continued studying the manuscript we were given whenever I could.

After the Spanish lessons ceased I asked Rosa if she knew of anywhere I might do volunteer work given my Social Work background. She enthusiastically replied, YES!, the Psychiatric Hospital, in los Santos nearby, operated by Dr. Olga Bouche de Romero. She then explained her own tragic situation of losing an infant to SIDS (crib death). She couldn't cope with the tragedy and was admitted to the psychiatric ward for treatment. Dr. Olga treated her and she recovered and is so grateful to her. She said she would love to introduce me to her, and did.

The next day we had an appointment with Dr. Olga at 10:00am, an appointment that impacted me so deeply, the memory is still with me today, thirty-five years later. The hospital was an older building housing Dr. Olga's office on the main floor, the Emergency Department consisting of three cots, for beds, no privacy screens or curtains in sight. On the opposite side were similar rooms with similar type cots as beds with one, two or several in each room. Then Dr. Olga took us to the basement which had several large rooms and cement floors with foam rubber mattresses, quite soiled, where male patients, many young, were lounging fully clothed.

Outside there was a large rectangular courtyard with a few buildings that serviced the Hospital. The courtyard was overgrown with tall weeds amongst shrubs and flowers with a few patients sitting out there.

When we sat down with Dr. Olga, a very intelligent and compassionate woman, she explained that funding was minimal and they had to do the best they could with what they had. In addition to the need for real beds and linen they could use help with medication, hospital gowns and new dishes as the metal mugs they served soup and beverages in often burned the patient's lips and created more problems. I asked her to please compile a list of needs and I would do my best to send help from Canada.

Thinking of the needy, weedy courtyard transformed into a basketball court for patients I asked her if they ever used volunteers to help with different projects – like lawn cutting and weeding.

She replied, "no, it wasn't a custom here."

I explained to her that in Canada volunteerism is a very popular and valued concept, used and relied on extensively. She seemed excited by the idea. I thanked her for the tour of the hospital and asked if we could meet once more for more discussion. I also asked for permission to take photos I could use in Canada to help explain the needs. She agreed. I left with many ideas about help swimming in my head.

I asked Rosa if she knew any prominent women in the community who we could meet to discuss volunteerism. She answered, yes, a lovely lady who owned an electrical business, is well known and liked by everyone. She said she would contact her and set up a first meeting.

CHAPTER 35

We had developed a friendship with one of the doctors and his wife at Joe's workplace – Dr. Pedro Gabriel Arosemenos and his wife Yanna. On weekends they would drive us to places of interest, beaches and even their cottage on the Azureo Peninsula. Dr. Pedro even loaned Joe one of his vehicles, a Jeep, to give us more access to the area which we appreciated greatly.

Finally a date for the volunteers meeting arrived. Dr. Olga, Rosa, I, the hostess, Marisa and her friend Estelle, another prominent member of the community, met in her living room.

I explained the concept of volunteerism in North America, its popularity and advantage to institutions. In terms of recruits it's an open field. The main component was their willingness to help with projects. Once recruited, they could very easily be trained. In terms of the

Psychiatric Hospital one possibility would be students to assist in clearing the courtyard square of tall weeds and turn it into a basketball area for patients – great exercise. Inside the hospital Dr. Olga said a coat of paint would help and wheeling patients into the sunny courtyard, befriending them and talking to them.

They all agreed to try to recruit friends and acquaintances and were excited by the prospect. I also explained that once a year we have a day when we show appreciation for our valued volunteers with a luncheon and speeches reflecting our appreciation for their services. After a cup of coffee and delicious cake we left the meeting full off hope and anticipation of what was to come. Dr. Pedro was impressed and a little amused when I told him about our meeting. He agreed it would be great if it worked. Good luck, he said. In the meantime Dr. Olga made out the list of needs that I would take back to Canada to Doreen Wicks and GEMS.

Joe's project was going very well and he and Stan Renton became friends, as did I and we exchanged home 'phone numbers.

Rosa then suggested she take me to a very unusual place, a residential school outside of Chitré in a mountainous area called Chepo de las Minas. Only Jeeps could go there, the terrain was so rough, two young men would drive and we would sit in the back. What breathtakingly beautiful scenery and complete wilderness, not a building in sight for miles. We stopped for a few minutes to walk about looking for the national flower, Rosa found one – a beautiful white orchid called 'Flor del Espizitu Santo' or the Holy Ghost orchid. It was chosen as a national flower in 1936. The national tree 'Stercula Apitala' was chosen in 1969 by Cabinet decree.

Back into the Jeep to continue the arduous journey. Rosa recounted to me that the residential school at Chepo de las Minas has a student population of about two hundred and serves about eleven villages in the surrounding area. The children walk those treacherous roads to school, some as much as 20km, many in bare feet as they cannot afford shoes. They reside in school along with the teachers from Monday to Friday and then go home for the weekend. The student population is rife with malnutrition due to poverty. There is no running water or electricity.

We finally arrived at our destination consisting of four very old buildings with tin roofs, surrounded by very high hills. I felt like I had been transported back a century or more but then we met the students and teachers. What an inspiring and uplifting experience that was. Despite the obvious hardships they were enduring they were bright, enthusiastic, outgoing, motivated, very friendly and all eager to learn. I had to keep turning to wipe my eyes I was so moved. They showed us the classrooms and the dormitories, one for girls the other for boys with one kerosene lamp in each when darkness came. The children slept on tin beds with old soiled mattresses and brought their own sheets and covers.

After many questions about Canada we received a lovely rendition of Panama's National Anthem and left to return to Chitré. I think I left half my heart with those beautiful, spirited, outwardly happy courageous young people and in my head, "we must help, we must help", A day I will never forget. The journey home was downhill and seemed somewhat easier. Dear Rosa, having suffered herself, loves and profoundly cares about her people and wants to help them.

I recounted my adventurous, moving journey to Joe over dinner and he was astounded but also excited and exhilarated and definitely agreed I should do my utmost to solicit help for them In Canada.

Joe's project at the hospital was coming to successful completion so the doctors decided to send us on a five day recuperation holiday to a vacation resort, on las Perlas Islands in the Pacific Ocean, during a farewell luncheon to

show their appreciation. We flew to Panama City where Enrique Williams, the CESO Agent, gave us a tour of the Panama Canal and then we flew on to las Perlas. It was a very quiet, restful resort with a lovely beach, much enjoyed. Then back to Panama City again and home to Toronto with much work ahead.

The Panamanian people stole our hearts, very warm and kind, they seem to love and enjoy life. Their national dance was the 'tamborito' (the little drums) dating back to the 17th century and the 'Cumbia', a mixture of African and Spanish. Their food was delicious, a lot of seafood from the Pacific and the Atlantic and plenty of tropical fruits and vegetables. I brought back many chicken and rice recipes as well as fish and seafood recipes that I use to this day. Panamanian's are known for their colourful national costumes and the men with their unique hats and shoulder bags. We will miss them. The return flight was smooth and uneventful as we anticipated a few busy weeks of work after our return.

CHAPTER 36

Home sweet home, it felt good to be back. The family were all well and looking forward to Spring. I telephoned Doreen Wicks, introduced myself and asked if we could meet. I told her I watched her documentary on CBC TV and was very interested in her and her work. She set up an appointment for two days later and said she was looking forward to meeting with me.

I gathered together my photos of the Psychiatric Hospital and Chepo de las Minas plus other photos of the country I thought she might enjoy. I drove downtown to GEMS and at last we were face to face, sporting big grins. As we were getting acquainted we found we shared so much in common. We were both poor as children, picked coal along the railway lines, both loved and admired our mother intensely and were both dedicated to helping the needy. She went through the photos with a teary eye and said she would definitely help the Psychiatric Hospital in Chitré. She would start collecting hospital beds first and go down the list. I thanked her profusely, we hugged with the promise she would call regularly to update me. I left feeling greatly optimistic about the project and so happy with my new-found friend.

As I look back to the day I watched the CBC documentary on Doreen Wicks I can't but think it was Divine intervention to connect Doreen, Rosa and Dr. Olga together, to change the lives of so many needy patients. "God moves in a mysterious way, his wonders to perform."

I also contacted Mr Joe Cashen, head of Easter Seals and president of the Rotary Club, Toronto and asked if we could meet to discuss Chepo de las Minas and their needs. He immediately gave me an appointment for the end of the week at which time I was able to outline the dire needs of the residential school at Chepo de las Minas, its students and staff, with photos to illustrate the challenges more starkly. Not only was he sympathetic but absolutely determined, with a tear in his eye, to do his utmost to get help. As we parted he told me he would be in touch with Rotary Club immediately and keep me posted on his progress. A man of his word; within six months, there was a plan to go to Panama, with his wife Yvonne, a school teacher and son Marc, aged ten, to complete an assessment of needs at the residential school in Chepo de las Minas – which he did.

Joe sent me a copy of his excellent report entitled, 'Report on a Community Development Project in the Republic of Panama, Community of Chepo de las Minas, Province of Herrara for the Ministry of Education, Government of Panama, under the auspices of the Canadian Executive Services Organization, the Rotary Club of Panama, the Ministry of Health, Panama in consultation with the Rotary Club of Toronto, by J. H. Cashen and Y. Cashen, December 1987 to January 1988.'

The report was thorough, concise and involved many long twelve hour days of work, with one to one interviews with all parties concerned in Chitré and Panama City. In the end Joe received authorized consent for the project from all concerned. To explain it from an emotional perspective it was a true 'crie du coeur' that was bound to succeed. However, fate intervened and due to the current President Noriega's misdeeds leading to imprisonment in the USA the Rotary Clubs cancelled the much needed project. Happily, not the end of the story or the Project as you will see in later chapters

I was so impressed and encouraged by the positive reception I received from both Doreen Wicks and Joe Cashen, two very special people whose energies gave me motivation to continue – and I did!

The next day I called CESO and informed Mr Dan Haggerty I was ready to discuss how I could help with his plans. He replied I could come in any time. As usual Joe submitted his post-project report and Dan said he already got word how pleased the hospital was with his excellent work. I made my appointment with Dan the following week.

CESO, with the approval of CIDA, was devising a strategy for the integration of 'Women in Development'. The goal was to enable participation of women in the development process both as agents and beneficiaries. In team discussions I suggested that we could begin the process with a Spouse Program. Many of the wives accompanying their husbands as CESO volunteers are retired from professions of their own and might be willing and happy to add a project of their own. For instance, retired teachers could teach English as a second language. Others, like myself, in the helping professions could expand the project at no extra cost. Having been well trained and well versed about volunteerism I was willing to take on the task of initiating the 'Spouse Program'. After a few meetings we decided to begin by inviting all CESO spouses who accompanied their husbands on projects to discuss the idea and get feedback. The first meeting was well attended, with great enthusiasm on the part of those present. We then designed an application form to learn more about the background of the spouse and the field of volunteerism they would be interested in. To keep the program informative we devised a Report Form for returning spouses to fill out regarding do's and don'ts of the host country which would better prepare future spouses going on assignments.

After months of intensive input by the team, the CESO representatives in the host countries were involved for information of potential placements that the spouse volunteers could chose from – matching volunteer to Potential Project. Several knowledgeable and experienced women were then put in charge of the Spouse Program to both supervise and monitor its success, at which time my role ended. Clare Bonnell, a CESO executive, wrote me a very heartening letter thanking me for my contribution. Valuing the concept of Volunteerism, as I did, and totally convinced it benefitted the volunteer as much as the beneficiary and recognizing the valuable contribution CESO was making in Third World countries, I felt honoured to be part of this addition to CESO's agenda. I should mention too that Doreen Wicks (GEMS) was invited as one of the speakers having had extensive experience in visiting and helping Third World countries. She was very helpful with ideas during the launching period.

Doreen kept in close contact for the next few months. I introduced her to Sid Renton, retired hospital administrator, who helped her with hospital beds for the shipment. When the time came to start packing the shipment to Chitré I invited my close Social Worker friend, Mary Benedetto, to come along.

She brought several unused sets of white sheets her Mother had tucked away and these were included in the shipment. Again, Doreen did her magic and put together a shipment beyond belief. It included thirty-three beds and mattresses, matching side tables, privacy curtain separators for the Emergency Dept., new plastic dishes and utensils donated by generous George Eaton of Eaton's, sheets, blankets, boxes of hospital gowns, disposable slippers, wheel chairs, soaps, creams and sanitizers, boxes of outer clothing and shoes, thanks to Bata Shoes, a basketball stand, net and balls for the courtyard, and on and on. Evergreen Shipping,a Taiwanese company started in 1968 by Chang Yung-fa of Taipei City, with a single vessel, transported the shipment in an international container free of charge. Today Evergreen owns 198 container vessels. GEMS and Rotary Toronto, J. Cashen CEO, donated $15,000 of medicines for the hospital.

I received a very moving letter from Dr Olga thanking me for my involvement. Also a photograph of the welcoming committee – Dr Olga, Mrs Ruth Denton, Honorary Consul of Canada, CESO representative Enrique Williams and the Rotary representative from Panama. Missing was President Noriega who was in deep trouble.

Both Mrs. Denton and Enrique Williams sent moving messages of gratitude. Enrique's lovely message arrived on my birthday May 12th. What a birthday present! Names and addresses for known contributors were passed on to Dr. Olga so she could thank them personally – which she did. Then the Creme de la Creme, dear Roseanna sent me a video they shot of the shipment arriving, being opened and unpacked, which really moved me to tears and still does.

The Final Result!

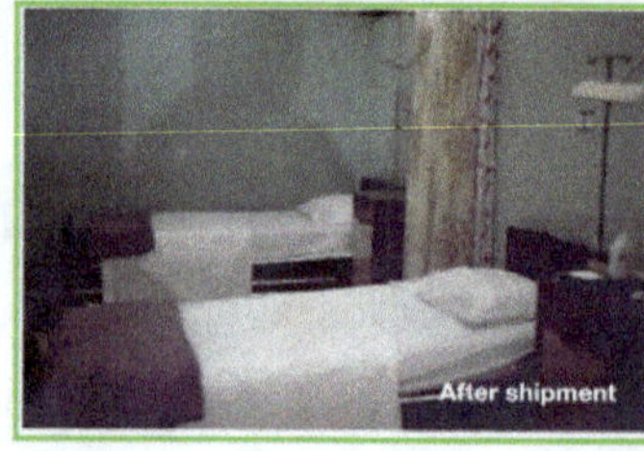

When Hearts and Hands Work Together to Help the Needy

CHAPTER 37

Joe's last assignment was a request from the USA form of CESO where they required a volunteer who spoke Russian. He fit the bill perfectly and left for his one month assignment which he completed very satisfactorily and deserves the thanks and praise from the US as well as CESO. However, he was missing for ten days and failed to inform his family or CESO that he took a side trip to the Kremlin touring various sites he had always been curious to see. Relieved at his return he worked a reprimand, as usual and the incident was eventually forgiven and forgotten.

In our personal life Joe and I seemed to reach a comfortable plateau. We respected each other and thoroughly enjoyed our work overseas helping Third World countries and even loved each other like brother and sister and that seemed to work well enough, with little bumps here and there. After I became an MSW and having studied marital therapy, I was convinced that Joe suffered from PTSD resulting from his wartime service as an air gunner. As with too many Veterans it was not diagnosed or treated. His condition played havoc in terms of the necessary behavioural patterns in a good marriage – emotional closeness, trust, sharing, fidelity etc. By the time I was aware of this it was too late to repair our marriage completely but we were able to live peacefully, respecting and caring for each other and our families for many years.

In terms of our spare time or 'vacation time', Joe continued his solo trips – most of the time – to places of interest and I began vacationing with one of my three daughters or one of the many close female friends I was fortunate enough to have over the years. This strange pattern in our marriage resembled 'widowhood' but we remained married.

My sister, Helen, continued having health problems after having had a thyroidectomy the previous year and was now in hospital awaiting surgery for pheochromocytoma, removal of the adrenal glands, serious surgery. Mother was so depressed that she couldn't go to be with her due to her own health problems, so asked if I would go.

"Of course," I replied. Not relishing driving alone I chose to go by rail, Gerry picking me up at the Ottawa station. I stayed with my sister for a week after her surgery. Our prayers were answered and she recuperated well but must take medication daily to survive, which she does. I reported back to Mother, pictures and all and she was happy I could be with Helen when she could not.

Sometimes I think life is like a rubber ball with constant ups and downs, for our next news was definitely up-lifting.

Shortly after our return from Panama we received word from our dear son, Peter, that he and Jocelyn Turner would marry in late summer. I immediately started a guest list for the bridal shower to be hosted by our family. It was a great success and fun as always. We were invited to Joan and Ed Turner's home in Guelph – Jocelyn's parents. Ed met Joan while serving in the armed forces in England during WW2. She was a charming woman, an accomplished artist with two other married daughters. Ed was retired after a very successful career in the Pet-Food business. They spent winters in their condo in Florida. The bridal shower was interesting especially watching Rachael, Andy's mother and Joan, both lovely Brits, interact. Jocelyn loved her gifts and meeting all the family.

Mother was unable to attend as she was having bad backaches. I noticed a significant weight loss in her on our return from Panama so I took her to her family physician, Dr. Marcus. He did tests and sent her to a dermatologist in Brantford but no results were available yet. I was going to Brantford on a weekly basis keeping a close eye on her and Father.

Peter and Jocelyn were married in St Margaret's Anglican Church on Avenue Road and Eglinton. His best-man was Mike Bagan, a friend from music days who was now a dentist and about to be married himself. A close friend of Jocelyn's was her Matron of Honour. It was a lovely, sentimental ceremony with a beautiful reception following in the Garden Room of the Old Mill. Peter and Jocelyn rented an apartment at Lawrence and Bathurst. He was employed with a printing company while she, a teacher, had a private tutorial business. We were all happy for them. We also met her sister, Jane and husband Jeff and their little son who lived in the USA. Nancy looked elegant and pregnant with little Jeffrey, another beautiful grandson!

After the wedding I went to Brantford to show my parents the pictures and tell them about the wedding. When I arrived I was shocked to see Mother looking so ill. I called her doctor the next day and he informed me that the dermatologist lost the sample lump he had excised from her back and wanted another sample. I told Dr. Marcus I wanted an appointment with a Specialist at Hamilton General. He agreed and within two days we had an appointment. He examined Mother thoroughly and said he was going to do a bone marrow test, which he did. After the appointment it was lunch time so I asked Mother if she would like to have lunch out.

"Yes!" she replied enthusiastically.

What a treat it was for her. Father always refused to go out for lunch or dinner. "Better food at home," was his excuse.

Mother thoroughly enjoyed lunch and before we left asked, "can we take Daddy some pizza?"

"Of course," I replied. Always thinking of others even when she was ill. That's my Mom.

I was back in Thornhill when I received the telephone call from Hamilton saying the tests were in. Mother had multiple-myeloma, cancer of the bone marrow. He didn't think there was much he could do for her.

I put the telephone down, sobbed my heart out. This can't happen, she's only eighty-one. I was alone in the house. Finally, I calmed down and got on my knees praying for help. I must take her to Princess Margaret Hospital Cancer Centre. Next day I made the appointment. I told them it was urgent and was lucky enough to get an appointment in a week.

I spent most of the remaining year in Brantford with Mom and Dad. During her appointment the doctor sadly confirmed the multiple-myeloma.

He asked Mother, "Matilda, how do you feel. Do you still enjoy life?"

"Yes, I do," Mother replied.

"Then I will give you this prescription for Prednisone that you must take each day. That will continue keeping you feeling good."

Mother and I thanked him, a very kind and gentle man. We both knew it was a matter of time – how long – that was the mystery. I stayed with Mother and Father until Christmas Day. I cooked Christmas dinner for the three of us – a sad Christmas dinner it was. No tree, gifts etc. just sadness. Mom never complained and didn't give in. She kept believing she would recover. After Christmas her face began to swell and she had a yellow pallor. On Boxing Day I went back home for a break and Nancy replaced me by going to Brantford. She telephoned me after Boxing Day saying she had to take Mother to Brantford Hospital as she was feeling very ill. She was admitted there and given excellent care.

I rushed back to Brantford and immediately telephoned my sister Helen in Ottawa to tell her to hurry down or she would not see Mother again. She got there in the nick of time to say hello and goodbye.

Mother's last words were, "take care of Daddy, don't leave him alone. Now, you girls go and get some sleep. I'll be alright."

We went home at 10:30pm to find Father despondent, pale and crying. At 1:30am we were awakened by a call from the hospital, "Mom passed away. She is no longer suffering."

She died on January 13th on my twin grandchildren's, Ashley and Shawn's, birthday.

We rushed to the hospital to see that Mother died sitting up in bed, propped against the pillows – always the strong one. We hugged her, kissed her goodbye and prayed. What a Mother, what an exceptional, courageous, fun-loving, kind, human being. Thank you God, for ending her suffering, peace at last. She is reunited with all her beloved family she hadn't seen for years and with her precious little baby Feri.

Early the next morning Helen and I made all the funeral arrangements including the funeral service at the Catholic Church where she was well known. During visitation hours people kept streaming in. Many were Smooth Rock Falls friends who were living in various parts of southern Ontario. I will never forget Mike Dubas, the young man she took in to live with us at his Mother's request and who literally became a part of our family. He came in with red weeping eyes, went to the coffin, kissed Mother and thanked her.

He then told everyone, 'this was my second Mother. She took me into her home and always treated me like a part of the family." We found ourselves consoling him, he was like a brother.

Two days later the service at the church was beautiful. I got permission from the priest to take Communion – I am Anglican. He also gave a lovely eulogy that included our immigrant history, which was very moving. He praised Mother's devotion to her religion and her kind and helpful nature. During a lull in the service a beautiful Hungarian voice started to sing, it was Zoli our young Hungarian friend. Then a chorus of other Hungarians joined in. It was a hymn usually sung at graveside before committal and since they would not all be coming to Thornhill for this, they honoured Mother with a farewell hymn here. I was moved beyond description. It brought back beautiful memories of our time in Szakasz and the Journey. It filled me with peace and calmed me. After the service everyone sat down to a lovely lunch prepared and served by the Catholic Women's League, of which Mom had been a member wherever she lived.

The hearse then moved on to Holy Cross Cemetery, Thornhill, where I had purchased their burial plots and six for my family. The drive seemed endless but we finally arrived. Mother was laid to rest with each family member placing a rose over her coffin to say goodbye. Holy Cross is located about a half mile from our subdivision in Thornhill so there were many visits with flowers, wreaths and prayers for the next year. By strange coincidence the grave next to her's and Father's is engraved with the name Wilson, like their first dear neighbours Maggie and John Wilson in Smooth Rock Falls.

I went into a severe depression after Mother's passing, couldn't get out of bed or answer the telephone, so I immediately sought help. Dr. Greta Rosenthal, a wonderful doctor, restored my health for which I am forever grateful.

The family had been taking turns visiting Father who was left alone in Brantford. Two weeks after the funeral I went over myself and was shocked to see him with the lights out, unshaven and listless and realized he was severely depressed. I packed his clothing and drove him to our home. He made no effort to dissuade me so I knew he was suffering badly. He was eighty-six at the time. Joe was very fond of my Father so agreed he should stay with us.

Father was a pleasure to look after. He generally slept until noon, ate breakfast then, weather permitting, sat under the mulberry tree on our front patio. He still had a good appetite and enjoyed his meals, with an occasional drink. He loved talking about the past especially his time in the USA.

With Spring approaching came wonderful news of the arrival of our fifth beautiful grandchild. Jeffry Kenneth Knox was born March 30th, 1987 weighing close to eleven pounds. Jessica was overjoyed to have a baby brother and we all welcomed him with love and gifts. After maternity leave Nancy found a young, competent Nanny, Alice, and returned to TV Ontario where she was employed as the Producer of a TV series about Canadian authors. Andy was commuting daily to Oakville, where he had a partnership in a law firm and little Jessica was happily attending school.

By mid-summer my right hip, which was injured in an auto accident on Hwy 401 began to give me trouble to the point that it made it difficult to climb stairs. I telephoned my sister and she suggested they take Father to live with them in Ottawa so that I could rest. I gratefully agreed. They came to Thornhill and we packed Father's belongings and off they went. Beautiful, affable dear old gent, Father, cooperated and was happy to be with his family wherever that may be. We missed his presence.

The pain in my hip did not subside so I telephoned my friend, Catherine Chalin, UoT days, for advice. She suggested I go to see her old doctor friend Dr. Salter, head of the Orthopaedic Department, Sick Children's Hospital in Toronto. He would recommend the best surgeon for the hip replacement. She arranged an appointment for the following week.

What an absolute privilege it was to meet dear Dr. Salter – a kind, gentle, compassionate and brilliant doctor. He examined my hip, after I gave him details of the accident and the treatment I received as a result. He explained that he invented a strategy called continuous passive motion or CPM, for joint injuries, which helped heal and regenerate the joint. The strategy has been in continuous use since 1978. Had I been put on that for treatment after the accident, chances are, I wouldn't be needing surgery now, which I do. He recommended Dr. David Hastings at the Wellesley Hospital or Dr.. Gross at Toronto General. Either doctor would do an excellent job at replacing my hip. I hugged him with gratitude and he wished me the best with the operation.

"Margaret, please let me know when you are having the surgery."

"I surely will, doctor," I replied.

I still marvel at my consultation with Dr. Salter and consider it the "miracle of miracles'. When I left his office there was no pain in my hip. The pain-free wellness continued for almost two years! I spoke to Catherine about it and was thoroughly convinced that this kind, compassionate doctor had a 'healing touch'. His whole demeanour exuded healing. As a matter of fact, he was awarded the distinction of being named, nationally, "Doctor of the Year" a few years later. Even prior to that, through his association with UoT (research orthopaedic) and then Hospital for Sick Children, he was chosen for countless distinctions and awards for his knowledge and his humanitarianism. In medical literature he is described as 'world renowned orthopaedic surgeon' and 'a medical giant'. All more than well deserved, I'm sure.

CHAPTER 38

There goes that bouncing ball again – this time it's good news. Peter informed me that Jocelyn was expecting a baby in April 1988. Our beautiful, precious, sixth and final grandchild, Jeremy Preston, arrived with love and celebration, uniting the various extended families.

Jocelyn, Peter and baby Jeremy moved in with us temporarily as Jocelyn felt she needed a bit of support. We were delighted to have them. After a week or so the baby, fed by bottle formula, was regurgitating quite consistently after each feeding. I advised them to call the doctor and have his condition checked. Dr Magee referred him to Hospital for Sick Children where, after a thorough examination, they found that his pyloric cavity wasn't open enough. A simple procedure corrected the condition and Jeremy was healthy and eating again.

They also decided a few months later to move from Toronto to Guelph where Jocelyn's parents lived. Peter had no problem in getting employment in the printing department of Guelph University. Jocelyn's parents wanted to buy them a house in Guelph so they could settle there. Being a university city prices were generally higher for houses so they had difficulty finding one for the price range they had in mind. Peter got a promotion to a better paying job at the university and Jocelyn became a stay-at-home Mom.

Janice, who was working as a cashier at Nortown, on Eglinton at Bathurst, decided to rent the apartment that Jocelyn and Peter vacated for it was closer to her work. We helped her move and furnish the apartment which was comfortable and quite attractive. I think she enjoyed the independence and is still living there to this day, a retired senior citizen.

In the meantime Father, living with Helen and Gerry in Ottawa, decided we should sell his house as he would never return there again. He wanted Helen and I to share the proceeds as he had sufficient money saved for his care for the rest of his life.

We put the house up for sale but the market was slow so I asked Jocelyn and Peter if they would be interested in buying Father's house, less the real estate fees. They were.

Joan decided to gift Jocelyn's share of the house, one half and I would give them a mortgage for the remaining half, interest free. On consulting Andy, my lawyer son-in-law, he thought I should charge them a minimal interest and give them a legal mortgage, which I did.

They loved the house and were excited about moving to their first home. On their first visit Peter looked for and found employment with a local printing company and Jocelyn would stay home with little Jeremy. Everyone seemed happy with the arrangement.

However, all stories don't end with a happy ending and I'm sad to say this one didn't either. Jocelyn found parenthood stressful and after irreconcilable differences she decided she wanted a divorce, moving into a women's shelter to help her case. The final decision of the Court was full custody of the child to the father with visiting rights to the mother. Jeremy was about seven years old at the time.

Peter found the house rental in Brantford so Jeremy could continue school and be with his friends. I can't say enough about what an excellent, kind and loving father Peter was to Jeremy. His heart and soul and energy were devoted to raising Jeremy who really wasn't bonded with Jocelyn, so he didn't see her much. Always an avid student, in his senior year in High School, Jeremy took up poetry writing and lo and behold won first prize for one of his many poems.

After High School they moved to Kitchener where Jeremy attended Waterloo University on a scholarship majoring in History and English and also became a gifted actor with a lead in 'Rocky Mountain Horror Show' which received rave reviews. He was also awarded scholarships for his Master's degree and PhD. What a brilliant young man, full of motivation, determination, courage and a golden character. Thank you Jocelyn for giving birth to our little angel. Thank you Peter for being such an exceptional, devoted and loving father. And thank you Jeremy for being such an outstanding grandson. But I have news – he is only number one. There are five others you will hear about later. Boasting grandparents are so intolerable but I can't control myself.

In late 1989 my injured hip was painful again so I asked our family doctor, Gary Magee, for a referral to Dr. David Hastings. I met with him and surgery for my hip replacement was booked for March 1990. I would be getting one of the new artificial ones with no screws or cement. He said I was a perfect candidate weighing only 120lbs. Dr. Salter was notified. I found Dr. Hastings very much like Dr. Salter, kind, gentle, compassionate and bright. I was in good hands.

I wanted Christmas 1989 to be very special celebration so we decorated the house early and made it warm and inviting. Following a Mexican tradition I filled a large aluminum paper bag full of mixed sweets, tied it with a ribbon that dangled to the ground. On Christmas Day we hung the piñata in an archway and had a 'magic wand' for each grandchild with which they could hit the magic bag and candies would drop down for them to eat – something different for them to remember. Each Christmas the grandchildren would stand or sit in front of the fireplace for their Christmas picture. I treasure the collection to this day. They were close, affectionate cousins and had good times together.

After a super turkey dinner we would all gather around Rachael, Andy's mother, who would bring out her special plum pudding, pour on the rum and light it – an annual tradition, then serve it with lovely sauce. One thing missing was Mother's special home made Christmas cake that we enjoyed for many years. We all missed her terribly! Father was with Helen and Gerry and I continued having Christmas dinner until my late seventies at which time the adult children would each bring a casserole and dessert and I'd just prepare the turkey and trimmings.

CHAPTER 39

January rolled around quickly and after it February and March, surgery time. I had written to all my out of town family and friends including my dear friend Ethel Lower in England about my upcoming surgery and received replies wishing me the best. The night before my admission to the hospital I had a fascinating dream. I dreamt I was in a large, square empty room with my friend Ethel Lower. She came and hugged me, took my hand and led me to an open field full of beautiful, colourful wild flowers of every variety. It seemed we were on a higher level of land.

Then she said, "this is where we'll walk through the flowers because it's safe. Not down there."

Down there was a sandy stretch of beach with open sea beyond it. Not being a swimmer I was always a little edgy around deep water. So the dream ended with Ethel and I walking hand in hand through the field of beautiful flowers, laughing and talking. When I awakened, ready to go into hospital, I was relaxed and filled with optimism that everything would go well and I would recover. That is exactly what happened.

Dr. Hastings and his wonderful team did a superb job replacing my injured hip with a new artificial one. I wasn't to stand on my right foot for six weeks and use crutches or a walker and hobble along on one foot only. If I put any pressure on the replacement hip it could undo the operation.

While I was recuperating in hospital we got word that dear Aunt Bertha had passed away in Cummer House at the age of ninety-eight. Sadly, I missed the visitation, the funeral service and committal in Carleton Place Cemetery with the rest of her family. I prayed a lot for her and during the time of the church service followed it in the Anglican Book of Prayer so I was there in spirit. My beloved Aunt, friend, hero, pioneer of so many events was gone but never, never forgotten. All our family attended the funeral in Carleton Place except Jani who insisted on staying so she could visit me every evening in hospital. Bless her generous heart, I appreciated it.

I was discharged after a week in hospital and chose home care for two weeks rather than spending the time in a public facility. Bruce, Judy's husband, put a piece of plywood under the cushions of the sofa in the family room to make it firmer and that was my bedroom for the next six weeks. The recovery was complete and wonderful as Ethel said it would be in my dream.

When I attended my post sixth-week appointment with Dr. Hastings he had three medical students with him and introduced me as 'my star patient with the new designed hip', she followed orders and her recovery is excellent. My new hip has never given me trouble and I'm now ninety-two. Thank you dear Drs. Hastings and Salter. I'm forever grateful.

In January of 1992 I received an invitation from my dear neighbours Olive and Wilf Neil to visit them on Jekyll Island, Georgia where they generally spent the winter months. I accepted with gratitude and flew to Jacksonville, Florida where they picked me up at the airport. We then drove to Jekyll Island together, a very interesting area of the United States. We arrived on the island where there was a guardsman with whom we had to check in – and also check out.

Jekyll Island is located off the State of Georgia, is one of the Sea Islands and also one of the Golden Isles of Georgia Barrier Islands, on the Atlantic coast between Savannah, Georgia and Jacksonville, Florida. St. Simon, Brunswick, Sea Island and Little St. Simon are also part of the Golden Isles.

In the late 1800s the island was an exclusive hunting club for the wealthy, like the Rockefellers, Morgans, Vanderbilts, etc. who conducted business meetings there including the birth of the US Federal Reserve. It is now a popular tourist resort with hotels, restaurants and home rentals.

Olive and Wilf rented a two bedroom bungalow close to the beach. They showed me a wonderful time on my two week vacation. We toured the island and all points of interest, explored the Golden Isles, including St. Simon which housed the first Episcopalian Church built in 1820 and rebuilt in 1884, whose many beams are the oak of wrecked ships. Behind the Church is an interesting cemetery one grave of which is for Eugenia Price, the famous author, who wrote St. Simon's Trilogy and other novels. We also visited the famous lighthouse of St. Simon's Island

The island is a little paradise for flower lovers, azaleas and camellias are everywhere. Also live oak, holly and cedar trees are prevalent. We had long walks on the beach daily, a few shopping trips to New Brunswick and many crab cake luncheons, a delicious treat in that area.

During my visit I received a most surprising telephone call from a very dear friend of many years, Doug Lower, telling me he and his wife Pauline, whom I met in our University days, were moving to France as she was battling cancer and wanted to spend the rest of her time there. I expressed my sorrow about Pauline's illness. He then asked if we could meet to say goodbye, would I be back in time? I answered of course, "I'll call you when I return."

The two weeks flew by too quickly and it was time to catch my flight back to Toronto. I thanked Olive and Wilf profusely and boarded my flight during a most colourful, beautiful sunset. Judy picked me up at Toronto airport. I telephoned Olive to let them know I had arrived safely and to thank them again for their wonderful hospitality.

The house was neat and organized and I spent my time unpacking and thinking. In the early 80's when my marriage was falling apart, I didn't have the courage or even the wish to break it up, I turned to decorating then adding new paintings as I learned more about art. I replaced my existing art with Picassos, Andrew Wyeth, C A Muñks and Daphne Odjig, a famous Native Canadian artist I discovered while visiting the Kleinburg Gallery. The children were young adults living their own lives so I felt a sense of freedom I'd never felt before. I also did another thing. I had an 'affair of the heart', a very deep feeling for a man other than my husband. He was exactly the opposite of Joe – he thought I was the greatest, loved my immigrant background, praised me for my numerous accomplishments. He also had a great sense of humour, was kind and generous, had travelled a great deal and was a journalist creating award winning documentaries. Perfect characteristics rolled up in one beautiful man!

He was the only one I didn't use my famous expression on, "never, you're like a brother to me". Now we were going to meet to say what we believed was a final goodbye.

"Affairs of the heart" are often very painful especially when both parties are married with children and grand-children involved. Sometimes they continue with miles between the involved parties. Often, "the heart has reasons the mind cannot always understand" and they somehow reunite! Now I'm meeting this wonderful man who is taking his ailing wife to France to enjoy her final years in an exciting country.

What might the future hold for us – heartache, boundless love or neither?

We decided to drive to Kleinburg, have lunch and then go to the Group of Seven Gallery, which we enjoyed so much. During the drive Doug accidentally ran a red light. An OPP Officer stopped us.

"Where are you going, Sir?" asked the OPP

"We're just going down Memory Lane, Officer," Doug replied

Frowning, the Officer replied, "Sorry, I'm not aware of that area, watch those red lights."

That was a bit of luck for us and we couldn't help laughing later about the "Memory Lane" bit.

We lunched, laughed and cried, had a great time at the Gallery, embraced and said our goodbyes. I never imagined, even in my wildest fantasies, that our paths would cross again.

I returned home to my art and decorating with plans, looking forward to a new beginning.

While I was away Joe decided he was too sedentary so booked a trip to Cuba – alone. He stayed at a resort in Havana and could speak Spanish so was able to communicate with the locals. He was away three weeks but didn't enjoy the beach because it was too windy. He recounted how he shared a taxi to a bar in Havana with a couple from Germany who openly tried to lure his ring from him. It was a very expensive gold ring with ruby inserts engraved with his initials – a gift from Dubois Chemicals at Christmas along with his performance bonus. The male asked if he could try it on. Joe declined several times smelling a rat in the request and they finally stopped asking. Needless to say he took a taxi back to the resort alone. He seemed extremely happy to get home arriving ten days after my return.

CHAPTER 40

Father, who was living with Helen and Gerry in Ottawa, had a severe stroke and could no longer climb stairs. We chose a Nursing Home as near as possible to their residence so they could visit him often. Father seemed content there for several months. Helen, devoted daughter, went in twice a day to feed him. The Home confined him to a wheelchair to avoid falls. His behaviour suddenly took a turn and he began shouting, "Mom, Mom," in a frightened voice – Mom, was his deceased wife, our Mother. This went on for some time. Finally my sister had a meeting with the nurses who looked after him and was informed he was taken off all his medication for high blood pressure, gout, etc. My sister was shocked and immediately arranged for a new, female doctor for him. She seemed very attentive, gave him a flu shot to begin with. However, the shouting behaviour, panic, continued.

I was with my sister when she took Father to the bathroom, waived her hand in front of his eyes and asked, "Dad, can you see my hand?"

"No," he replied crying, "I can't."

That was how we discovered Father was blind all those weeks, and shouting for Mom to help him. None of the staff or doctors detected it!

At this point Father had lost a lot of weight, wasn't eating or Drinking properly. His body was so thin they had to use a medical hoist to turn or lift him to avoid pain.

I returned home to prepare for the inevitable and it came. Our beloved Father passed away November 4th, 1994. His body was transported to Kane Funeral Hone in Thornhill for visitation. Many of his friends and family from Brantford attended. The Funeral Service was conducted at St Luke's Roman Catholic Church in Thornhill. The priests there would not allow eulogies during the Service so Gerry, my brother-in-law, delivered a beautiful eulogy after lunch which was served at the Church to those attending. Father was then buried bedside the love of his life, Mother, at Holy Cross Cemetery.

Mother and Father had their ups and downs in their long marriage but they had a deep abiding love for one another that was stronger than their differences. What was unique about them was their deep empathy and caring for their family, friends and their community. They were participants always there to help when there was a need.

Consequently they were loved wherever they lived and missed when gone, I'm sure.

Earlier in 1993 my beloved sister-in-law, Thelma, Currie's wife, returned from her vacation in Florida with her girlfriends, lay down her luggage, stretched out for forty winks after a tiring flight home and passed away in her sleep. A great reward for a life well lived.

Thelma and Currie's marriage was somewhat similar to ours. They had one beautiful, loveable daughter, Linda and in later life chose to take separate holidays. Currie loved attending race-car events alone, while Thelma enjoyed Myrtle Beach with family and Florida with her girlfriends. She was a good woman, fun to be with and had a hearty laugh. Linda is so much like her and we all love her.

Dear Thelma was laid to rest in the family plot at Carelton Place Cemetery in Spring. A beautiful lady, never forgotten.

The following year Currie, who had had a heart by-pass some years ago, required another one in 1994 which he booked and informed all the family. We received a call from Linda who was married to a young man named Philip Young. They were living in a wonderful home in Markham, Linda working at IBM and Philip, at the time, was an author. Linda recounted how her Father had been visited at the hospital daily by a lawyer who was a member and representative of the Salvation Army and eventually coerced into leaving his entire estate, home, house and all to the Salvation Army, disinheriting her completely. Thelma's family inheritance was included in this give away! As an aside Thelma had been complaining that Currie was too generous to several charities and she was worried about the consequences – shortages they might suffer in their old age. Joe and I talked it over and decided this was cruelly unfair to Linda and she must try and reverse it. He advised her to call her Father in hospital and tell him it was Mom's money and house involved and she would be horrified at what he was doing. She went on to say she would call him back, record the call while he reverses his decision in the Will leaving everything to Linda, their only off-spring. Currie agreed and it was accomplished that afternoon with Linda possessing the recorded conversation.

Next Joe asked Andy, our son-in-law lawyer, to recommend an excellent lawyer in Ottawa that Linda could retain to handle the whole thing – which he did. Linda went to stay with her Father a couple of days before the operation and was very grateful for the advice from Joe. At eleven a.m. the day of the surgery there were serious complications. The Surgeon was faced with extensive scar tissue from the previous by-pass and as he proceeded to remove it Currie began to haemorrhage severely and lost consciousness. We had gone to Ottawa to be with Linda and Currie so she tearfully asked if we could stay and sit with Currie while she returned to Markham for her appropriate clothes for the funeral. Of course we agreed and she left immediately. We sat with Currie, one at each side, and the critical care nurse informed us that we should talk to him as patients in that condition can hear you to the end. So I held Currie's hand and recited the Lord's Prayer. To comfort him I said he would be reunited with Thelma and his Mother and Father. Suddenly, Joe in a very anguished tone said, "I can't do this any longer, I have to leave." PTSD? Is it that? I told him to go to the cafeteria and I would remain with Currie until the end. The nurse informed me she would pull the plug when his pulse reached a certain point and he would pass quietly. For thirty minutes more I kept talking to my brother-in-law recounting how much we all cared for him and would be there for Linda when she needed us. Then the nurse pulled the plug and he was gone. She hugged me and I left the room, my eyes full of tears and somehow found my way to the cafeteria to tell Joe.

The funeral was held in St James Anglican Church and Currie was buried in Carleton Place Cemetery beside Thelma in the family compound. The most abhorrent thing happened during visitation. The Salvation Army lawyer came and as Robert greeted him at the door the lawyer asked, with a grin, "what did you think of Currie's Will leaving everything to the Salvation Army?"

Robert replied, "you can leave right now, you're not welcome here." He did.

A week after the funeral the legal case over the Will commenced. It was finally resolved with Linda receiving her rightful share but the Salvation Army retaining about $75,000. We were delighted to be able to help our beloved niece and still keep in touch with her to this day. I have always held the Salvation Army in high regard and still do, one bad apple does not spoil the whole barrel!

The past two years were filled with sadness and heartache, parting with so many loved ones but as Christians we believed we will joyfully reunite with them. In the meantime prayers and hard work eventually brought to us a new normalcy – life without so many beloved family members.

Joe surprised me by offering to accompany me to Hungary and Romania to see my remaining family. We booked our three week trip with the first stop a few days in Paris, France. Sitting under an umbrella at a Parisian café immediately brought back memories of 1933 and my first stay there, before heading for our new home in Canada.

We stayed at the Hôtel du Brésil, close to Luxembourg Gardens. A brass plaque on the outside wall of the hotel proudly announced that Sigmund Freud had stayed there at one time. We enjoyed the tasty French food, the people and the sites which included Luxembourg Gardens, the Louvre, Musée d'Orsay and Notre Dame Cathedral. A pleasant memory was hearing the Nuns at a nearby Nunnery singing hymns in their angelic voices each morning.

Our next flight was to Budapest, Hungary, returning to the land of my ancestors. We stayed at an hotel in downtown Budapest which had a large balcony overlooking the main street and a large inner courtyard on the other side of our room, on the third floor. Our first venture out on the streets of Budapest stunned me. I always considered myself a staunch patriotic Canadian, as per Father's instructions to Mother and me on our arrival. But as we walked along I could hear my mother tongue being spoken everywhere, laughter, friendly voices and I could understand it all! Next, hearing beautiful Hungarian music, mostly violins and songs my Mother used to sing in our home, moved me very deeply, a feeling I didn't expect.

We were fortunate to attend the Budapest Opera House, a Bach symphony concert, Hero's Square and the Hungarian Parliament building, a most impressive site on the banks of the Danube. Joe enjoyed speaking Hungarian, which surprised me no end.

We both loved Budapest, Buda and Pest with the Danube between. Now we were travelling to Szakasz by train to the current home of my ancestors. We got our first shock when we were happily seated on the leather seats in our little compartment we suddenly felt them getting hotter and hotter, heated seats in the middle of summer! Something obviously malfunctioned, so we changed seats.

We arrived in Satu Mare, the Romanian version of Szatmar, where my cousin Margaret and her husband Steven met us with a mixture of tears, laughter and excitement. They kindly invited us to stay with them which served as home base while we visited our various relatives. Margaret's husband was a builder who proudly showed us the apartments and banks etc. he built. They lived in an up-scale condo but had a beautiful two story house in the country which he built himself and where they spent most weekends.

The family members consisted of my beloved fraternal grandparents, now deceased, who moved to Cleveland in 1912 with my Father, then age eleven. In her late forties Grandmother gave birth to two additional sons, Joni and Bela, found she couldn't cope with the stress and the whole family, including my Father, returned to Europe. He was immediately conscripted into the army where he served as an assistant to a General because he spoke perfect English.

However, Father couldn't tolerate life there and moved to Canada in 1928 a few months before I was born. Mother and I followed in 1933. The rest of the family remained and endured untold hardships, WW2, take-over by the Communists and a life of relative poverty and suffering until 1989 when the communists were ousted. My sister, Helen and I, put together money for each family and took gifts of coffee which was in short supply. I also took wreaths for the graves of my grandparents and uncle Joni, who had passed away. As I tearfully placed the wreath on my grand-parent's grave it brought back memories of our tearful farewell at the train station many years ago. Sadly I thought, *"kedves Nagymama,"*! I did come back to see you. I look different but still love you and will forever until we meet again.

Although I was overjoyed to meet all the families I was heartbroken to witness how poorly they lived. Obviously my dear Grandmother made a horrible mistake moving back with dire consequences for the family.

Prior to WW2 the American Consul had contacted my two uncles, who were born in Cleveland but they refused to return to the U.S. and leave behind their parents and girl friends. Parents always want the best for their children but sometimes things backfire and the result is sad for everyone concerned.

Uncle Bela, my favourite uncle, who was about fourteen when I left for Canada, had a son and daughter, each with one child. Both family's were prosperous and modern by European standards. Joni's family, however, was very large and lived in relative poverty with their Mother, Joni's widow.

Two events helped to brighten up the trip, somewhat. Two adults, one female, one male appeared to inform me that we were playmates before our departure, The female was a teacher and the male worked on the family farm. I remember them and welcomed their visit.

The second event was our numerous visits to the family wine cellar where drinking was accompanied by Hungarian music, violins again and songs, many of which Mother sang in Smooth Rock Falls. After a week of visits, including the graves of my grandparents and uncle, two days at Margaret's country home, most enjoyable, we packed preparing for our return to Budapest to catch a flight home. Joe enjoyed the trip, his second one there, because he could join in the conversations speaking Hungarian. I found it more sad than happy and thanked my Mother for moving us to Canada when she did. Bless her beautiful soul.

We took many pictures during the reunions until my uncle Bela died ten years later.

I often question myself about my positive and emotional attitude about Budapest and the opposite about Romania. After much thought decided that although I was born in Romania, the part of Hungary awarded to Romania after WWI by the Treaty of Trion, I never learned to speak Romanian, never attended school there and identified more as a Hungarian – thus the emotional feeling about Budapest, which was lacking in Romania.

The flight home was pleasant and home never looked so good. We wrote thank you letters, exchanged videos and photographs etc. and kept in touch until my uncle died, absent but not forgotten.

CHAPTER 41

We barely had time to unpack when Joe decided he would visit South America – Venezuela and Rio de Janeiro, Brazil. While he was gone I accepted Rachael's (Andy's mother) kind invitation to join her and spend a month at her condo in Naples, Florida. I had never met Andy's Father Ken for he had passed on before Nancy and Andy were married. However, Rachael talked about him often and would get extremely depressed at Christmas, the anniversary of his death. She sadly recounted to me how even her best friend would not allow her to discuss how much she missed him or anything about him which unfortunately prolonged the mourning period. Having studied Death and Dying and the Mourning Process at University I thought and hoped I could help Rachael with this painful problem.

I flew to Fort Meyers where she met me and we drove to

her condo in Naples which was situated across the street from the beach and ocean. A two bedroom condo with a lovely living room, dining room and kitchen and two bathrooms. A corner unit, it had plenty of windows so was bright and cheerful. In the courtyard there was a good sized pool surrounded with tables, umbrellas and chaise lounges. She had close Canadian friends across the street, a retired couple Agnes and Ernest. I was introduced to them at a lovely luncheon hosted by Rachael at the Ritz where we enjoyed cocktails and soft piano music. The outing was delightful as were her friends, Agnes and Ernest. When I questioned Rachael about the luncheon tab it turned out to be hefty so I insisted on paying half and did so despite her resistance.

Agnes and Ernest were a lively retired couple who earlier in life had adopted a daughter, now a school teacher and a son. They had a lovely home in Toronto and a summer cottage in Muskoka. They encouraged and helped Rachael and Ken find and purchase their condo in Naples. Each day we would walk along the beach and sit under our umbrellas enjoying the view and beautiful weather. Our weekly routine included shopping trips, visits to the local library, concerts and eating out. This trip cemented our friendship as we exchanged stories of our lives and really got to know each other well. Rachael was born in Yorkshire, England, joined the WRENS during WW2 where she met Ken. After the war she attend Oxford where she read law and graduated. Ken became a chartered accountant and operated his own business. They had one child, a son AnDrew, born in 1947.

I was really impressed with her outstanding accomplishments both in England and later in Canada. She worked as a representative of "Save the Children" during which time she travelled to several countries meeting dignitaries everywhere. Wanting to broaden their opportunities she and Ken decided to emigrate to Canada, settling in Acton, Ontario for a few years and finally to a new home Oakville, Ontario. She served as the Registrar of the Ontario Bar Admission Course, the second of the two women appointed to that position. She had a distinguished career with the Law Society of Ontario until her retirement in 1969.

Husband Ken had a successful business as a Chartered Accountant until heart problems ended it. Rachael's parents also emigrated to Canada and lived with them, helping to raise little Andy.

I encouraged Rachael to keep talking about the good and not so good she experienced and it soon became a daily occurrence where she had a listening ear, a lot of empathy, understanding and praise for her good works.

A few years after her trip Rachael confessed she no longer suffered the deep depression and anxiety connected to Ken's death at Christmas. She became a beloved member of our extended family and at Christmas dinners she was in charge of making and serving the plum pudding for dessert. The children always enjoyed gathering around her for the lighting of the 'pudding ceremony'. Over the years we developed a deep friendship visiting back and forth, including Rachael's beloved dog Dom, always celebrating birthdays and special occasions like Christmas, Easter etc.. I will never forget her wonderful compliment to me sitting beside our fireplace in Thornhill, "you my dear are the glue that keeps this family together."

As I look back I cannot believe the many exceptionally intelligent and outstanding women friends I had, both young and old. Rachael was in that category. Apart from family I think good friends, both male and female, are such a blessing for they enrich your life and expand your world greatly. All mine certainly did!

In 1980 Rachael found it necessary to sell her house and move into a Retirement Condo Hearthstone by the Lake, in Burlington, Ontario. It had two bedrooms, living and dining room, a kitchenette and two bathrooms. She could cook her own meals or eat in the Dining Room that had a super Chef, which we can attest to. Her balcony faced south so she had a wonderful view of Lake Ontario.

On her eightieth birthday Rachael hosted a party to celebrate the happy occasion that was held In the Party Room, enjoyed by all attending. She made new friends and took part in the social life at Hearthstone until the fateful day, New Year's Eve, when friends picked her up to attend a Bridge game, she loved Bridge. As she was about to enter the back seat of the car with the door still open the driver mistakenly backed the car up thinking she was already in it. She was badly injured and hospitalized.

After her discharge she was in a wheel chair and found it impossible to carry on by herself in the condo. Sadly the family moved her to a Nursing Home in Oakville where we visited her often. Her health continued to decline until she had to be hospitalized for a second time.

The last time I visited her was the day before she died. The ladies of St Jude's Anglican Church were singing hymns and saying prayers for her. It was a tearful visit and as I was about to leave she clung to my hand as though she had a premonition. I stayed a few minutes longer and finally kissed her and headed toward the door where I looked back to waive to her. She smiled weakly and said, "I love you". I repeated the compliment with tears flooding my eyes. My beloved friend Rachael died the next day, October 6th, her birthday at age eighty-three!

A beautiful, intelligent, devout most accomplished woman, always thoughtful and giving of herself and who always loved and put her family first. I miss her, even today but I know we will meet again amidst angel voices.

As I reminisce my beloved friend Ethel Lower, mentioned in a previous chapter, comes to mind. We first met when I hosted a bridal shower for her granddaughter Susan and for a quarter of a century corresponded regularly until her death in 1996. Ethel, like Aunt Bertha, was 'one of a kind'. In her early years she was an activist before it was a label and an old time socialist who attended rallies in Trafalgar Square, Parliament Square and Hyde Park Speaker's Corner in London, England, a time honoured tradition among the UK's young and politically aware.

Her socialism was centred on men like George Lansbury and other persons of wealth and privilege who believed the industrial era had spawned a legacy of gross inequality and neglect writ large on the general population, the 'great unwashed' critics sarcastically chided. The downside of the political left arguing for change, was a fragile coalition between socialists, genuine theorists and activists, the cooperatives, wholesale/retail trader groups, and Trades Unions that were becoming daringly disruptive.

Ethel joined the Jarrow Death March, a group of NE coal miners, unemployed and starving, neglected politically, who by the time they reached London two hunDred miles away, where she joined them, numbered thousands of supporters. On arrival in Parliament Square they were never greeted but brutally dispersed by police on horseback. Ethel was grabbed by a policeman and told, 'get on 'ome with your kid," her first born, Jean, in her arms.

Later she joined the protests against a Marie Stopes birth control clinic in north London when early right-to-lifers, mostly religious zealots, tried to destroy the building.

There was much social unrest in early XIX and XXC

UK with unsure, insecure elites lashing out under the guise of responsible government.

Fairness and justice were an integral part of Ethel's makeup. She was an avid reader and her daughters complained they couldn't keep up with the her demand for books to read.

Our correspondence continued during my volunteer days in Central America delighting her with the work I was doing. Her history of marches and participation for justice eventually made the world a better place for many. I shed many tears after her death in 1996 and still miss her. An outstanding, intelligent woman with a passion for life and justice who practiced what she preached!

Then there is beloved Doreen Wicks (GEMS), married to Ben Wicks, the famous cartoonist we all loved. She and Ben emigrated to Canada in 1957 going to Alberta first, then finally settling in Toronto where Ben established his new career. He also had a Pub on Parliament Street frequented by media people. Doreen, as I stated earlier was a Head Nurse at Sunnybrook Hospital when she decided to leave in 1982 to open a highly revered Charitable Organization GEMS to help the poor and needy (especially women) in Third World Countries.

We became fast friends after our first meeting regarding the needs of the Psychiatric Hospital in Panama, for we found because we had so much in common we instantly liked each other. The friendship deepened each time we saw each other, consequently she invited me to her B'nai

Brith award luncheon held in Toronto. But that wasn't her only award. In 1989 she was honoured with the Order of Canada which Ben had already received in 1986. One of the few couples both receiving it! Then in 1997 she was appointed Citizenship Judge and reappointed the following year. All well deserved. But her outstanding achievement and what embedded her in my heart forever was the incredible shipment she sent to the Psychiatric Hospital in Panama – unforgettable! Consequently she joins the list of my admirable, beloved, exceptional, heroic women.

Sadly Ben passed away in 2000 while I was overseas and I sent condolences by mail. Then we were all shocked and saddened when beloved Doreen passed away March 1st., 2004. I was one of the mourners at her well attended funeral where I had the pleasure of meeting her three children, Susan, Kim and Vincent.

On the subject of remarkable women, I would be remiss not to mention Gertie Gowan, who happened to be my granddaughter Lisa's husband Brad's maternal grandmother. She spent her life in the Creemore, Ontario area, married raising seven beautiful children. One would believe that was a full-time job but not for Gertie. She was very involved with her Church, St Luke's Anglican, in Creemore. She served her Church devoutly all her adult life being an active member of the ACW and major organizer of all Church events, holding various positions within the Church Council. In 2015 she was awarded the Order of the Diocese of Toronto for her extensive contribution to her Church and Community. She was a Cancer Society volunteer for fifty years, Olympic Torch Bearer for the 2010 Vancouver Olympics and received the Senior of the Year Award in 2006 and 2010.

Sadly she passed away December 11th, 2020 at the age of 89. Her life was a shining beacon of love, for family, friends and Community and will be greatly missed by her fifteen grandchildren, eighteen great grandchildren and ALL who knew and loved her.

What a privilege and honour it is to have known these exceptional women who never stopped giving and caring. They made the world a better place for many and also served as great role models for the next generation. I should mention I could easily add to the list at least ten more of these exceptional women/friends.

CHAPTER 42

———

A Grandmother's Prayer
Joy to the World, a special gift from Above
Our first precious grandchild
To nurture and to love
And give purpose, meaning and joy to our lives
As we love, teach, guide and watch her grow and thrive
Dearest Lisa we are so happy you are here
You make life more precious and fill our hearts with cheer.
As you mature and choose your life path, this is my fervent prayer
That you live life fully, love truly and work persistently
To make the World a better place for Everyone to be

My grandchildren (and my children and great-grandchildren) are the greatest blessing and gift of my life. They are my heart and soul and I love each one dearly and am pleased and grateful for the wonderful human beings they have become. Therefore, I'll take the liberty to prove my point by devoting this chapter to my six beloved grandchildren.

The first arrival, Lisa, was born to Judy and Bruce Smith on June 28th., 1979 in York Central Hospital, Richmond Hill, Ontario. A beautiful blue eyed, blonde haired, baby girl with smiles galore.

Four years later on January 13th., 1983 the surprise of our lives twins Ashley and Shawn were born (twins don't always skip a generation!), in the same hospital under Dr Bate's excellent care. They were grandchildren three and four.

On July 9th, 1981 our second beloved grandchild, Jessica, was born in Mt. Sinai Hospital, Toronto to our wonderful elder daughter Nancy. Despite the tragic circumstances (later divorce) the whole family rejoiced and celebrated her arrival. The paediatrician invited "Grandma" (me) masked and gowned into the delivery room and I was honoured to be the first relative to hold the little bundle of joy and that she certainly was and still is. She was born a day after my Father's birthday.

Our beautiful fifth grandchild, Jeffery, born to Nancy and Andy Knox weighed in at nearly eleven pounds, born by Caesarian section, a robust, brown eyed, brown haired and chubby little cheeks. Nancy and Andy were overjoyed as were we all. He was born March 30th., 1988 a day before my Mother's birthday.

Finally our sixth beloved grandchild, Jeremy, was born to Jocelyn and Peter Hawkins on April 30th., 1989 amidst great celebration. A beautiful little angel, long limbed and lanky. Unfortunately he had minor surgery of his pyloric cavity, to open it more, at Sick Children's Hospital when he was a week old. He survived and thrived growing into a wonderful young man.

A little side line here is imperative. My beloved Mother always welcomed the great-grandchildren with beautiful crocheted bonnets, sweaters and a lovely wool crocheted blanket of their own. Sadly she passed away before meeting Jeremy and Jeffrey but they also received their beautiful clothes and little blanket which she prepared before she died. Consequently I nick-named her the beloved fairy-grandmother – may she rest in peace.

So Joe and I entered another phase in our lives filled with fun, laughter, joy and gratitude to God for his blessing, as I say in my poetry. Despite a busy household – I had just graduated from York University with a BSW and formed my own company 'York Counselling Services' and worked with the Ministry of Correctional Services as a probationary officer. Joe was completing his BA at Atkinson, York University nevertheless we looked forward to many happy visits with our beloved grandchildren. There were also numerous weekend dinners when we would all unite at our house and the grandchildren had many good times together. Many photos were taken in the garden in the summer and in front of the fireplace in the winter. I looked at cooking as a labour of love and did a lot of that with pleasure.

I often picked Jessica up and brought her home for the weekend to give Nancy a break while she was child rearing alone before her second marriage.

As the children grew and thrived each had their unique personalities and exhibited multi-varied talents. One thing they all had in common was they were all fun loving, happy and genuinely cared for each other deeply. They all had loving parents who were great role models and also grand-parents on both sides who were warm and loving.

Judy and Bruce's children were enrolled in total French immersion and were bi-lingual at the end of Grade 8. In school the children all performed extremely well, above average.

At the end of Grade 8, Jeremy (Peter and Jocelyn were now sadly divorced and Peter had sole custody of his son), exhibited great talent for drama and writing poetry and was awarded first prize for one of his many poems called 'Purpose of Being'.

We are mesh, a network of decisions,
Slightest, simplest most specific
Can it be predicted?
Or is it spontaneous?
Destiny or individual choices
Sculpt the intricate process
                Jeremy Hawkins

What deep and complex thoughts for a young teenager! His family all loved him and marvelled at his writing skills.

The teen years went by smoothly with most of the grandchildren preoccupied with studies and part-time work just as their parents did a generation before. Lisa started part-time work with Richmond Hill library, where her mother worked and had a lucrative position there all through her university days.

Shawn was into sports, ie. hockey and at the point we were convinced he would end up with NHL. Not so, he had more interesting ideas.

Our grandchildren had the good fortune of having great parents who loved, guided them and showed endless interest in their welfare. Also loving parents (themselves adult students) attending university, as role models (which helped overcome obstacles created by tragic family events such as divorce, health problems etc.). After high school graduation each miraculously continued on to university.

Lisa Smith was the first to graduate with a B.A. in Psychology from York University. Then on to Seneca College for a Diploma in Early Childhood Education. And finally a B.A. in Education from Brock University in St. Catherines. At the present time she and Brad are parenting three beautiful children- Carter, Quinn and Shawn and she is a highly competent and popular teacher of Grade students employed by the Oak Ridges School Board. Her dedication was exemplary when she spent a summer studying Autism and therefor has several Autistic students integrated into her class, which makes my heart leap with delight.

Her interests beyond teaching are endless. She is a very gifted photographer, painter and gardener. Growing fourth generation peonies in her garden. Not long ago I gave her a huge bagful of my late Mother's knitting and crocheting material containing books, needles and wool material. In a few months she taught herself to knit and crochet and now makes beautiful unique crocheted Sesame type animals and can hardly keep up with the orders she receives from parents. I secretly have nicknamed her "Angel Hands" for anything she touches is a great success.

Jessica Knox is the next little miracle skipping grades through the early years she was a little over sixteen when she attended Queens University and then changed to McGill in Montréal where she graduated with a Bachelor of Science in Neuro Biology with a scholarship to continue her studies. However, after graduation she chose to take a year off to do volunteer teaching in the North-West Territories – a great experience and eye opener in many ways. She then used her scholarship from McGill to attend Riverside University in California where she obtained a Master's Degree in Bio-Chemistry.

Returning to Canada she continued taking extra courses in the Digital World and finally accepted a position with a company in Toronto providing learning services to companies of various disciplines, i.e. pharmaceutical, manufacturing, scientific and universities. With her extraordinary skills she managed to double the business in the first six months. After a few years the Owners decided to sell the business which she purchased and now has twenty-two employees in different disciplines to oversee. She is also a loving Mother of two year old Evander and seven year old Alyssa, a little step-daughter, whom she parents with her wonderful partner, Mark.

Jessica has been attending a yearly conference in the USA called "Life Science Trainers and Educators Network" for eight years and in 2021 was named "Member of the Year", a well deserved honour!

Ashley and Shawn Smith, are amazing twins. Ashley attended McMaster University in Hamilton where she received a B.A. in Sociology then on to York University for a Bachelor of Social Work Degree like her Nanny Margaret – me! She's employed by the Ontario Ministry of Community & Social Services serving disabled children and families. Recently Ashley was promoted to the Policy Division which she enjoys greatly. She and Scott have two beautiful

little children, Hailey and Smith in pre-school. Ashley has always been kind, thoughtful and considerate so will be an excellent social worker and parent.

The other half of the equation Shawn, decided to attend Ryerson University where he received a Bachelor of Aerospace Engineering. In his first position with Bombardier he was sent to Lower Siberia where they were doing studies on planes in extreme cold weather. However, Shawn left Bombardier and is now employed by Pratt & Whitney. He and his lovely wife, Christina, a high school teacher, have a little beautiful son, Alexander. Shawn is also a great help to his widowed Mother when needed.

Jeffrey Knox, who at age three placed his pet cat in a filing cabinet drawer so it wouldn't run away from him, attended Western University in London, Ontario and received a Bachelor of Engineering and Geology Degree. He then attended Humber College where he graduated as a Program Supply Chain Manager. Jeffrey is very successful in his present work. He and his lovely wife, Jenn, are happily married. Jenn is a prime salesperson with Nintendo. Jeffrey being a bit of a digital expert is very much in demand by his family members and always good natured about helping.

Now we come to the last precious member of the group, Jeremy Preston Hawkins (my poet laureate!). Jeremy and his father Peter moved from Brantford to Kitchener, Ontario where he attended Waterloo University with great success. He studied English and Drama graduating with a Master of Art Degree and a scholarship to continue studying for his PhD. Not only did he excel in poetry but proved to be somewhat of a Drama Prince applauded greatly for his various roles on stage (by the way, Jeremy's maternal grandmother, Joan Turner, is an accomplished poet and artist!). I was informed Jeremy went on to complete his PhD successfully for which the family and I applaud him and his Father, Peter, who helped him greatly.

Perhaps you will understand why I had to include this chapter about our precious, outstanding grandchildren who not only worked tirelessly to achieve their academic goals, but are employed in work that benefits others and "makes this world better place for everyone to be", a grandmother's prayer answered. It's also worth noting, with pride, that each young couple own their own home.

CHAPTER 43

Families:

Families are a Treasure, pure Gold
Sent to us to love, to have and to hold
Always be loving, kind and giving
And life will be joyful and really worth living.

I expressed myself about 'families' in the little poem above. Of course, families are not always perfect but we can always try harder to create harmony, peace and a loving environment in the family circle (and in the world!). So as Matriarch of the family I enjoy sharing guidelines to achieve that and, of course, try my utmost to follow my own advice.

My sister, Helen, and her retired husband, Gerry, moved from their home in Ottawa to Oakville in 1999. Gerry purchased a beautiful two story, four bedroom home without Helen seeing it – turned out to be a lovely surprise. Their children, James, a High School teacher, Nada, his wife and their family live in Oakville. Patrick, a successful lawyer and wife Jan, a physician and their family live nearby in Mississauga. John a lawyer with the Department of Justice, his wife Katie and their family live in Toronto. Therefor it was a happy move for all concerned as it brought the family closer together. We now celebrated birthdays and anniversaries and visited each other more often.

The Hawkins' family reunions – hosted by sister-in-law Isobel and me – stopped as the members aged and a few died. Joe's sister Alma who we saw frequently died in the

Nursing Home in 2002, at age 88. We visited her twice weekly and missed her when she was gone. Sadly I was away in England when that

occurred. She had two lovely sons, Paul (and lovely wife Christine) and David. I looked after baby Paul when David was born! Alma was a good, hard working woman with a fun loving side – she loved attending Saturday night dances at Harborfront. She was a devoted mother to her two boys.

Bessie (Fee) died in 2005 at the age of 91. Husband, Art, a WW2 veteran suffered repercussions from the war and was institutionalized in Kingston where he died. They had two beautiful daughters, Barbara and Lorraine, who reside in Carleton Place.

Joe's youngest brother, Robert, whose wife was beautiful Isobel, died May 15th, 2010. They have two lovely children, Douglas, and his wife who operates a successful shoe store in Carleton Place and Karen Mantel, who is employed by Guelph University. She and husband, Matt, also have two outstanding sons, Matt and Chris, who reside in Guelph.

I had great admiration for Robert and Isobel. Besides a good marriage they were kind and helpful to Mom Hawkins. Robert also honoured Isobel In his Will, unlike some of the other brothers. He broke the negative part of the Hawkins saga toward women and treated Isobel with love and respect!

My loving friend Isobel moved into the Nursing Home in Carleton Place shortly after and let her grandson move into the family farm home. Douglas had built a new home across the road from the family home. Isobel and I were close and cared about each other. As mentioned before, they spent many Thanksgivings with us in Toronto so when she died in May 2019 I was greatly saddened. I could not attend the funeral because I was just discharged from the hospital after a short stay. However, dear Karen dropped in with Matt on their way home to Guelph and we had a lovely reunion and visit.

So the Old Folks move on and a new generation take over. Making the poem 'Families' even more important in order to live a satisfying and happy life – God Bless them All!

Meanwhile . . . .

Joe completed his studies and could speak Hungarian
and Spanish fluently. However, 'the itchy feet syndrome'
hit again and he informed me that he had booked a trip to

Argentina for a month. I asked him if it was a good idea to take such a long trip alone at his age. He seemed confident it would be safe. When his departure date arrived I offered to drive him to York Mills subway station where there was a connecting bus to the airport. He adamantly refused, stating he could take the bus there.

When he was away for long periods of time I usually occupied my time with the family, if they were available or with girlfriends of which I had many. So the time went quickly. This time I was still sad and upset over the death of my dear friend Ethel, in England and wasn't in the mood to socialize. However I received an urgent call from my close friend Susan Lower, who had gone through her divorce and was living with her young son Nicky in the Beaches area. She received word that her mother, Pauline, was gravely ill in England where she was hospitalized and that she and her brother Marc were planning to leave as soon as possible to see her. Could I possibly take care of Nicky until she returned? I didn't hesitate a minute. Of course I would be glad to go to her residence and be a pleasure to look after little Nicky. I packed a small suitcase and got there pronto.

Sadly Sue and Marc didn't make it in time to say goodbye to their mother as she died before they arrived. Marc couldn't stay for the funeral but Sue did, joined by the rest of the family. I followed the service in my Anglican prayer book which I did for all my friends when I couldn't attend a funeral.

Nicky was a pleasant, well behaved little boy and a pleasure to look after. Susan returned In a little over a week, sad but grateful that her mother was no longer suffering. She had lived eight years with ovarian cancer, which is quite a record. She was a courageous Soul. God Bless Her!

Time seems to fly by and Joe reappeared again. He sat with the family to talk about his trip to Argentina showing us pictures that were taken of him with a man and a woman. He explained that his Spanish teacher, the obnoxious caller harassing Jani and me, is Argentinian and asked him to call on her parents while he was there, After his death I discovered evidence that she also accompanied Joe on the trip and they both stayed with the parents when they weren't touring. Now his reluctance to have me to drive him to York Mills made sense. He was meeting her there for the trip to the airport! Quite a thank you for ripping up the divorce papers to let the 'poor old fellow' live out his life in peace and comfort ! ! ! All that remained in terms of 'respect' on my part was his service during WW2 and his unrelenting attempt to better his educational standing and improve his qualifications for work. Let God deal with the rest.

Nancy my eldest daughter and I planned a mother daughter trip to France. We received a kind invitation from Doug Lower to visit him in Le Patis de Fontenio, in Brittany, while we were there – which we did. We met his French friends, admired his beautiful home and garden and toured the area in parts of southern France, which was exciting, ending our memorable vacation with several days in Paris. There were strong indications that the 'affair of the heart' was alive and well which elevated my mood considerably.

We arrived home to be greeted with the sad news that Peter and Jocelyn were divorced and Peter was granted full custody of darling little Jermey, age seven and that they were staying with Joe in Thornhill to discuss future plans. Peter found and rented accommodation in Brantford where Jeremy would complete public and high school as the family home was sold. A sad time for the whole family, to be sure, but a positive move for Peter and Jeremy in terms of their future.

As for me life felt strange and surreal with Joe away so much – at times two major trips a year to far away places and in between trips to the US and different parts of Canada, I felt somewhat like a widow but had the burden of worrying about the safety of an elderly husband wandering alone to strange places around the globe.

To cope with the stress I finally decided to take a few trips of my own and accepted Doug Lower's many kind invitations to visit his home in France. On one occasion my sister, Helen and her husband Gerry, who worked at CBC TV and knew Doug, spent their vacation time with us which included a trip to the moors in England.

Another time we joined daughter Nancy and Andy and my beloved grandson Jeffery in the southern part of France where they were vacationing. We had a memorable family vacation together and that certainly relieved some of the stress.

Eventually Doug decided to sell his home in France and return to Canada where he temporarily resided with his daughter Susan. Precious memories of Le Patis de Fontenio, its beautiful garden and the lovely friends I met will remain forever.

In 2006 we were shocked and saddened to be told that Andy, Nancy's husband, had been diagnosed with multiple myeloma, the cancer that took our beloved Mother from us. He was being treated at Princess Margaret Cancer Hospital where they recommended a stem cell transplant. Doug stayed with him for the required twenty-four hour period and the surgery was successful. He survived and recovered, faithfully adhering to health rules along the way. Nancy and Andy had just purchased a lovely condominium on Bloor Street West and Doug and other friends and family helped with the move.

They have made many good friends in their 'condo' and have been extremely generous throwing Christmas Dinner parties in the Party Room for many years. Also, I would be remiss not to mention the fabulous ninetieth birthday party they hosted for me. Family and friends from near and far and Nancy and Andy's hard work made it an absolutely unforgettable occasion.

Sadly another terrible family tragedy occurred in 2011. Bruce, Judy's husband, was diagnosed with cancer in the mouth and admitted to Mt Sinai Hospital to have it removed. After a lengthy operation by a very competent surgeon the cancer was successfully removed. While he was in the ICU, after a tracheotomy they removed the monitor too soon thinking he could breathe on his own and he lost consciousness. Judy and the children sat with him hoping for the best but he died after five days. The surgeon explained he had never lost a patient that way and if Judy needed him he was ready to testify.

A profound gloom set over our family and Bruce's as well. I wrote a beautiful eulogy praising Bruce recounting the countless times he helped us with house repairs, building patios and planning and planting the garden. He had a wonderful funeral with relatives and friends attending and was buried in the Elgin Mills Cemetery. We didn't tell Joe as he was in the nursing home and probably couldn't deal with the bad news. Judy and her children have gone to Bruce's grave every anniversary with balloons and wreaths and take a family picture together near his grave each year. It's difficult to forget a good husband and father. Judy continued to work at the Richmond Hill Library until retirement and remained in the same house with many renovations and is a wonderful, loving grandmother to her six, soon to be seven, grandchildren. She has not remarried.

CHAPTER 44

Joe began having health problems that were worrisome. He gave up driving earlier when he hit the rear end of a truck stopped at a red light while driving my car with Janice as a passenger, but no one was injured.

I took him to Dr Magee for a checkup and the news was not good. Dr Magee's diagnosis was that Joe was suffering from high blood pressure and also dementia. He has two bad falls, one waiting for the bus and the other in the garage following his sister Alma's pattern of falls. Her forehead was bandaged when she entered the Nursing Home. She also had dementia. Dr Magee prescribed medication for his blood pressure and recommended a referral to a psychologist regarding the dementia. Joe refused the latter and continued the falls that were nerve wracking.

On advice from close friends I started looking for

possible nursing homes in case the dementia became a problem. The areas included Thornhill, Aurora and finally Sunnybrook Veterans Nursing home on Bayview Avenue. I then slowly took him on a tour of each one. His response to most was, "it's like a morgue, so quiet I'd die of boredom! No thank you". Then we visited the last one, Sunnybrook and had the grand tour. It was filled with mostly male and some female veterans, well staffed with good programs including a huge music room where various groups entertained every day of the week. He loved the atmosphere, the people and especially the music every day. So we filled out the application with a very pleasant Intake Officer who said he would be in touch with us 'soonish'.

We returned home, informed all the family members and waited. Within a week a female nurse from Sunnybrook appeared, talked at length with Joe then whispered to me, "I don't think he has dementia." She left, promising they would be in touch.

I immediately telephoned Dr Magee with the news and he was disgusted. "She's not competent to diagnose. So I'll refer him to a psychologist and we'll have the proof." Within a few days I told Joe we have an appointment with a specialist that will confirm you have dementia.

A few days later we kept our appointment with the psychologist in Markham who seemed very competent and thorough. He kept shaking his head with every question he asked Joe. He finally ended with, "Mr

Hawkins, do you know why you're here." Joe innocently answered, "No, I don't". After I explained to him at least three times where we were going and why. He diagnosed Joe as having moderate, going on severe dementia and advised that the nursing home placement would be appropriate.

On our return home I immediately telephoned the Intake Officer and corrected the nurse's assessment for which he apologized.

Life continued at a slow and sad pace. Joe appointed Nancy and Judith as Executors of his estate as he was no longer able to manage his accounts. Veterans were entitled to help in the house and outside, gardening and snow removal, which was a big help.

While I was visiting my sister, Helen, in Oakville I got word from Janice, who was visiting for the weekend, that Joe opened the 'fridge door and something in his back snapped. They called an ambulance and he was taken to York Central Hospital for treatment. I hurried home and went straight to the hospital where they were doing diagnostic tests on his back, which turned out to be a severe pinched nerve in his back. After a week and half of treatment he was ready for discharge. Meanwhile I was in touch with Sunnybrook about the possibility of an admission. The hospital would charge $90 a day to keep him there, and the VA would pay. Within a few days I got word that they had a bed for him at Sunnybrook. With the help of my sister and brother-in-law who drove me to

Sunnybrook, Joe was transported by ambulance to his new home on the Main Floor of the Veterans Nursing Home in a semi-private room. It was June 2009 and Joe was in his 91st year and very frail so I was very grateful that he would now get good care and be happy there. Despite our alienated relationship my tears flowed for several days.

I developed a pattern of visiting Joe at least three times and usually four times weekly. Some times alone, some times with family members, especially on anniversaries when we had parties with cakes and balloons and singsong. I also thought it was imperative to attend each Medical meeting to review and give and receive input on his health. The Medical group was aware that Judy and Nancy had power of attorney for their father and that my name was absent. One of the observant female doctors, Dr Bennett, questioned him about it. "Surely Mr Hawkins, you don't object to Mrs Hawkins knowing about your health condition, do you? She attends every meeting faithfully and is concerned about your welfare" Joe meekly answered, "no I don't mind". Embarrassing to be sure but he agreed to one thing. By the way,

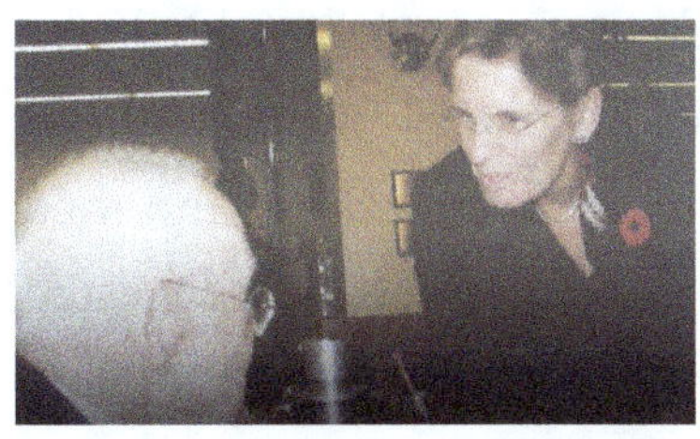

the girls never attended the Medical conferences so it was important for me to do so!

I can't praise Sunnybrook Nursing Home enough. It was a wonderful, friendly, well equipped and cheerful setting. Joe loved it from the beginning and right to the end.

He was first placed in a room with two other patients but the room was walled and constructed to give each one privacy. After three months during which time he was mostly in a wheelchair they moved him to the second floor and removed the wheelchair. He attended the musical programs daily and enjoyed them immensely. I joined him for many. Sometimes there was a full orchestra, other

times individual singers, musicians and groups. All very enjoyable. On special occasions like holidays and Remembrance Day etc., the Premier of Ontario, Kathleen Wynne and other government official attended. They always seemed to stop and talk to Joe. I snapped

pictures when they did.

The food was reasonable, not home cooking but nourishing, no complaints from Joe. He spent five years there and enjoyed it right to the end. About the third year the family gathered to celebrate his ninety-fourth birthday in the party room. We sang, played music and had birthday cake. During the singsong someone suggested singing "White Cliffs of Dover" and he suddenly exploded into tears, crying out loud. That was the moment something clicked in me and I was convinced he had PTSD from WW2 and had suffered many years, could not talk about the war. He also had a strange continuous blink

when I first met him. The only thing he was treated for was loss of hearing when he was middle-aged and they blamed it on the war. It dawned on me that perhaps that was the reason for all the other strange behaviours during our marriage and why he found it so difficult to consider divorce.

Joe attended Chapel every Sunday, I was told by Chaplain Wes. On November 30th., 2014 while the girls were attending an outdoor barbecue with Joe he had a severe stroke and sadly died before I could even get to the hospital.

CHAPTER 45

———

Joe had a lovely funeral conducted by Chaplain Wes with prayers, beautiful hymns and touching eulogies with relatives and many old friends attending. As the coffin was lowered I forgave him for all the misdemeanours and asked God to be kind to him. He was buried in Elgin Mills Cemetery where he had purchased six plots – for himself, me, Jani and Peter and Jeremy. When my beloved Mother died, she and later my Father were buried in Holy Cross Cemetery in Thornhill, just north of our home and at that time I purchased six plots, for myself and any family member who wished to be buried there. Jani and Peter have indicated they wished to be buried there.

Shortly after the funeral I received complaints from Peter about Joe's death notice in the newspaper and the fact that he was not asked to write it despite wanting to. I replied that I had absolutely no recollection of him asking to do that. I reminded him that he only visited his Father once in five years claiming he found it too difficult to see his Father in that condition. He then wrote me a very hurtful letter stating he needs a break from me and the whole family. Furthermore, he and Jeremy have nothing in common with the family and he will notify me when he wished to continue the family relationship. It was a very heart breaking event for me as I could not think of one thing I did to ever hurt them. I always gave them both, love, support, encouragement and substantial financial support to get Jeremy through his studies. It was like a blow to the heart, very cruel and very undeserved. I began and still do leave telephone messages saying we all love and miss them but no response! My conclusion is that he suffered a breakdown when his Father died and needs help. My latest effort towards reconciliation is the following poem that I wrote and sent him.

Ode to Peter

THE JOURNEY

On a cold and frosty winter's morn
Our precious baby son was born
With blonde hair, brown eyes and chubby cheeks
We arrived home after a very busy week
To a loving welcome from little sister so excited
With her new baby brother to at last be united.

As a scholar he excelled beyond our dreams
Also tried swimming, hockey and baseball teams
Then a gift of a guitar came into his life
As beautiful music and song filled the house
An excellent musician he soon formed a Band
With regular gigs in Toronto and Midland.

Then love came at last pulling at his heartstrings
He and his love soon exchanged wedding rings
Next came the birth of a precious bundle of joy – a little son
But after a few years of bliss now tragically there was none
Father was granted full custody of his beloved Son
Peace and tranquillity ensued and the music played on

Our Son's life as single parent was nothing short of a miracle

With all his heart and soul he dedicated his life to this worthy role

From the tender age of seven to the present day
He was there for his Son in every way
With loving support family members joined in
To celebrate endless occasions of their beloved kin

Our grandson thankfully grew and thrived
Until High School graduation time arrived
He won an award for 'Best Poetry' written
'Purpose of Being' proved by the Arts he was smitten
A second award a University Scholarship was granted
By our Grandson's dedication we were totally enchanted

The pinnacle he reached after arduous years of study
Brought to light many talents – for the world he was ready!
What greater gift can a Father give his Son
Than love and devotion and the motivation to go on
We all admired your determination and selflessness
And crown you 'Father Like No Other' with a heartfelt kiss.

You've always been a loving Son considerate and kind

So this alienation since your Father's death is a harsh blow to the mind

Let the music in your soul guide you rather than hide you from us
Then you will understand how much we all love and need both of you

To be 'One Big Happy Loving Family' as in the days of yore
My fervent prayer – that you agree 'It's The Right Thing To Do'.

No response.
The saddest part of this alienation is that Jeremy is left

with no relatives on his maternal or paternal side to turn to, when in reality he has many aunts, uncles and cousins who love him dearly and miss him so much. Another problem that only God could solve!

CHAPTER 46

As mentioned before, Nancy and Judy were named executors of Joe's estate and were given Power of Attorney to look after his investments. Neither had experience nor were they adept in that field so for several years his investments lay dormant or were reinvested at low interest rates by the banks concerned. Joe also had stock in Dubois Chemicals, where he was a vice-president, which had grown to a substantial amount over the years but because Joe ignored them and refused to cash them they ended up in the Company's bank in the USA as unclaimed property. When we tried to retrieve them the grand sum of $99.00 was sent to me, a loss of at least $100,000.

Tax-free savings amounting to $30,000 in total were purchased by Judy the last year he was in the nursing home. I inherited some cash and the house, of course. The greatest insult Joe perpetrated had to do with his inheritance from dear Aunt Bertha. He inherited $24,000 – as did the other nineteen nieces and nephews – invested, it grew over the years to a substantial amount. He left the total amount to be divided amongst our four children, including my share which was the interest, necessitating me to go to the lawyer's office and sign away my share. Off course no mother would withhold any benefit to their children so I signed off and each of the children received $13,000 in cash, instead of the $6,000 they were entitled to legally. That was a true punch in the gut from a heartless husband. I loved Aunt Bertha dearly and looked after her when none of the other Hawkins relatives would, making sure she was safely placed in care in Cummer House. That was his thank you from the grave. Reminiscent of another mother, Mum Hawkins, whose only inheritance from Dad Hawkins was the rent from 12 acres of the family farm. Nothing else!

I don't entirely blame Judy and Nancy for going along with Joe's strange behaviour after the devoted care he received from me, right to the time of his death. They were inexperienced and had serious family problems of their own to deal with. However, had I been in their shoes I would have said to Joe, "Dad, Mom's name should be added to ours as PoA and Executrix. She knows more than we do about investing and her hard work enabled you to save what you did. So she should have some say". Of the four children, Janice, the most needy gladly offered to give me her whole amount but I refused. I would never let money come between me and my children, I love them too much. Slowly, hurts fade away and stop hurting.

After Joe's confinement in the Nursing Home and his death I did spend time redecorating, partially to get rid of bad memories but mostly to create a more cheerful environment because I felt sad. I infused brighter colours in the cushions, added more cheerful pictures and switched furniture around to make it look different.

Helen and Gerry's proximity to Thornhill was very convenient as I visited more often and stayed a few days. It gave me the opportunity to strengthen our relationship and to get to know the extended family better. Gerry was battling prostate cancer and receiving chemotherapy regularly. Despite this he would, as usual, play old tunes on the piano and cheer everyone up.

Although Helen and I were very close early in our lives a few blips existed in our relationship. She did not attend my wedding in 1948 claiming she had exams to write in High School. I had turned Anglican before my wedding and that bothered dear Helen as she was a very devout Roman Catholic. I attended their wedding, as did Joe and the children and we all enjoyed it. Also they celebrated a special anniversary at a little Inn near Tillsonburg that left me and all my family off the invitation list. Even Nancy, who was a bridesmaid at her wedding, and should have been there. They also did not accept the invitation to Nancy's second marriage to Andy that was held in a Protestant Church. I was very hurt by these omissions which I am sure had to do with religion. My view of religion, in contrast, does not exclude people due to their faith.

However, the move to Toronto did bring us closer and we had some wonderful times together both at home and on trips to France and England. We also made some good friends through them including Mary Anne Barrie who studied law with Gerry and Rudi Vezér, a beloved Hungarian friend, also a lawyer and his lovely family. We still keep in touch with Rudi and have beautiful memories of cabbage roll dinners he used to bring to share with us before the Covid epidemic.

We'll never forget the lovely retirement party we attended when Rudi turned 65 where we met more friends from his university days at UoT. Again, Doug produced a touching video tracing Rudi's family journey from Hungary to Canada and their amazing achievements in education and business. Rudi is a devoted and loving father and just recently we received a lovely surprise – a picture of his beautiful grandchildren.

More memorable times with Helen and Gerry included Susan, Doug's daughter, and Henry's wedding which took place in Ancaster where they had purchased a new home. Of course, we'll never forget celebrating Helen's 70th and 80th birthdays, one held at Jan and Patrick's beautiful, outstanding home and the other at Jamie and Nada's lovely home in Oakville. Doug made videos for each of the family. In later years Patrick and Jan had Helen and Gerry for dinner every weekend and were extremely kind and thoughtful. John and Katy and family lived in Toronto so visits happened but less frequently.

As Helen and Gerry aged Helen was plagued with continuous health problems caused by her lack of adrenal glands and thyroid. Also her knee replacement was causing pain and the surgeon who completed the operation was deceased. So she was attending her regular practitioner for help and didn't get it. We finally convinced Gerry to let us help by finding specialists in Sunnybrook and St Michael's Hospital, which we did many times and she received some relief.

Despite being a close loving family a strange phenomenon existed in Helen's family – a couple of them denied that Helen had any illness rather, "she was just looking for attention". This callous attitude appalled and surprised me because my sister had real health issues!

On July 18th, 2019 my beloved sister called me to say she was in the family room and Gerry was at the pharmacy to pick up prescriptions and that each time she stood up she was extremely dizzy and couldn't walk. I told her to sit down, (fearing a fall) and as soon as Gerry returned call an ambulance to get to the hospital and be checked. Gerry returned because the pharmacy didn't open until 10am. I begged him to call an ambulance as I believed Helen was very ill. That didn't happen until later that afternoon when she was taken to the hospital in Oakville. I phoned Jamie and Patrick's iPhones that Helen was very ill, please come home. They arrived and sat with Helen until the early morning hours. The attending doctor thought she had a heart attack and said they would investigate in the morning. We motored to Oakville Hospital to give Gerry a printout of Helen's medical history which was compiled after the many visits to Sunnybrook and St Michael's Hospital. Never dreaming I would never see my sister alive again. We were utterly shocked and saddened to receive word from Gerry that Helen died of a heart attack at 4am. My beloved little sister, who I adored for so many years, is gone, joining all her departed loved ones. My mind was in a haze for days. With the Covid pandemic there were rules and limitations regarding funerals. Doug put together a touching video tribute of Helen's life for the family and friends at the visitation.

The funeral took place in the Roman Catholic Church they attended. Then the procession continued to Caledon Cemetery where Gerry's family members are buried. The Cemetery was established in 1830 in a beautiful hilltop area. Everyone placed a single rose on her coffin, a Hungarian tradition. Just weeks before she died Helen confided in me, "I told Gerry I love daisies and would like them on my coffin when I die". I told the family about her wishes and they complied. I sat at home with my granddaughter Lisa and my daughter Janice and wept and prayed for my sister. I just could not make it to the cemetery at ninety-one. I know she will understand. For months my darling sister's sudden death haunted me and made me ill but I am a devout Christian and know we'll meet again. Following the family tradition her life was one of loving and giving, to Gerry, family and community. God bless her soul.

Gerry is happily ensconced in a Chartwell Nursing Home in Oakville and misses Helen terribly, as do we.

CHAPTER 47

———

Real Miracles do Happen! Earlier, in Chapter 36, I wrote about my dear friends Joe and Yvonne Cashen and their ten year old son, Marc who went to Chitre in response to my heartfelt plea for help for the residential school in Chepo de las Minas. They spent endless days between December 1987 and January 1988 compiling a remarkable report outlining the necessary changes needed to make life more tolerable for ALL at the residential school. A copy was then sent to many of the relevant parties and institutions in and out of the country – Panama and Canada including Rotary International. Meetings were also held in Chitre and Panama City and finally authorized consent was received for the Project from all concerned. However, Panama's President Noriega's misdeeds led to prison in the USA and Rotary had to cancel the whole Project. How terribly sad for all concerned. They returned to Canada with broken hearts. We must remember that Good People all over the World don't give up easily when it comes to helping the Needy.

In 2012 Rotary Panama and Rotary International revived the Project which was beautifully completed by eager Volunteers (many days numbering ninety) in 2015. The Residence was rebuilt and now included electric lighting, running water, new interior, school supplies etc. The Outer Buildings (the Service Buildings) were also modernized and equipped. Also a paved highway was constructed so the children would not have to use the dangerous mountain paths walking to school any more. I also learned that the Volunteers assisted the neighbouring farmers who were very poor and needy. When I tried to contact Joe and Yvonne I was absolutely unsuccessful. I finally looked in the Obituary and found the heart-wrenching notice of my dear friend's death in the Ottawa paper. He passed away October 27th, 2016 in his eighty-sixth year. The obituary also mentioned that he sent a shipment of much needed medication to a hospital in Panama (Dr Olga's hospital) typical of his kindness, may His Soul rest in Peace. He was an Angel. I haven't given up finding Yvonne and Mark who are somewhere in Mississauga, to tell them the wonderful news of the completion of the Project.

Another miracle occurred regarding Rotary clubs – they have 1.5 million members in 46,000 clubs and donate 16 million volunteer hours a year globally. How impressive is that? Rotary's core values are – 1. Service programmes bring greater understanding and peace. 2. Fellowship, individual efforts focus on individual needs but combined efforts serve humanity, diversity, integrity, leadership. The main motto of Rotarians is "service above self and one profits most who serves best".

Rotary International's mission, according to Google is, "we provide service to others, promote integrity and advance world understanding, good will and peace through our fellowship and business". And more importantly, "Rotary is partnering with other service organizations to inspire volunteers around the world to participate in – International Week of Service, March 25th to March 31st., 2017. Other organizations include Lion's Club, Optimists International, Kiwanis International and Y's Men International to name a few.

This weekly drive each year recruits volunteers, raising funds for projects and helping millions in dire need globally. My favourite motto regarding Volunteering which I have been involved in for decades is "Volunteers get back as much, often more, than they give". The experience teaches you so much about the world, people, conditions, new skills, new friendship and could be the greatest personal growth experience in your life. I highly recommend it.

CHAPTER 48

The journey isn't over yet. The last, or present, part has to be told and that includes my dear friend Doug, who happens to be my partner in life also.

Our amazing friendship goes back decades to the early 1970's when Pauline, his deceased wife, and I were attending York University, Atkinson College as mature students. Over time the individual friendship grew into 'couple friendship' that included three or four other couples. Then Pauline and Doug purchased a bungalow and moved to the street just behind us, so we saw each other more frequently. Eventually I met the extended family – Pauline's mother, Doug's mother and two sisters Jean and Grace and we all became good friends.

Doug spent his early years at sea as a Deck Officer (M aster FG) and travelled the globe. A fascinating life as a single person but incompatible with marriage.

So he gave up the sea and tried various careers as a dj in Luxembourg GD, then working with BBC as a Program Host and finally deciding to make the great move to Toronto, Canada with Pauline, Susan and Marc following shortly after. Starting at CBC producing a radio program, his success and advancement were phenomenal. In a relatively short period of time he was with CBC TV as E xecutive Producer of three weekly network programmes plus filming d ocumentaries o n a variety of subjects, domestically and globally. Over the years our friendship grew to mutual adoration. Who wouldn't adore a brilliant, worldly man who had a way with words and handsome too! But that wasn't the whole story, he also was intrigued by my Hungarian heritage, wanted to hear the whole story and admired my Mother's courage making the journey to a new country with her little five year old girl and learning English. He eventually met my dear Mother at my B.S.W. graduation party, hosted by my eldest daughter, Nancy. He also insisted calling me by my Hungarian name, Margit, quite a contrast to Joe's attitude which was to try and hide my ancestry, implying he was ashamed of it?

Val Hancock ~ Nancy ~ Paulette Bernardie

But there is more. Doug had a great respect for women and admired their accomplishments. He constantly praised me for mine. Lastly, he is the kindest most generous man I have ever known. He just never stops giving, nothing is too much. Strangely enough we tend to have similar traits. Total validation, acceptance and celebration of who you are! That's what my beloved friend, Doug, gave me.

When we were finally able to see each other again, after our tearful *au revoir*, we were both still hurting from various wounds life inflicts but felt so good and natural to be together again. Eventually very healing. With healing comes harmony which has a tendency to release hidden talent and it surely did as you will see.

My few visits to France impacted me greatly. The beautiful French countryside with fields of sun flowers, lush green pastures, stunning wild flowers, ferns and berries that filled the roadsides and chestnut trees heavy with blooms are all unforgettable. I found it uplifting, body and soul . .

Then the result: my poem

THE JOURNEY

Will you walk with me for an hour or three
Along roadsides lined with lush green ferns
Where roses spew their fragrant perfumes
And banks of mossy wild flowers
Adorn our ankles as we stop to call
Bovine friends who rush to greet us
Their eyes forlorn as we depart
Around the bend past deep cool forests
into heady scents of new mown hay

Will you talk with me for an hour or three
Of things that are and never should be
The amazing friendship of feline and frog
How birds glide through the air with wings aloft
And moules grow on farms under the sea
The wonder of sunrise on sheltered coves
And the magic of moon light in a misty shroud
The moors' haunting beauty and the noble tors
The crumbling remains of King Arthur's abode

Will you dance with me for an hour or three
To the bitter sweet rhythm of life's serenade
Hold me and whisper sweet words in my ear
Kiss away sadness and drown all despair
With dreams of the Danube or even the Nile
Then the tango we'll dance under striped canopy
And let the joy of existence penetrate deep

347

Set our spirits soaring and our hearts ablaze
To sustain us as the music fades

Likewise the country-people in France were wonderful. We made many close friends with whom we still correspond. The whole experience filled a void – loneliness, despair etc – and created a *"joie de vivre"* I hadn't felt for a long time.

With Nancy we spent time touring old castles, beautiful cathedrals, art galleries and then parts of Paris. Art galleries were outstanding and most enjoyable. Luxembourg Gardens full of beautiful lush trees became a favourite. We had the good fortune to witness a lovely symphony concert there performed by a touring American student orchestra. Such a short time but so memorable, again the result, my poem.

What wonders did my eyes behold
As you touched my hand and gently led me
Through major landscapes both old and new
Where rolling hills form patchwork quilts
Of rare design and multi-hued greens

Reach up and touch soft azure skies

What wonders did my mind unfold
As you led me on to look within
Through abbeys housing hearts of Kings
Where silence is ripe with memories of lives
Cloistered behind ancient vine covered walls
And bells once heard peeling we hear now

What wonders did my mind unfold
When your eyes met mine in a steady gaze
And we marvelled at fields of golden sunflowers
All turning their head to be kissed by the sun
Those caves in the hillside, magnificent shores
Our hearts enchanted by sunset on the Loire

What wonders my senses did unfold
As our hearts entwined and the world stood still
Hearing angel voices at evensong
Or beholding a masterful work of art
While violins sing in Luxembourg Gardens
Our ecstasy swells to a new crescendo

What wonders did my soul unfold
As our hearts touched a new world emerged
A garden expanded and filled with blooms
A slow mist rising with birdsongs at dawn
My heart is so full and my soul so content

You are my soulmate, my trusted friend.
Each visit raises my consciousness about the empty life
I'm living at home alone. Doug's contribution – his poem

Watch a spider weave its web, listen as bees suck nectar

Hear the last drop of rain to fall, soak up this fresh, clear spectre

Trace butterflies in the dance of life,
Lambs and piglets suckling free from strife
Marvel as the sunflower greets the sun
See? Creation stands renewed each day and so must we

Our love, like steel tempered in the heat of learning

Draws new breath and seeks new knowledge growing each day

The Journey

In a universe full off wonder love stands singular
Above all laws and understanding
It's written in the stars they say, oh yes
It's written in stars alright – and bright

In galaxies of worlds both red and white
I see the twinkling of my love
Oh of my love – unique self, mischievous and laughter
And tears both glad and sad
But near the centre like a super nova bursting
Is the moment of reality where my soul sees truth
A timeless forever without bounds. Infinity,
No beginning no end, the firmament but a shroud
Whisking us to eternity and endless love,
the sun forever risen
So there you are

And when it was time to leave, he wrote –
Each caress is a million stars put to account
A galaxy of dreams to draw on
No shooting stars for us that flare and fade
Our love is the next day's sun
Rising. Warm and rising.

Mourn not the separation tis only space
Mourn not the parting tis only time
For time and space we have unto eternity
And we shall draw upon that stock

In time our lives will twine, rapturous and free
Kindred spirits in a quest for life, a sight for all to see
Til then we'll snatch our moments of delight
And put the fears of doubt to flight
Je t'aime cheri, je vous adore.

That is what our undreamed of reunion produced. We brought out the poetry in each other. I am a keen gardener so each visit the existing beautiful garden was made breathtakingly beautiful with more colour, more variety of plants until it became 'a showcase'. The Locals brought their friends and visitors to see, *"le jardin d'Anglaise"*. We thanked them for their kind words and good taste! Doug's house sold within a couple of days while we were with Nancy, Andy and Jeffrey in the south of France. I think the garden helped as the new owners loved gardening.

I finally decided it was time to sell our home in Thornhill, after making several improvements it was time to 'List'. The house sold very quickly at a good price. They even wanted to buy all the contents but that was a no-no.

The result, my poem

Ode to the crew

On a sad and dreary September morn
The decision was made to sell our family home
But how do we deal with years of accumulation
Call our Andy an organization sensation!

Skip and crew he quickly assembled

THE JOURNEY

Bruce, Bradley and Shawn,
Scott, Jeffrey and Eli
Princes of clean-up on them to rely

After pizza and beer, aching muscles, sore backs
Steph. Ashley and Judy joined in with more trips
Chairs, boxes and rubbish finally the wretched skip
But alas, it's not the end of the story yet
Andy in his wisdom says, "another skip needed."
Jeff and Eli the frantic call heeded

Then paint brush and rollers were put to the task
Peter and Jeremy tackled basement floors and walls
Jess, Eli and Lisa the bathrooms and halls

Next came the laying of floor by the yard
Eli and Jeffrey worked superbly hard
The Siren's call beckoned loud and bold
The broadloom must go if the house is to be sold
Judy tackled the hall and Jeffrey the stairs
Behold the hardwood's in A1 condition

Bruce pruned the garden with care and ease
Jan and Judy planted flowers and future trees
Back came Ashley and Scott to seed the lawn
At last our beautiful home was done
What more could a grateful Grandmother ask?

Nancy, Jessica, Jude, Jan and Lisa packed with vigour
The Merry Maids pulled their magical trigger
And low and behold with our house up for sale
It sold in three days and we nearly went pale!
This tale is not about a realtor's deed
But a family's love in a time of need.
And as I count my blessings one by one
You each are the greatest, like a warm rising sun
And I thank you each from the bottom of my heart

Each member of the crew received a copy of the poem and my heartfelt thanks for their help.

I moved to Oakville into rental accommodation to be nearer my sister and family. In the meantime Doug was looking at houses to buy in Ancaster, Ontario where Sue & Henry bought a home. He asked me if I would help in the search and I replied that I would be more than happy to – thinking I may buy one too.

Ancaster is a small, affluent community, a suburb of Hamilton off Hwy 403. It is actually part of the Niagara escarpment so is very scenic and beautiful. There is easy access to Toronto and the Niagara area.

It wasn't long before he found a perfect lot sitting on the edge of lovely, wooded conservation land which included a small lake. One of the neighbours kindly showed us through his house, told us the builder's name and within a few days Doug ended up purchasing the end unit which was beginning to be constructed. This gave him the opportunity to make significant changes to suit his lifestyle and also improve the model. In a few months the two story, brick, three bedroom house was complete. Marble counters graced the kitchen and recess lights added to the kitchen and hallway areas. Beige broadloom covered the living room, dining room and bedroom floors. Huge windows provided a wonderful view of the wooded conservation area and the side field was covered with beautiful shrubs and wild flowers. He was thrilled with his purchase and looked forward to moving in. Within six months he added a deck off the dining-room, which all the neighbours did later.

The front garden was planted with a variety of shrubs, hostas, ferns and perennials. The town planted a large tree at the end of each driveway.

As soon as it was feasible Doug decided since we've known each other for decades, adored and trusted each other, it made sense to share the house and spend the remainder of our lives living happily together. I agreed and enthusiastically moved my household furniture out of storage and hung my art collection on the walls. Home never looked so good, nor so inviting! We had a signed agreement leaving all our worldly goods, furniture and investments to our children and looked forward to a wonderful future.

Result, my poem –

Could this miracle be happening to me?
At four score and six I feel twenty-three
I rise each morning and spring to my feet

With my whistle and song only sweet birds compete.

What could this mysterious malady be?
That only sunshine and rainbows I see?
My feet want to dance my heart wants to sing
Could I be a victim of Cupid's sting?

Alas my love the answer is clear
My cup runneth over when you are near
The world is so joyous cos you love me
And I return that love tenfold to thee

CHAPTER 49

———

Our new life together was nothing short of magical. We met some of the neighbours, one being Caroline, our pharmacist, her husband Fred and family and had fun times socializing. Also regular family visits back and forth were enjoyable. Both Ancaster and Oakville have some super restaurants so Helen and Gerry joined us and we them, frequently eating out.

We also made annual visits to Oceanport, NJ where Doug's son Marc resided with his lovely wife Jodi and children Kathryn and Eric. Jodi's mother, Joan, became a dear friend we enjoyed so much. The shopping there was phenomenal! More clothes!

We also spent a few winter vacations in Florida, Sarasota was our favourite place, with a beautiful beach and endless sources of entertainment. We attended a memorable concert there featuring Chris Botti, the famous trumpeter and his group. We've been an avid fan of his ever since. For a more intellectual night there were always lectures offered at various hospitals and universities that we looked forward to attending. Interesting trips and most enjoyable.

Back home spring was an invigorating and happy time for gardening. The backyard became our workplace until the end of summer. We planted attractive flowering shrubs down each side of the backyard. Ornamental grasses and forsythia across the bottom to blend in with the conservation area. The garden was then dug across the top and filled with beautiful annuals and perennials, tiger lilies and day lilies predominating on one side. Two round beds were dug in the centre of the lawn with a concrete stairway dividing them. A special place for hydrangeas, the prominent flower in Doug's French garden. Purple clematis was planted along the wooden wall separating us from the neighbours. They climb and bloom each year and now cover the wall. Then the *"piece de résistance"*, we planted wisteria in the corner of the wall and the house, It is covered with dozens of white blooms each summer and now covers the complete back wall of the house rising higher each year and along the whole side of the deck. Astonishingly beautiful! But we're not done yet. Every spring, long planters are filled with beautiful greens and flowers and placed on the railing around the deck.

We're surrounded by beauty all summer, how could we not be ecstatic? We're still able to garden at age 93 and 90.

Thanks be to God! Doug has made a beautiful video of this garden and also the one in France – (Chris Botti and French music and some poetry.) We give copies to close friends including my beloved physician who just retired – after being our family doctor for over fifty years, bless his heart

Result – my poem . . .

Come into my garden and leave your cares behind
While sweet bird songs with music fill your mind
Tarry here a while and in nature steep
Let peace and contentment penetrate deep
Then as you depart know you're loved and so dear
Now my garden is more precious because You were here!

While overseas I met Doug's cousin, Heather (couzies she called us), a delightful, talented woman who had a career as a Graphics Artist until she retired at age sixty. Heather has a home in Suffolk, England and is an exceptionally talented artist. We have several of her paintings on our walls so we think of her often. She also is an avid bird watcher and has travelled different parts of the globe including Antarctica, to enhance her knowledge of art and birds. Like us, she also has and loves her beautiful garden.

We were delighted when she accepted our invitation to visit us in Canada. She stopped to visit an old friend in Montréal for a few days so we motored to Ottawa where we picked her up and stayed to sightsee. We toured and showed her the Parliament Buildings and went walking around the marketplace, attended a symphony concert then headed home.

Susan, Doug's daughter, took Heather to Pelee Island for a few days, a favourite bird watching venue. When she returned to us we took her to the MacMichael Art Gallery in Kleinburg and the Art Gallery in Toronto. Then, on the way home, we stopped at Helen and Gerry's in Oakville for a singsong.

We had a wonderful time with dear 'couzy' and were sorry to see her leave. She sent us one of her beautiful paintings as remembrance of our time together once she retuned home.

A second lovely visitor was our dear friend Madeleine from France. Alain her husband had died and she was living alone. We met her at the airport in Montréal, stopped to show her around Ottawa and even took a boat cruise on the St. Lawrence, which was quite pleasant.

Madeleine used to play tennis in France with Pauline and they became good friends. We toured interesting parts of Toronto with her, also attended a concert and visited family members. We still keep in touch and received lovely pictures of her growing, beautiful grandchildren at Christmas. Madeleine will always be one of our dear friends.

Both Doug and I love cooking. He is a *'chef extraordinaire'* so before Covid we entertained with dinner parties for family and friends. But we have an extraordinary friend who insists in bringing dinner to us – Helen and Gerry usually joined us. Dear Rudi (Hungarian like me) had brought tasty cabbage-roll dinners (Hungarian favourite), and Rachael, his dear friend and ours would bring dessert. We shared a lot of good times and cannot wait for this pandemic to be over and do it again.

As we age we slow down a little but I think we are doing remarkably well. Doug is an ardent reader. We spend many hours talking about many subjects and both enjoy writing. He has written two books, 'Bagatelle' (fiction) and Just a Lad, an autobiography. He is now working on fiction number two, Bagatelle's sequel called 'Pachinko'. No serious signs of forgetfulness – yet. Thank God.

I cannot conclude this book without mentioning my kind, loving and loyal family. For years Nancy and Andy have hosted a dinner party in their condo party room around Christmas and Hanukkah. All friends and family were invited totalling at least fifty people. What a brave endeavour and much appreciated by everyone. It gave us an opportunity to get to know their friends, have a lovely evening and delicious turkey dinner! Nothing since Covid, of course.

They also hosted a memorable ninetieth birthday party for me with all the same people plus my dear friend Irene and her son Robbie, from Bonnie Brae days some sixty years ago. I'll never forget their kindness and generosity.

Result, my poem . . .

My daughter

On September 1st 1949
God blessed me with a baby girl divine
Her presence brought joy and made each day shine
Newspapers she could read at the tender age of three
With love she welcomed baby brother and held him on her knee

Then adorable twin sisters she welcomed with glee
Babies, more babies excitement mounting daily

  As time went by she excelled in every way
Piano, dancing, baton twirling and school
A scholarship for university, she's no fool
Then overseas to gain a worldwide view
On her return to Media and Broadcasting she drew

Highlighting Canadian Authors for me and you

Then romance crept in far and away
And our darling Jess was born on a summer's day
But fate decreed she meet and marry her true love
A handsome and gentle man surely sent from above
Then precious Grandson Jeff appeared one Spring
Filling our hearts which made us sing

Through all your ups and downs and you've had a few
You've never lost your love and kindness and compassion too
Always thinking and doing for others and always there
Nothing makes the World better than love and care
That's why I feel so Up at ninety-two
Because I have a loving caring daughter, You
Happy seventy-first birthday, darling daughter.

Likewise my twin daughters, Jani and Judy are kind and thoughtful and always there when I need them.

My beautiful twin daughters
One in five million a birth, so unique
Hoards of doctors gathered the answers to seek
How two different blood types in one cosy space
Survived long enough to win the birth race
A Mother's deep devotion and prayers to God above

And a close bond between tots, a true act of love

Modern science intervened turning yellow skin to pink
Life's a mystery and a miracle, I think

You've lived a good life and survived tragedies too
But one thing is clear, that whatever you do
If hard times come your way pull together
For you are survivors, a bond that's 'forever'.

How fortunate I am to have a such a loving and caring family for all these years. God is Good.

Doug's daughter, Susan, who recently sold her business and retired, has been a close friend for decades – sort of my other daughter. She and her husband Henry now live in a beautiful home that Henry continues to beautify with his endless talents. We keep in close touch by 'phone or personally just as we do with Marc and Jodi, who recently moved from Oceanport to Florida. On Susan's last birthday in October we celebrated at their home.

Result – my poem . . .

She came, she saw, she conquered life's hurdles and prevailed
When hard times came she refused to give in
Mounted a lofty balloon and through blue skies she sailed
A beloved daughter, wife, mother and cherished friend
Her extraordinary achievements seem to have no end
So on this special anniversary we want to say
We love and admire you forever and a day
Happy, happy birthday, never lose that passion for life, it's you.

CHAPTER 50

I know I've talked too much about the joyous, interesting, exhilarating times we've had in our new partnership. And that is good, but we cannot forget the sad times that are a part of life as we age.

Jean went back to England to help look after her dear mother, Ethel, who died in 1996 then stayed on to help her sister Grace and husband Allan. She was a most compassionate, caring daughter, sister and sister-in-law. She was also a close friend of mine during my University days. I admired her courage moving from Britain to the USA, travelling by bus to California and finding secretarial work in no time. Then to Australia as a model, then back to Washington DC.

Sadly, in 2002, Allan passed away. Jean agreed to stay with Grace in her Devonshire country home until she died in 2009. Doug felt Jean should not stay alone in England so persuaded her to be in Ancaster with us where he found a lovely Seniors apartment nearby. We helped her furnish and decorate it with fabulous results – very comfortable and most attractive. She made friends easily and spent five enjoyable years there, including many dinners and parties with us. When it became obvious she needed more care she moved into an upscale nursing home in the area where she received excellent care. I'll never forget our last day with her, I was holding her hand and Doug had his arm around her shoulder. She laughingly pointed to her cheek and we each kissed her and this is what she said, "I'm so glad you two are together, you are so good for each other." Dear Jean died the next day. After a lovely, well attended funeral, Doug, accompanied by Susan and Henry, flew to England to scatter her ashes near her Mother's on a high point of Cornish moorland. Due to health problems I could not make the long journey but as usual I was here with my prayer book saying goodbye to my courageous friend. We miss her so much but have a lovely reminder of her each day. We gave Jean a beautiful coloured print by the Group of Seven which now hangs in our dining-room where the sun's rays sparkle on it each morning, reminding us of her.

They were away a week or so .

The result – my poem . . .

You are my heart and soul
Without you I am not whole

I need your joyful smile at sunrise
To fill the day with fun and surprise
Your love and kindness make my heart quiver
Our love is forever like a Deep River

I really missed his presence, life wasn't the same without him.

I lost other close friends, dear Gordon with the laughing face, my dear friend Irene's husband and also precious David, their son who was a childhood friend of our son, Peter. Irene and I are the only females left of the wonderful Bonnie Brae gang. We talk regularly.

Then my beautiful sister-in-law, Isobel, and my beloved sister, Helen, died suddenly. Time to stop, there are too many. We have to remember they all have peace and tranquility and no pain, that's comforting. Bless all their Souls!

With Doug, Susan and Henry returned, life continues but at a slower pace. We are fortunate to have beautiful neighbours, Frank, Caroline's brother who bought their house when they moved elsewhere and other kind individuals who always rush over with their powerful snowblowers and clear our driveway after a snow storm, before Doug can get at it.

At ninety-three and ninety we live a busy life always with something to look forward to. At the moment Spring, when I can tackle my three planters for the deck and Doug the garden work. Since I've been plagued with minor health problems (which seemed to have begun after my sister's sudden death) Doug has been exceptionally kind, taking over many of the chores I attended to. No complaints, just a big smile and laughing eyes. My girls call him the 'Saint', An Angel, and Perfect Man – he deserves all the praise he receives.

Result – my poem . . .

How lucky can a damsel be
To have a partner who can see
The wonder and beauty of each day we share
Dark clouds always have a silver lining
Your love is a miracle that keeps me smiling
A love so special, forever and a day
I'll love you eternally, what more can I say?

As I reflect on the obvious contrast of 'life before' (my marriage) and 'life now', I feel a deep sense of sadness that Joe and I failed to experience the same '*joie de vivre*' in our life together. I admit it's never, or seldom, just one person's fault but in this case I'm convinced his 'WW2 war wounds, PTSD' played a major part. I'm still thankful for his service to his country, the volunteer work we did in Third World countries, my four beautiful children and feel he did the best he could given his condition. God bless his Soul!

CHAPTER 51

___

What an Absolutely, Extraordinary Journey from Szakasz at the tender age of five with my dear Mother, to my beloved Canada where I was given endless opportunities, by exceptional mentors, to become who I am today. After marrying at an early age and raising four beautiful children, mostly alone, I pursued higher education and a career in Social Work, never dreaming where it would ultimately lead me.

I am extremely grateful to so many people beginning with my beloved parents and 'Nagymama' (grandmother) for their love and for instilling, by rote and by example, those important values – love thy neighbour and always help those in need and the importance of education.

The same value system was continued by my extraordinary teachers in public and high school – again, the importance of education, I believed them and always excelled in my studies. The Afghan we made for children in Residential Schools, knitting socks and scarves for the Red Cross during WW2. Showing exceptional kindness to a little immigrant girl – me – who received a punch in the nose from an aggressive student. I am most grateful and thank all those wonderful teachers for their special influence.

Now on to higher learning from a B.A. to an M.S.W. I am extremely grateful to all the teaching staff at both York University and University of Toronto, especially Dr Wilson Head who gently nudged me into Social Work. I am thankful for the scholarships that helped propel me to receive an MSW, which certainly made the journey exceptionally interesting and worthwhile. It provided guidelines for my life

Social Work enabled me to obtain a most interesting career in Probation, forming my own company, many thanks to Mr H. Roy Hawkins, a superintendent in the Provincial Ministry of Correctional Services. He encouraged important and positive changes in the lives of young offenders through new, more humane policies. I considered it a great privilege to work with him and such a worthy cause.

CESO (Canadian Executive Services Overseas), was the Government Agency that provided such unique opportunity to serve the poor, sick and needy in Third World countries, to make their lives more tolerable. Mr Dan Haggerty was an excellent head of CESO and helped advance and expand their programs significantly. I originally went overseas as a spouse of a CESO volunteer which meant sitting around the swimming pool and enjoying one's self while your husband worked all day – certainly against the grain of a Social Worker, so I undertook volunteer projects for hospitals and institutions wherever I could, the greatest being projects in Chitre, Panama, Central America which involved a Psychiatric Hospital and Residential School for children in Chepo de las Minas.

I would be remiss not to give my heartfelt thanks to all the 'hands on' people who made Projects possible. First would be my beloved friend Doreen Wicks who formed her company GEMS that helped the poor, sick and needy globally for many years. She was in charge of compiling the incredible shipment to the Psychiatric Hospital in Chitre, shipped free by Evergreen (thank you, thank you!). She is deceased and I'm sure one of God's angels, always helping whenever needed. My love and gratitude to all her children. Others I want to thank, Syd Renton, CESO volunteer, was with us in Panama, and procured many of the hospital beds as he was a retired hospital administrator in Etobicoke. Mr George Eaton, who contributed sets of plastic dinnerware so patients wouldn't suffer burned lips drinking from tin cups, deserve great thanks. My dear friend Mary Benedetto who contributed sets off sheets and helped with the packing.

The Rotary Club and Mr Joe Cashen, deceased, and

wife Yvonne who tackled the difficult task of assessing Chepo de las Minas and the needs of the Residential School. The fabulous work was finally completed in 2015. Heartfelt thanks to Yvonne.

Lastly, sincere thanks to Dr Olga Bouché de Romero, head of the Psychiatric Hospital, a wonderful compassionate psychiatrist, who proudly wrote me that they had the best equipped hospital in Panama after the shipment was received. Many thanks also to dear, sweet Rosa, Chitreana Roja, the interpreter, who, in the first place, led me to the Psychiatric Hospital where the needs were so great. Keep up the superb work Rosa. God bless all the helpers.

These Projects will always hold a special place in my heart. Being a devout believer, I thank God for guiding me in that direction.

Perhaps my mantra should be – Try Volunteering, it will change and enhance your life forever!

Finally, for everyone who loves Springtime, my poem is for you –

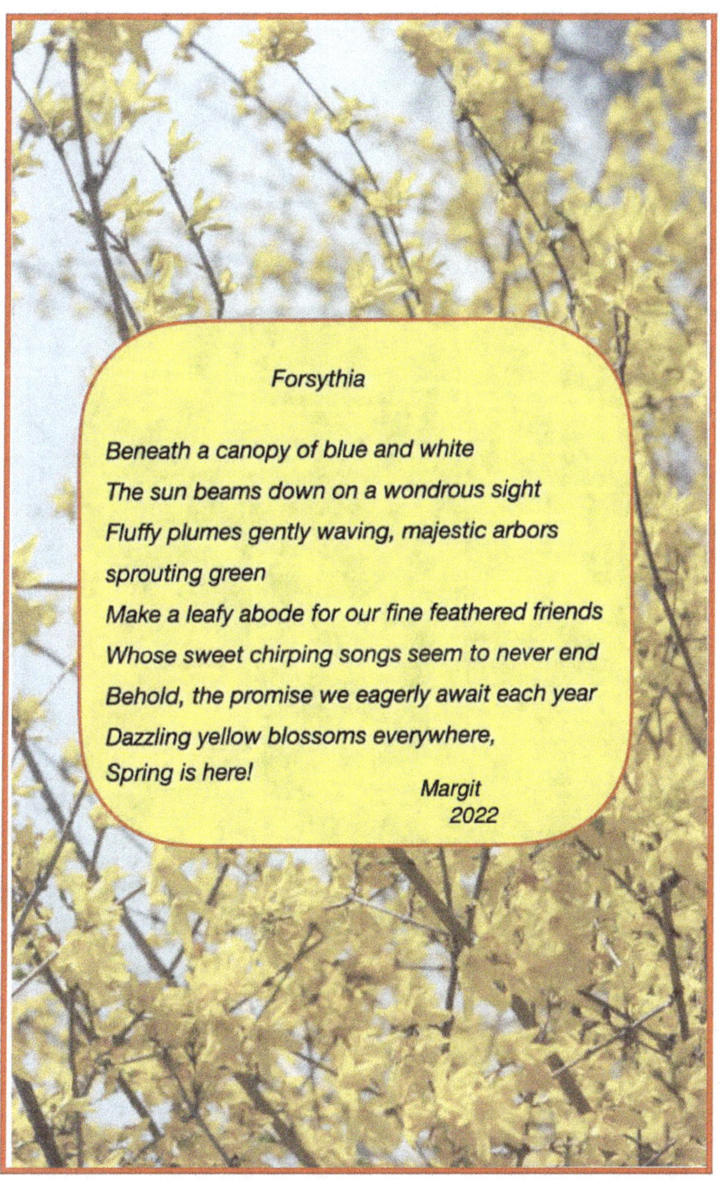

Forsythia

Beneath a canopy of blue and white
The sun beams down on a wondrous sight
Fluffy plumes gently waving, majestic arbors
sprouting green
Make a leafy abode for our fine feathered friends
Whose sweet chirping songs seem to never end
Behold, the promise we eagerly await each year
Dazzling yellow blossoms everywhere,
Spring is here!
Margit
2022

The Beautiful Fruit
of Our Labour of Love

Dra. Olga Bouche de Romero
PSIQUIATRA
Apdo. No. 29 - Chitré, Herrera
República de Panamá

Los Santos, 15 de Mayo de 1987.

Mrs.
Margaret Hawkins
20 Rothsay Rd.,
Thornhill, Ontario
Canada, L3T 3J,

Dear Mrs Hawkins:
My first lines is[are] for you sincere, cordial and affectionate greeting.
How are you, your husband and Mr Renton?
I am fine and very, very happy for your presents for Psychiatric Hospital of Azuero. I don't find the words or manner to express you our thankfulness.
Your efforts are very important. Today, The Psychiatric Intensive Care Unit is the best ward psychiatric in Panamá Republic, thanks to you and your group. The

THE JOURNEY

Canadian Consulate

Consulat du Canada

Box 3658

Balboa, R de Panama

May 25.1987

Mrs.Margaret Hawkins,

Toronto, Ontario

Dear Mrs.Hawkins:

How I wish you could have been with Enrique Williams, our CESO man here, his son and I on May 2 when we went to Los Santos for the dedication of the medical supplies you sent to the hospital. Thank you so much.

They arrived late at night and patients as well as staff unloaded the containers, set up the beds, made them and spruced up the salon so that they could go ahead with the Ceremonies as planned. I felt you would have felt like weeping, as I did to see the joy you made possible. I found the Dra.Olga a very caring person and anybody who gets to that hospital will receive all the professional care he or she needs besides a positive attitude to life in general.

I trust that if you or your husband returns to Panama you will get in touch with me here at the Consulate or at my home.

Sincerely,

Hon.Canadian Consul

LRW/RVD

MARGARET HAWKINS

Canadian Executive Service Organization Service Administratif Canadien aux Organismes
CESO, Suite 2000, 415 Yonge Street, Toronto, Ontario, Canada M5B 2E7
Tel: (416) 596-2376 WATS LINE: 1-800-268-9052 Cable: CANEXSO Telex: 06-20583

November 17, 1987

Mrs. Margaret Hawkins
20 Rothsay Rd.
Thornhill, Ont.
L3T 3J7

Dear Margaret:

I was so pleased to see you again at the beginning of the month,
and am also pleased to say I am enjoying working with Joanne who
has the reins of the Spouse Program solidly in her grasp. Thank
you for taking the time to come in and ease Joanne into the role
that you created (albeit with a little nudge from Dan at the
start).

Until we spoke on the phone in late October, I hadn't realised
that your contribution as a CESO office Volunteer (we must find a
better way to distinguish these Volunteers from VCs) had come to
an end. May I take the opportunity now to thank you for all the
time, thought, creativity and commitment that you gave to the
establishment of a program for CESO Spouses. We have already
experienced the practical benefits of some spouses being better
prepared for projects through the phone calls you made, others
who wanted to share their experience of being a spouse having the
chance to do just this by volunteering to run the program with
you, and the beginnings of a practical tool that any spouse can
use in any country if she wishes to teach conversational english.
I share your belief that this program will develop into something
that opens up possibilities for spouses to make significant
contributions to organizations and people in the developing
countries CESO serves. It will help to shape CESO's policy in
many ways as it becomes a reality that we recognize and foster.
Everyone at CESO is grateful to you for the pioneering work you
have done in this area, and Susan, Mercedes and I enjoyed
developing the program goals with you and Nancy.

I am sure Joanne will keep you informed of progress. Nancy has
been to CIDA and discussed the english teaching materials, and
Susan has been talking with them about the Spouse Module of the
CIDA Briefing. The Directories are in for typing and Joanne is
contacting networks to gather information about opportunities in
developing countries. We are at an exciting stage but it all
takes time and consistent effort to bring ideas to fruition.

Thank you again Margaret for the commitment you demonstrated to
the program, especially in the rather isolated first months when
you were working alone, and thank you too for sharing your
experience of working with volunteers with me. You know the
results of that!

THE JOURNEY

350 Ramsey Road, Toronto, Ontario M4G 1R8
Phone (416) 425-6220

November 13, 1984

Mrs. Margaret Hawkins, B.A., B.S.W.
York Counselling Services
20 Rothsay Road
Thornhill, Ontario
L3T 3J4

Dear Margaret:

Since we last spoke I have had an opportunity to represent
the needs of the Asociación Dominicana de Rehabilitación
Inc. to the International Services Committee of the Toronto
Rotary Club.

There was in general a high level of interest and support
for providing assistance. The budget available to this
committee, however, requires that we be very precise in
the kind of support required and fairly accurate as to costs
involved.

If you could provide me with this kind of information, it
would assist the committee greatly in arriving at a decision
as to what they can provide in terms of dollars or indirect
support.

I'll look forward to hearing from you soon.

Yours sincerely,

J. H. Cashen
Director of Services

JHC:AL

TELEX 0121
MAY 11/87

ATT MARGARET HAWKINS

RE HOSPITAL SUPPLIES FOR HOSPITAL PSIQUIATRICO DE LOS SANTOS
PLEASE BE INFORMED THAT GOODS WERE DELIVERED ON APRIL 30TH
AND FORMALY RECEIVED ON MAY 2ND IN A SMALL BUT EMOTIONAL
CEREMONY. PRESENT WERE TWO REPRESENTATIVES FROM THE PANAMA
ROTARY CLUB, THE HONORARY CANADIAN CONSUL MRS RUTH DENTON AND
MYSELF ON CESO AND YOUR BEHALF. QUANTITY AND QUALITY OF
DONATION YOU OBTAINED WERE BEYOND EVERYONE'S EXPECTATIONS AND
GAVE EVERYONE INVOLVED A SPECIAL PRIDE TO BE A MINUSCLE
PARTICIPANT IN AN OTHERWISE GIGANTIC ENDEAVOUR. ON BEHALF OF
PANAMA MY HEARTFELT GRATITUDE. WILL CONVEY DETAILS PERSONALLY
GOD WILLING IN TORONTO. REGARDS
ENRIQUE

CC DAN HAGERTY, PRES.

Acknowledgments:
Special thanks and appreciation to Doug, my loving friend, for his relentless encouragement.

He believed it was important for me to share my story, particularly the volunteer work, to inspire others to do the same.

And thanks to my wonderful granddaughter Jessica for her generous contribution of publishing and printing this book for me.